Indifference Arguments

B

Issues in Ancient Philosophy

General Editor: *Jonathan Barnes*

1 Plato and Platonism   *Julius Moravcsik*
2 Indifference Arguments   *Stephen Makin*
3 Aristotle on Moral Responsibility   *Susan Sauve Meyer*

Indifference Arguments

———————◆———————

STEPHEN MAKIN

BLACKWELL
Oxford UK & Cambridge USA

Copyright © Stephen Makin 1993

The right of Stephen Makin to be identified as author of this work has been
asserted in accordance with the Copyright, Designs and Patents Act 1988.

First published 1993

Blackwell Publishers
108 Cowley Road
Oxford OX4 1JF
UK

238 Main Street,
Cambridge, Massachusetts 02142
USA

British Library Cataloguing in Publication Data

A CIP catalogue record for this book is available from the British Library.

Library of Congress Cataloging-in-Publication Data

Makin, Stephen, 1955–
Indifference arguments / Stephen Makin.
p. cm. – (Issues in ancient philosophy; 2)
Includes bibliographical references and index.

1. Atomism. 2. Logic, Ancient. 3. Reasoning. I. Title. II. Series: Issues in ancient
philosophy (Cambridge, Mass.); 2.
B193.M33 1993 160—dc20 93–9799 CIP

ISBN 0–631–17838 4

Typeset in 11 on 13 pt Garamond by Pure Tech Corporation, Pondicherry, India
Printed in Great Britain by T. J. Press Ltd, Padstow, Cornwall

This book is printed on acid-free paper

for alyson

Contents

◆

Preface   ix

1 Introduction   1

1.1 *Indifference Arguments*   1
1.2 *Presocratic Atomism*   8
1.3 *The Importance of Logical Analysis*   14
     Notes   15

2 The Eleatics   17

2.1 *Why Zeno Needs Indifference Arguments*   18
2.2 *Where Zeno Uses Indifference Arguments*   24
2.3 *Parmenides and Division*   28
2.4 *Indifference Reasoning in Melissus?*   33
2.5 *Eleatic Indifference Reasoning*   41
     Notes   42

3 The Atomists   49

3.1 *Indifference and Indivisibility*   49
3.2 *Indifference and Variety*   62
3.3 *Indifference and Epistemology*   65
     Notes   84

4 Some Other Indifference Arguments   98

4.1 *Preamble*   98
4.2 *Anaximander's Earth*   101

4.3 Aristotle against the Void   105
4.4 Agents and Patients   115
4.5 Closing Remarks   122
     Notes   123

5 The Form of Indifference Arguments   129

5.1 Two Types of Argument   130
5.2 Reasons and Modalities   134
     Notes   157

6 Epistemological Indifference Arguments   160

6.1 Are All Indifference Arguments Epistemological?   160
6.2 Ou Mallon and Ancient Scepticism   167
6.3 A Democritean Argument   170
6.4 Sorites Arguments   178
6.5 Arbitrary Objects and Quantification   197
6.6 Conclusion   200
     Notes   201

7 Indifference Arguments without Epistemology   208

7.1 The Non-Epistemological Reading   208
7.2 An Argument for a Weak Principle of Plenitude   212
7.3 The Democritean Arguments   219
7.4 Looking Back   224
     Notes   229

Appendix   231

Bibliography   233

Index   239

Preface

◆

My hope is that this book will be of interest both to readers with a special interest in presocratic philosophy, and to those concerned with the analysis of informal modes of argument. Some basic decisions about style have been made with that hope in mind.

The volume can be read by philosophers who have no knowledge of Greek, and who are not overly familiar with presocratic and other ancient writings. Passages that are discussed are quoted, and quoted passages are translated in the text. For the referential convenience of philologically adept readers who are specialists in ancient Greek thought, the Greek text of quoted passages is for the most part reproduced in the notes. Translation of the Greek of presocratics is particularly contentious and fraught with difficulty. If I were to offer my own translations I would inevitably be obliged to provide justification for anything that might be original. Philological issues would be off-putting to a section of my intended readership. The best solution seemed to be to offer translations from a source with which a majority of Greekless readers might be familiar. Translations of presocratic texts follow the second edition of *The Presocratic Philosophers*, by G. S. Kirk, J. E. Raven and M. Schofield. If Kirk, Raven and Schofield do not provide a translation of the passage in question, as in the case of some of the Democritean passages cited, the source of the translation is given. Presocratic texts are identified by reference to *Die Fragmente der Vorsokratiker* by H. Diels and W. Kranz, which is a widespread system of reference. In the case of Democritus, reference is also made to the more comprehensive collection *Democritea* edited by S. Luria. I have not typically provided Greek text for later authors. Quotations from Aristotle follow the translations in the Clarendon Aristotle series, or in the Revised Oxford translation, unless the passage in question is found in Kirk, Raven and Schofield, in which case I give their translation. Quotations from Hellenistic philosophers are taken, where possible, from *The Hellenistic Philosophers*, by A. A. Long and D. Sedley.

It is a pleasure to give thanks. I am grateful to my publishers for their patience as months turned into years. Jonathan Barnes, as the editor of this series, has been encouraging at every stage. I am indebted to Elizabeth Anscombe, who first aroused my interest in indifference reasoning. I have discussed topics from this book with friends and colleagues too numerous to mention. I would like to thank particularly those who read, in whole or in part, the penultimate version of this book. Peter Smith gave me valuable advice on mathematics and the need for clarity. Nicholas Denyer's comments were as stimulating as ever. Finally, Robert Wardy was generous with his time and energy: his acute comments saved me from many an error – though undoubtedly many others remain – and encouraged me to think harder about what I was saying. Many thanks!

My deepest thanks are due to Alyson: to say anything else here is impossible.

Sheffield,
December 1992

1

Introduction

◆

This book starts from the fact that there are arguments concerning *indifference* and ways of thinking involving *symmetry* which resonate strongly with us. Such arguments and ways of thinking are found in ancient philosophical sources, and are of particular significance in the presocratic atomism of Democritus and Leucippus (whom I do not distinguish). They occur also throughout subsequent philosophy and in everyday thought. They should puzzle us. We should be puzzled about quite how they work and about whether any of them are good arguments. We should wonder whether our being struck by considerations of symmetry and balance is indicative of some deep metaphysical commitments – and if so, what they are – or whether it is really of little further significance. We should be interested also in what the systematic use of arguments of this sort by Democritus tells us about the nature of the atomic theory propounded by him.

1.1 Indifference Arguments

What is to be discussed is a general form of argument. However, it is, usually particular examples that seize the attention and motivate interest – the less complex the example, the better. Consider the following argument. Other galaxies are observed to be moving away from this one. Since there is nothing special about this galaxy, there is no more reason for galaxies to be receding from this one than from any other. So it is a reasonable conclusion that all galaxies are moving in the same manner away from one another. That is an appealing indifference argument. The thought behind it is that the Milky Way is *no different* in relevant ways from any other galaxy.

There are two sorts of claim which could be found underlying that argument. First, there is a view about *reasons*. There will be some explanation of why other galaxies are moving away from this one. That explanation will appeal to very basic features of the universe. Suppose there were a fundamental asymmetry between this galaxy and every other. Then that asymmetry should be explicable in very basic terms. Yet at that basic level the Milky Way appears to be no different from any other galaxy. The reasons which explain why other galaxies recede from this one are equally reasons why they will recede in the same way from one another. In consequence, if the other galaxies are moving away from this one all galaxies will be moving away from one another.

Second, there is a distinct view about the *rationality of belief*. It is more rational to believe what is more likely. It is extremely improbable that the Milky Way should occupy a privileged position in the universe, such that the motion of all other galaxies relative to it is quite different from their motion relative to one another. It is far more probable that the way galactic motions appear from this galaxy is typical of the way they appear from elsewhere. So it is rational to believe that all the galaxies are moving in the same way away from one another.

Indifference arguments, then, have something to do with *reasons* and something to do with *rational belief*. The first thought is reminiscent of a familiar metaphysical claim, the Principle of Sufficient Reason. As stated by Leibniz, that is the principle 'that no fact can be real or actual, and no proposition true, without there being a sufficient reason for its being so and not otherwise, although most often these reasons just cannot be known by us'.[1] The Milky Way cannot be fundamentally distinct from every other galaxy because there is no reason why it should be *this* galaxy that is unique in that respect. It might be supposed that the main interest of indifference arguments lies in their connection with a Principle of Sufficient Reason. That is what is suggested by their being commonly referred to as Principle of *In*sufficient Reason arguments. The second thought above suggests, in contrast, that indifference arguments are primarily epistemological arguments, whose appeal is to be explicated by reference to principles of rationality. Whether or not this galaxy is fundamentally different from others, it is overwhelmingly rational to believe that it is not.

Neither of those approaches, taken on its own, gives the complete picture. Not all intuitively appealing indifference arguments concern the rationality of belief. A charged particle will remain suspended at an appropriate position in a magnetic field. If it were to move it would have to move in some direction. There is a position at which it has no more reason to move in one direction than in another. So, at that position it will not move, but will remain suspended in equilibrium. That argument *could* be put in terms of the rationality of believing that there will be no movement in any direction. It seems appealing, however, in that it offers an account of why a particle does not move, rather than why it would be reasonable to adopt a particular belief.

Another example illustrates the same point. The level of intelligence presently manifested among living things is obviously limited. There could be organisms with greater intelligence, and over evolutionary time intelligence levels have increased. Now, it seems impossible that there should be an arbitrary stopping point to that increase, that for no reason there should just never be living things with intelligence above a particular level. If there is no reason for one level rather than another to be the upper limit of intelligence there is no such limit, and so organisms will continue to develop and increase in intelligence. Again this argument does not appear to concern the rationality of belief. It offers a type of explanation of *why* intelligence should continue to develop. The thought that there is no reason for the development of intelligence naturally to cease at one point rather than any other is the thought that nature is indifferent to limits. The consequence which is claimed to follow is that, on a large enough time scale, nature will continue to develop.

If epistemological issues concerning the rationality of belief are not always the central issue, the conviction might be strengthened that it is the Principle of Sufficient Reason that is significant. Appeal to that principle will turn out not to be of primary importance, although it is useful to say something more about the matter. The two arguments offered above are appealing only to the extent that they concern cases in which there is no mere inexplicable contingency, and in which an application of the Principle of Sufficient Reason is accepted. If the charged particle is to move it has to move in some direction, and there has to be a reason for its moving in that direction rather than any other. Hence if there is no reason for it to move in one direction rather than in any other it will not move. Clearly that line of reasoning would hold no appeal if it were allowed that a particle could move in a particular direction for no reason.

Suppose it is objected that the argument above about intelligence development is very poor, as is obvious from the following parody. Mice vary in length. There seems no reason why one length rather than another should be the upper limit of mouse size. Hence there either were or are or eventually will be mice of whatever size you care to mention. That conclusion is plainly unwarranted. Everything we know about animals suggests that there are limits to the development of a species. What that suggests, however, is that the premiss of the parody argument is not true. There will be a reason why some length is the upper limit of size for the species; for example, concerning the relations between body size and the maintenance of a stable body temperature or the mechanical properties of the endoskeleton. The conclusion of the argument is ludicrous precisely because the premiss is unacceptable, and the premiss is unacceptable because of the conviction that there will be a sufficient reason, perhaps not presently known, for one size rather than another to be the upper size limit for the development of the species. The argument about intelligence development might elicit a similar response, that there will be a reason for there being one limit rather than another to intelligence development: for example, some reason concerning the evolutionary pressures which drive intelligence development. Responses like that bring the Principle of Sufficient Reason into play. The arguments are thought to proceed from false premisses because it is believed that there is a sufficient reason to be provided for there being particular limits to intelligence development or mouse size, or whatever.

In mischievous mood someone might try to make the mouse argument seem more forceful, by attempting to rehabilitate the premiss. Suppose one proceeds stepwise, considering lengths one-tenth of an inch apart. Of any such pair there is no reason why one rather than the other should be the upper limit of mouse size. Hence it appears that it could eventually be shown that of any two lengths you care to pick there is no reason for one rather than the other to be the upper limit of mouse size. While no one would take that argument seriously, it does illustrate a connection of interest between indifference reasoning and sorites arguments, by focusing on the point that the sorts of reasons which could explain the limits of species size are insensitive to sufficiently small size variations. There will be more to say about sorites reasoning later.

For the present we should return to the Principle of Sufficient Reason. Contrary to what may have been suggested by earlier examples, reference to that principle tells us very little of what we want to know about indifference arguments. The Principle of Sufficient Reason is a principle of general application. The fairly typical claim cited from Leibniz was that in *no* case does there fail to be a sufficient reason for whatever is so being so. One does not, however, have to believe a universal principle of this kind in order to find indifference arguments appealing. Indeed, hardly anyone *does* believe a full-blown Leibnizian Principle of Sufficient Reason, yet indifference arguments of one type or another are of widespread appeal. Even if I were committed to an instance of the universal Leibnizian principle concerning any case in which I found indifference reasoning appealing, to point that out would not constitute much progress towards a more general understanding of indifference arguments. The general structure of indifference arguments would remain an open question. Does a claim about the need for reasons occur as a *premiss* in any good indifference argument? Certainly one might try to rewrite any indifference argument so as to include as a premiss the requirement that reasons be provided in the case under consideration. Yet it is not clear that such a strategy would be particularly revealing, either of the force of the argument in question or of its connection with other arguments. Indifference reasoning is found in many different areas. There are the arguments of ancient atomism. There are other ancient arguments which will be mentioned later. There are the examples cited above. As well as sorites arguments there are techniques of mathematical and logical reasoning which involve appeal to the arbitrary. A proof that an arbitrary number has a certain property justifies the conclusion that all the infinitely many numbers have that property: appeal to the arbitrary number serves in some way to establish that there is no more reason for one number than for another to have the property. What needs to be brought out is the most general and enlightening way of relating these and other arguments. In order to do that it is necessary to discuss precisely *what* the connections are between, on the one hand, such notions as the balance of reasons, evidence that is indifferent between alternatives or symmetrical explanatory factors, and, on the other, the conclusions typically derived from indifference arguments. What is required is an account of a unifying *formal* structure, to which various indifference arguments can be related and in terms of which they can be understood. The significance or otherwise of the Principle of Sufficient Reason, in whatever guise, can only be appreciated in the light of such a structure.

Provision of a satisfactory general account of indifference arguments should enable one to distinguish between good and bad instances of indifference reasoning. It is a commonplace that a particular argument can be criticized as bad on two sorts of grounds. First, it may be invalid. There may be a flaw as regards the form or structure in virtue of which the premisses of the argument are reckoned to support the conclusion. Second, it may be unsound. One or more of the premisses of the argument may be untrue, and so the argument will provide no good grounds for accepting the conclusion as true. It is natural to ask here whether in distinguishing good from bad indifference arguments one is making a point about the *soundness* of particular arguments or about the *validity* of a common argument form.

This is not so clear-cut an issue as that simple dichotomy might suggest. An indifference argument typically contains a premiss concerning symmetry, which I will call its indifference premiss. Commonly this will be a premiss of the form: there is no more reason for . . . than for. . . . Consider a set-up of which an indifference premiss would be true, but to which the application of an indifference argument would be ludicrous. Take a case in which no one would believe the conclusion that the indifference argument would appear to justify. There is, let us suppose, no more reason for Annabel to purchase this bottle of Pouilly Fumé than another bottle of the same vintage, from the same vineyard, at the same price, and so on. Still, there does not seem to be a good inference to the conclusion that she either purchases both or purchases neither or hangs like Buridan's Ass suspended between them. That case differs from one in which an indifference argument is *unsound*. Suppose one were to argue that a body could move infinitely fast, on the grounds that there is no reason for the upper limit of velocity to be one speed rather than another. That argument would be bad because it is unsound. The indifference premiss is false, since there *is* reason for the speed of light to be the upper limit of velocity.

On the other hand, one might not want to criticize the argument about Annabel's wine-buying as *invalid*, as unacceptable due to a flaw in the form in virtue of which the conclusion is taken to follow from the premisses. For there are other arguments which are perfectly cogent, which share a common form with the wine-buying argument. The argument cited earlier was a case in point: at the appropriate position in a magnetic field the charged particle has no more reason to move in one direction than in any other, and so since it cannot move in all directions at once it will not move. An example like that generates a tension. Since that is a good indifference argument there is some indifference argument structure which can be set out as a valid form. Yet there are indifference arguments which *seem* to be of the same form, such as that about Annabel the wine-buyer, and which have true premisses but false conclusions. Of course that is not possible. There are alternative ways of responding. One would be to deny that there is any form common to the arguments in question, in virtue of which both arguments are reckoned to be valid. Yet in this case that does not seem very plausible. To the extent that the argument about Annabel is engaging, it just does appear to share some logically significant structure with the argument about charged particles in a magnetic field. Another response would be to claim that, while the arguments are of a common form, in virtue of which they are both valid, and while in each case the indifference premiss is true, there is some other suppressed premiss which is false in the one case and true in the other. That would be to say that, when the form of the argument about Annabel's wine-buying is made clearer, the argument is seen to be unsound. There is nothing in principle to rule against expanding on that response, and providing the argument form in question. That approach would not be inconsistent with the alternative strategy I prefer. That strategy is to say that the conclusion to which the argument about Annabel *seems* to lead and which is false, that she will buy either both bottles or neither bottle, is not the conclusion justified by the valid argument form which is shared with the argument about charged particles in magnetic fields. Further, since that common argument form is valid, and since it allows for just one premiss, and since that premiss in the case of Annabel's wine-buying is true, there is some other conclusion about Annabel which *is* true, and which *is* justified by a valid and sound indifference argument.

It will emerge that the conclusions justified by the indifference premiss, and which are true of Annabel in the case imagined, are equivalences between modal claims: it does indeed follow that Annabel *must* buy the one bottle if and only if she *must* buy the other, and that she *can* buy the one bottle if and only if she *can* buy the other. Quite how such conclusions follow validly from an indifference premiss is a matter for later discussion. It is worth pointing out here, though, the role this approach gives for the Principle of Sufficient Reason. There is a gap between the sort of conclusions that an indifference argument validly supports – that it *must* be that p if and only it *must* be that q, and that it *can* be that p if and only if it *can* be that q – and the sort of conclusion that an indifference argument is often used to support – that it *is* the case that p if and only if it *is* the case that q (which is to say that *either* both p and q *or* neither p nor q is the case). In some instances that gap can be closed. In those cases there are further sound arguments leading from the first conclusions to the second. In other instances there are no such further arguments. Which of those is the case depends on the particular features of the argument in question. In many, though not all, cases in which there is a further argument which closes the gap, the requirements of the Principle of Sufficient Reason are acceptable. In such set-ups it is reasonable to accept that nothing occurs, or is true, without a reason for it, rather than anything else, occurring or being true. In cases where there is no defensible supplementary argument the demand for a reason is not acceptable. Yet all that is extraneous to an account of *indifference* arguments, for it concerns the feasibility of bridging a logical gap between the conclusions which follow validly from an indifference argument and some further conclusion. What is of primary interest is the move from the indifference premiss to the first set of conclusions.

It should now be clearer why it is useful to raise questions about the general structure of indifference arguments. Only if a general structure is made perspicuous is it possible to see what sort of conclusion *is* justified by an indifference argument with true premisses. In the course of giving an account of that structure very general relations between notions of reason, cause, explanation and modality come into view. As a consequence some insight is likely to be gained into indifference arguments whose status is genuinely opaque. It is, of course, those arguments that tend to be the most interesting. The indifference arguments associated with presocratic atomism are just such arguments.

1.2 Presocratic Atomism

Nothing that has been said so far gives reason to think that the discussion of indifference arguments should involve particular attention to ancient philosophers. It is true that there are plenty of examples of indifference arguments to be found in ancient writings, most transparently *ou mallon* arguments which typically have a premiss containing the phrase *ou mallon...ê...*, meaning 'no more...than...' or 'not...

rather than...' Yet there are also plenty of examples of indifference arguments to be gathered from other periods. What makes indifference arguments a topic of such relevance to *ancient* philosophy is the importance of their systematic use in presocratic atomism.

Indifference reasoning underlies the Zenonian arguments about plurality which I take to be the primary stimulus to Democritus' atomism. The same sort of reasoning explains the indivisibility and the basic properties of Democritean atoms. Those claims will be made out in more detail in what follows. It is helpful to say something more general here about the perspective in which presocratic atomism will be set.

The distinction between scientific and philosophical theories is not a wholly clear one, and its application to presocratics is anachronistic. Yet some anachronism is unavoidable in writing about the presocratics, and so long as the distinction is made clear in advance there should be no danger of confusion. It is a commonplace that, in one way of taking the term, Democritean atomism is not a *scientific* theory. It is not a theory based on empirical evidence and grounded in observation. Claims made about the atoms are supported by *a priori* argument rather than by appeal to experience. Granted that obviously correct view, there is, however, a further and more contentious question about how Democritus should be approached, which it is tempting also to set in terms of a distinction between the scientific and the philosophical.

The issue here concerns the way in which different aspects of Democritus' thought should be related together. There is evidence that Democritus expressed views on a huge range of topics. In addition to the existence and properties of atoms, these seem to have included astronomy, cosmology, cosmogony, meteorology, agriculture, diet, medicine, anatomy, perception, the mind, language, poetry, epistemology, mathematics, religion, ethics and politics. Of the works that are attributed to Democritus some, no doubt, are not genuine. Further, these divisions between topics need not reflect disciplines which Democritus himself recognized. What is more, we know practically nothing of the content of most of Democritus' thought. Nevertheless, the fact that it was wide ranging is sufficiently evident to generate a question about its overall structure.

Some abbreviation will be useful in what follows. What I call the *basic atomic theory* comprises Democritus' views on the existence and intrinsic features of the atoms: for example, their number, shape, size, motion and variety. What I mean by Democritus' *theory of nature* are his accounts of various aspects of nature at the macroscopic level. The theory of nature thus includes his cosmogony, anatomy, account of perception and the like. A further distinction can now be set out between Democritus as a scientific and as a philosophical thinker. This is a distinction which concerns the view to be taken of Democritus' dialectical strategy in response to the arguments of Zeno and Parmenides, and which can best be made out in terms of the relation between the basic atomic theory and the theory of nature.

Two characters are to be described – the scientific Democritus and the philosophical Democritus – whose motivations, and relations to Eleatic argument, differ significantly. It need not be supposed that either one or the other of these pure types is the historical Democritus. Democritus is reported not only to have been of polymathic inclination, but also to have lived a long life. We have no idea, and there would seem no way of finding out, when Democritus developed the different strands of his thought, the order in which he wrote the works attributed to him, whether or how he revised his views and whether he had anything to say about an order in which his thought should be taken. Nevertheless the distinction between the scientific and the philosophical Democritus serves a purpose, since any particular account of presocratic atomism will tend to emphasize one of them over the other. That is not a *mere* difference of emphasis, however. Where an exegete lays the emphasis goes along with particular views taken of the nature of Democritean atoms, of the status of Democritus' views about the macroscopic world and about the relation of presocratic atomism to Eleatic thought.

The scientific Democritus is someone concerned primarily to defend a theory of nature against the threat posed by Eleatic argument. Parmenides, bolstered by Melissus and Zeno, appears as posing a fundamental challenge, stopping pre-Eleatic cosmic speculation dead in its tracks. Any post-Eleatic theory of nature needs to provide an answer to the Eleatics. Democritus' fundamental move here is the introduction of void. The justification for that move is that it rescues the macroscopic world which is the domain of the theory of nature from the Eleatic threat. The introduction of void gives rise to the basic atomic theory, which constitutes Democritus' response to the Eleatics. Once the Eleatics are answered the way is open for Democritus to offer a theory of nature, helping himself, where appropriate, to the world view provided by the basic atomic theory. In some areas the theory of nature will be practically independent of the basic atomic theory. For example, views about the properties of atoms will be in the main irrelevant to an account of the development of societies or of language. More commonly the basic atomic theory will constrain but not determine the theory of nature. Two adherents of the basic atomic theory could agree that perception is ultimately the movement of atoms, but nevertheless disagree about a great deal: for example, about whether there are atomic films which move from the perceived object to the perceiver or whether atoms produce impressions on the atoms of the intervening medium, whether any atoms leave the eye in the course of visual perception, whether the atoms that arrive at the perceiver actually enter the eye or whether they merely produce movement in the atoms of the eye, and so on. The same point could be made *inter alia* about atomist cosmology, biology and meteorology. In summary, the scientific Democritus is primarily a theorizer about nature, and it is the theory of nature that is the *raison d'être* of the basic atomic theory.

In contrast the main concern of the philosophical Democritus is not the provision of a theory of nature. The philosophical Democritus is rather someone who is impressed by forms of Eleatic – particularly Zenonian – reasoning, but who recognizes that the conclusions drawn by Eleatics are self-stultifying. The introduction of void is the minimal move required to render possible creative and serious use of Zenonian indifference arguments. The basic atomic theory is what results from the defensible use of indifference reasoning. There is then quite a different view of the significance of the theory of nature. It is not part of the justification of the basic atomic theory that it is a prerequisite for an acceptable theory of nature. The philosophical Democritus is not offering a grand unified explanatory structure, with the basic atomic theory as the roots and the theory of nature in all its variety as the branches, in which resides the primary value of the whole. The theory of nature is more loosely related to the basic atomic theory. The philosophical Democritus does have a lot to say about nature, but it merely goes along with rather than gives point to the basic atomic theory. There are therefore options for the philosophical Democritus which are not open to the scientific. One is that the philosophical Democritus should not be wholly committed to the theory of nature associated with him. Maybe the theory of nature is Democritus' illustration of what a good account of natural phenomena would be like if such an account were possible: if, however, there should for whatever reason be a conflict between the basic atomic theory and the project of providing a theory of nature then it is the latter that would have to go. Perhaps the relation of the philosophical Democritus' theory of nature to the basic atomic theory just is no more clear than is the relation of the Parmenidean cosmologies to Parmenides' way of truth.

Most accounts of presocratic atomism emphasize the scientific Democritus. This is so both in the ancient world – most influentially in the Aristotelian picture – and among contemporary commentators.[2] The philosophical Democritus is a less popular type.[3] The account that follows of presocratic atomism lays more emphasis on the philosophical Democritus than is typical. Much is made of the continuities between the basic atomic theory and Zenonian argument. The basic atomic theory is presented as a monolithic theory, generated by a single type of reasoning found also in Zeno. Democritus appears as primarily an indifference reasoner rather than as a theorizer about nature. In consequence the account that will be given of atomic indivisibility is a departure from the more usual alternatives, and a proper weight is given to aspects of the basic atomic theory, such as the claims that there are extremely large atoms, which are more commonly found an embarrassment.

It might seem in advance, however, unwise to place any great emphasis on the philosophical Democritus. What recommends the account that will be given of Democritean atomism is charity. The indifference arguments which generate, and practically constitute, the basic atomic theory are cogent and stimulating arguments, and one should so interpret a philosopher as to attribute the more cogent and plausible positions to him. Yet at first sight the philosophical Democritus seems conceptually unattractive. In comparison with the scientific type, his thought seems deficient in unity of structure and purpose.

There are a couple of points which it is relevant to make. The first is that it is important to be wary of begging the question here. An appeal to charity will recommend a preference for overall unity of structure and purpose only if they are counted conceptual virtues. Yet they should be accounted virtues only if the theories they characterize are intended as unified explanatory theories. But whether Democritus' atomism *is* intended in that way is just what is at issue between the scientific and the philosophical approaches. Hence that appeal to charity will not give reason to prefer one of those approaches to the other. Of course *consistency* is a conceptual virtue, regardless of the approach to Democritus that is emphasized. However, that will not tell in favour of one approach rather than another, since there is no suggestion that the philosophical Democritus is any more inconsistent in his views than the scientific.

That leads to the second point. If the scientific Democritus is reckoned to be more appealing because his combination of basic atomic theory and theory of nature is a reasonably *good* response to the Eleatics,[4] then it had better *be* a reasonably good response, at least in the eyes of Democritus. The more that there are obvious problems in taking the basic atomic theory to underpin a theory of nature applying to the macroscopic world, the less should charity recommend a preference for the scientific Democritus. But there are problems which seem sufficiently obvious to lead to the conclusion that considerations of charity should not straightaway recommend the scientific over the philosophical Democritus. One is emphasized by Wardy. If the basic atomic theory is offered as a means of evading Eleatic arguments against the possibility of genuine coming into and going out of existence, then macroscopic complexes of atoms cannot be genuine objects since they *would* come into and go out of existence. It is exceedingly *un*charitable to suppose that Democritus should have been sufficiently aware of the problems concerning existential change that he was motivated to construct a basic atomic theory to evade them, while at the same time being sufficiently unaware of their power not to see the danger of their applying to the macroscopic world. Another problem concerns the account that will be offered of atomic indivisibility, as based on homogeneity. As will emerge, that would be a cogent account for someone to offer who had a perceptive appreciation of the problems posed by Zenonian arguments. Yet it does not sit well with the picture of atoms colliding and hooking up with one another, and in general ever coming into contact so as to form continuous masses of atomic stuff. It is not at all clear how someone who saw the power of the account of indivisibility could fail to see that once atoms come in contact with one another they should by parity of reasoning become continuous, and so indivisible, masses of atomic stuff.

The moral to be drawn here from both these cases is the same. We do not *have* to conclude that Democritus denied the existence of macroscopic objects.[5] It would be extremely implausible to suppose that he denied that atoms come into contact, although a report that Democritus did take just that view is found in Philoponus some 900 years later. It is enough to note that there are problems in marrying the basic atomic theory to the theory of nature which are sufficiently obvious problems to remove any presumption of charity in favour of the scientific Democritus. Whether emphasis on the scientific or the philosophical Democritus is preferred, his response to Eleatic argument is going to be flawed in some respect. Neither the scientific nor the philosophical Democritus appear to have much of a reply to Zeno's paradoxes concerning motion. So both are in much the same position as regards appeals to charity, and there are not immediate and overwhelming considerations of charity ruling against an emphasis on the philosophical Democritus.

1.3 The Importance of Logical Analysis

Emphasis is laid on the philosophical Democritus because of the absolutely central importance given to indifference arguments in the basic atomic theory. It is not simply that there is a single argument structure to be identified underlying the basic atomic theory, nor that the structure is common to the Zenonian arguments to which the basic atomic theory is a response. It is also, and importantly, that the indifference arguments are plausible, stimulating arguments, and that the basic atomic theory which results is engaging and subtle. If those claims about the role of indifference arguments in Democritus' atomic theory are to be made persuasive there is no alternative but for discussion to be conducted in quite a particular way.

On the one hand, the extraction of common argument structures from presocratic and other texts requires exegetical work, on Democritus, Zeno and, to a lesser extent, Parmenides and Melissus. On the other hand, in order to generate sympathy for the arguments as *good* arguments it is necessary to engage in the sort of logical analysis of indifference arguments that was introduced in the first section of this chapter. The first task requires the second for its completion. The second task – as well as being of interest in itself – has a connection with ancient philosophy because it is required for the first. Since what is of significance is a common form of argument it is unsurprising and unavoidable that there should be some formalization of arguments. If the appeal of arguments of that form is to be brought out it is inevitable that there will be engagement with the abstract issues raised by indifference arguments. It is highly likely that discussion of those issues will involve analytic techniques that are historically very distant from presocratic philosophy. That is just what is required by reliance on the principle of charity in exegesis. One need not fear that the results of such discussions are in consequence bound to be essentially ahistorical.[6] Still, I attempt in what follows to avoid *unnecessary* reference to and reliance on formal logic. In the chapter dealing with the indifference argument form it is, to some degree, unavoidable. To a lesser extent it is helpful in the chapters that follow, in which there is some assessment of indifference arguments. Any symbols that are used are, for the sake of convenience, explained in an appendix.

In summary, what is to come is this. I will first substantiate claims about the importance of indifference reasoning in Zeno, and say something about the position of Parmenides and Melissus (chapter 2). That will lead on to consideration of the significance of indifference reasoning in atomist thought (chapter 3). Some occurrences of indifference arguments in other contexts are discussed in Chapter 4. The analytic core of the book is the semi-formal account of indifference arguments in chapter 5. Chapter 6 considers the thought that whatever force indifference arguments have is connected with questions of knowledge and justification. Chapter 7 concentrates on assessment of the Democritean indifference arguments about the properties of the atoms as a paradigm instance of non-epistemological indifference reasoning.

NOTES

1 Leibniz, *Monadology*, §32, translation as Rescher (1991).
2 A typical characterization is that of Barnes (1982), who says (p. 344) that the atomic theory of Leucippus 'was indeed a scientific one, in the old Ionian fashion; it was not a myth, nor an abstract philosophy. But its foundations, unlike the foundations of modern atomisms, were solidly philosophical.' Compare also Sorabji (1983, 350f); and the approach encapsulated in the title of Furley (1987); *The Greek Cosmologists: The Formation of the Atomic Theory* . . .
3 An extreme form of the philosophical Democritus is presented in Wardy (1988), from which I have learned a great deal.
4 For a typical example of the place of this assumption in presentations of the scientific Democritus, see Guthrie (1969, p. 389): 'Atomism is the final, *and most successful,* attempt to rescue the reality of the physical world from

the fatal effects of Eleatic logic by means of a pluralistic theory' (my emphasis).

5 Compare note 2 above. The view of Democritus in Wardy (1988) is extreme in that it is resolute about Democritus' acceptance of this conclusion. I will say more in Chapter 3.3 about the question of Democritus' ontology.

6 For a far more sustained clarification and defence of the role of the principle of charity in philosophical exegesis, see Makin (1988).

2

The Eleatics

◆

A striking consequence of the importance of indifference reasoning in presocratic atomism is the continuity revealed between atomism and the Eleatic arguments to which it responds. Before turning to Democritus some attention to his Eleatic predecessors is called for.

In *GC* 1.8 Aristotle presents atomism as a response to Eleatic thought. The story Aristotle tells is familiar. Parmenides had argued for a stultifying monism, an absence of plurality and change. While the arguments of Parmenides' poem might appear compelling, their conclusions are incredible. The challenge is then to find a way of avoiding Parmenides' arguments, and saving something approximating more closely to a world of plurality and change. Another familiar story from the beginning of Plato's *Parmenides* brings Zeno into the picture. It is tempting to make a robustly commonsense response to Parmenides. His arguments are so abstract, and his conclusions so absurd, that bewilderment is a more appropriate response than belief. Zeno's arguments are presented as redressing the balance in favour of Parmenides. Unexamined concepts of motion and plurality harbour far greater absurdities than do Parmenides' conclusions. Faced with Zeno's offensive it is no longer so easy for Parmenides' opponents to rest on the patent acceptability of the commonsense outlook. Zeno's arguments call for a defence of key concepts of plurality and motion, and so stimulate a creative response to Parmenides. Democritean atomism is one such response.

This story has been challenged at various points. Some have denied that the atomists are primarily reacting to Eleatic arguments.[1] We have already seen room for disagreement about precisely what the atomist attitude to Eleatic thought is. Others have challenged the view of Zeno

as a defender of Parmenides.[2] What follows is something of a boot-
strapping exercise. The standard view of the relation of Zeno to Parmenides will be accepted, as well as the view of Democritus as concerned
to avoid the anti-pluaralist consequences of Parmenidean and Zenonian
reasoning.[3] If a cogent and philosophically stimulating account of the
Eleatics and atomists results from those assumptions, that provides some
justification on grounds of charity for having accepted them. We will
start with Zeno. If indifference reasoning is found in Zeno one might
naturally wonder whether it is derived from Parmenides, and whether it
appears also in Melissus.

2.1 Why Zeno Needs Indifference Arguments

Before looking in any detail at Zeno's arguments against plurality, we
should start with a question. It is clear enough that Zeno aims to
generate problems from the idea that things are *divisible*. Pluralists should
be worried if he succeeds. To believe that there are pluralities is to
suppose at least that there are collections which are divisible into a
plurality of components. What is less clear is how Zeno aims to get
problems about divisibility going. In particular, should we suppose that
Zeno's arguments start from a *premiss* about divisibility, that *every*
magnitude is (by definition) divisible into magnitudes, that magnitudes
are infinitely divisible?

Here are two reasons why we should. First, there is textual evidence.
For example, in reporting an argument of Zeno's Simplicius *says* that it
proceeds by appeal to infinite divisibility,[4] and other doxographers make
similar points.[5] Second, if the infinite divisibility of magnitudes were a
premiss of Zeno's arguments, and Zeno's opponents were committed
to that premiss, then it is easy to see how the arguments would create
problems for them. Zeno would have to succeed in deriving absurdities
from the infinite divisibility of magnitudes, and that is just what he
attempts to do.

However, there are also reasons why we should not take Zeno's
arguments to start from the *premiss* that magnitudes are infinitely
divisible. First, if the infinite divisibility of magnitudes is a premiss of
the arguments, they will be powerful only against opponents who accept
that premiss. It might be that, as a matter of fact, Zeno's opponents
did so. Yet the arguments would have more weight if they appeared to

force pluralists to accept the infinite divisibility of magnitudes than if infinite divisibility were an unsupported premiss. Second, the arguments prompted a sophisticated reaction from atomists precisely because a simple denial of the infinite divisibility of magnitudes was not an option. Yet a bare rejection of infinite divisibility would be as good a reaction as any other, if infinite divisibility were an unsupported premiss of Zeno's arguments. Third, from the point of view of the standard story about the relation of Zeno and Parmenides, it would be preferable if Zeno's arguments did not raise problems for Eleatic views. There would be problems, however, if they involved a premiss which ruled out the possibility of there being an extended yet indivisible magnitude, for it seems that some Eleatics did hold just that view. According to Melissus, what-there-is is an infinite magnitude, which is one and undivided or indivisible.[6] Parmenides' position is less clear. His claim that what-there-is is like a ball or sphere might suggest that it is extended,[7] but this is contentious.[8] Still, it would be preferable so to understand Zeno's arguments as not to rule out as a possible reading of Parmenides that what-there-is is extended.

Proper weight would be given to these opposed considerations if the infinite divisibility of magnitudes were not a *premiss* of Zeno's arguments, but would seem to Zeno's opponents to follow from the premisses of the arguments. The later atomist response to Zeno would then be to avoid commitment to infinite divisibility.

Is there reason to accept that Zeno's arguments against plurality *can* be read in that way? There is some evidence that they can in the fact that the arguments Diels and Kranz collect as Zeno's B fragments do not *assume* the infinite divisibility of magnitudes. On the contrary, reference there to the infinite divisibility of magnitudes is always conditional. The position Zeno endorses is that *if* there is a plurality *then* any magnitude is divisible.

The argument of Zeno's B2 and B1 is that those who suppose there are pluralities are committed to asserting contraries. In particular, they are committed to asserting that the same things are both large and small – in fact infinitely large, and of no magnitude whatever. One limb of the argument is summarized in B2 by Simplicius. Zeno has first proved (in an argument given in B1) that[9]

[each of the many] has no magnitude, since each of the many is the same as itself and one.

That argument is often expanded with reference to partlessness, along these lines.[10] If something has magnitude it has parts. If it has parts its identity depends on the identity of those parts – it would not be too misleading to put this by saying that it is not the same as *itself* but as some collection of other things, namely its parts. Further, if something has parts it is not one, but a collection or plurality – namely, of those parts. So it would follow that if something *is* the same as itself and *is* one, then it has no parts, and so has no magnitude.

So far, so good. But there is more to the argument attributed to Zeno in B2:[11]

what has neither magnitude nor solidity nor bulk would not even exist.

Now there is a danger that the One of Parmenides or Melissus would be vulnerable to this argument. It will be the same as itself and one, and so should have no magnitude, and so should not exist. This sort of worry, no doubt, lies behind the tradition which sees Zeno as a paradox monger, making trouble for all and sundry. Simplicius sees the problem, and *says* that Zeno's purpose is to raise problems for pluralists, rather than for monists. Could that be more than wishful thinking on Simplicius' part?

Simplicius' remarks succeed in making a substantial point because Zeno's argument – that if there are many things then each thing is so small as to have no magnitude – when correctly understood, makes trouble *only* for pluralists. It does not rest on a general claim about parts, but on the principle that any plurality requires a unit, of which it is a plurality.[12] Zeno's opponents believe, on the basis of some criteria, that there are pluralities. Then they also have to suppose that there are units which are units *by the same criteria*. It may seem odd to speak of believing that there are pluralities on the basis of criteria at all. It seems rather to be straight away *obvious* that we live in a world which contains pluralities.[13] That thought should not worry Zeno. What is it, he might ask, that is so obvious? One thing that seems obvious is that the world is extended, and that in consequence it can be differentiated into at least a minimal plurality of what is over here and what is over there. If Zeno can reasonably press that thought on his opponents, he can claim that the unit they require would have to be *non-differentiated* into one part over here and one part over there, and so *non-extended*. That gives precisely the argument of B2. If you are going to introduce pluralities, you are committed to units which have no magnitude, since each is the same as itself and one, as opposed to being further differentiated into a further plurality. But units like that with no magnitude would be nothings. So since there can be no such units there can be no such pluralities.

That argument does not rest on the premiss that *whatever* is a unit has no magnitude. Hence it does not threaten the One defended by Eleatics. It rests rather on the premiss that whatever is a unit *by the pluralists' criteria of what is a plurality* has no magnitude. That is a premiss which will make trouble only for pluralists.

If the first limb of the argument of B2/B1 proceeds on the assumption that there is a plurality, we should expect the second limb – that things will be so large as to be infinite – to do so also. In that case the argument will not need the *premiss* that all magnitudes are infinitely divisible.

It is, however, less easy to see how Zeno can avoid creating problems for his supposed Eleatic allies by the argument offered in the B1 fragment:[14]

> But if it is [a plurality], it is necessary for each to have some magnitude and thickness, and for the one part of it to be away from the other. And the same argument holds about the part out in front; for that too will have magnitude and a part of it will be out in front. Indeed it is the same to say this once and to go on saying it always; for no such part of it will be last, nor will there not be one part related to another. Thus if there are many things, it is necessary that they are both small and large: so small as not to have magnitude [argued in the passage previously discussed], so large as to be unlimited [argued here].

Commentators are pulled in either of two ways. First, there is the thought that the Eleatic One is not vulnerable to this argument because it is *partless*. Alternatively it might be said that a One which was finite and extended *would* be vulnerable, and that that is what motivates Melissus' view that the One is infinite. However talk of partlessness is not helpful here.[15] Nor would Zeno's argument tell against the view that what-there-is is one, finite and extended.

The argument of B1 proceeds to its conclusion – that things are so large as to be unlimited and infinite – from the assumption that there is a plurality. If there is a plurality then some division is possible, namely the division into a plurality. The core of Zeno's argument is that once division is allowed to get going it could never be stopped. That is the point of Zeno's assertion that 'it is the same to say this once and to go on saying it always; for no such part of it will be last, nor will there not be one part related to another.' Yet no support is provided for that claim, and some support might reasonably be demanded by those attacked by Zeno.

Something supplementary is required, and it is here that the need for an indifference argument becomes apparent. We can tell the sort of conceptual resources available to those whom Zeno is attacking by seeing what is new in the response made later by Democritus and Leucippus. Their innovation was the introduction of void, in opposition to Parmenides' strictures on the inadmissibility of what-is-not. The consequence of that innovation was to evade Parmenides' charac-terization of what-there-is as *homogeneous*, as something which is all alike insofar as it is considered under the most general description as what-is, which description will apply indifferently and in the same way to whatever it is one attempts to talk about.[16] If that is the atomists' innovatory move, the pluralists Zeno is attacking will not be admitting the existence of void, and so could have the homogeneity of what-there-is foisted on them by Zeno. Given their position, a merely finite division of what-there-is would be wholly arbitrary. If what-there-is is homogeneous – if it is everywhere alike describable in the same way just as what-is – then, Zeno can allege, there could be no reason why it should only be divisible up to this point rather than up to that point. If no merely finite division of what-there-is is possible two alternatives remain. Either what-there-is is *in*divisible or it is *infinitely* divisible. Zeno's opponents are pluralists, and so will not accept the first alter-native. So they seem committed to infinite divisibility. An Eleatic monist, on the other hand, would welcome the conclusion that what-there-is is indivisible. It would be possible to hold that there is a single indivisible yet extended thing – of either finite or infinite extent – and not to be worried by the argument of Zeno's B1.

The fragment B1 does not include the compressed indifference argument, that if a magnitude is divisible and homogeneous then it is infinitely divisible. Yet that is what is needed as a premiss, rather than the claim that magnitudes are infinitely divisible. Only if it has that conditional premiss does the argument that spans B2 and B1 raise problems for Zeno's pluralist opponents while not threatening an Eleatic position. Further, if the argument of B2/B1 is read in that way the atomists make a cogent and perceptive response. Explication of the argument of B2/B1 in terms of indifference reasoning is therefore recommended on grounds of charity.

The argument of Zeno's B3 is that those who believe there is a plurality are committed to asserting that the same things are limited and unlimited:[17]

> If there are many things, it is necessary that they are just as many as they are, and neither more nor less than that. But if they are as many as they are, they will be limited.
>
> If there are many things, the things that are are unlimited; for there are always others between the things that are, and again others between those. And thus the things that are are unlimited.

This argument too involves considerations of homogeneity. The second limb of the argument rests on the thought that a plurality must be a plurality of distinct and therefore *separate* units. Grant that thought for the moment. Then the argument is fairly straightforward. A and B could only be separate if separated by something, say C. Without reference to something distinct from A and B which separates A from B, Zeno's opponents would be hard pressed to say what the difference is between being separated and not being separated. Yet if C is to separate A from B then C must itself be distinct and separated from both A and B, and so there must be something which separates C from A, and so on *ad infinitum.*

Why, however, *should* it be granted that distinct things have to be separated from one another? Zeno might more reasonably expect to push that on to his opponents as a plausible claim, if all that his opponents can appeal to are *homogeneous* things. If A and B were homogeneous and not separated from one another they would be parts of a homogeneous whole rather than distinct members of a plurality. Yet Zeno's opponents cannot happily rest with the thought that A and B are distinct though non-separated parts of a homogeneous whole, since in that case they open themselves up to the regress of B1. It will not be A and B that are the distinct things of which a plurality is composed, but *their* 'distinct' though non-separate parts; and then not those parts but *their* further parts, and so on to infinity. Zeno could at this point have drawn the consequence of B1, that in that case there will not be any genuine units which are sufficient to compose a plurality. It suits Zeno's purpose in the second limb of B3, however, to emphasize instead the consequence that this series of separators will go on to infinity. If any plurality has to be a plurality of units a plurality of homogeneous units would have *per impossibile* to be composed of units which are both distinct *and separated.*

An atomist, in contrast, need not be so worried by this argument. Having introduced void, there is heterogeneity sufficient to stop the threatened regress at the first step. What renders one atom distinct from another is that there is void in between them, that they are separated from one another by the void. What makes one atom distinct from the void between it and a nearby atom is that atoms and void are hetero-geneous.[18] There is not the same conceptual pressure to come up with something else which then *separates* an atom from the void.

Now it is all very well to suggest that Zeno's arguments need to appeal to homogeneity, and that in doing so they will import considera-tions of indifference. They would be better arguments if they did so. It is also, fortunately, possible to find attributions of indifference reasoning to Zeno.

2.2   Where Zeno Uses Indifference Arguments

The following argument against plurality occurs in a report by Simpli-cius:[19]

> For of course (1) since it is everywhere the same (2) if it is divisible it will be divisible everywhere in the same way, and not [divisible] here but not there. (3) Then suppose it to have been divided everywhere; (4) then it's clear again that nothing remains (5) but it will have vanished, and if it is put back together it will be put back together from nothings. (6) For if something does remain, it will not yet have been divided everywhere. (7) So it is obvious from these considerations too, he says, that what is will be indivisible, partless and one.

Simplicius quotes this passage from Porphyry, who attributes it to Parmenides. Yet the style of argument makes a Zenonian origin more likely. Further, attribution of the argument to Zeno enables us to provide what discussion of Zeno's B1 revealed to be required: an *argument* in support of the view that once division starts it can never be brought to an end. I will take it, then, that the argument can reasonably be attributed to Zeno.[20]

What is of particular interest about this argument is that no *premiss* concerning infinite divisibility occurs in it. The only premiss is (1), which is an explicit and non-hypothetical claim about homogeneity. The benefits of supposing that Zeno argued from such a premiss were rehearsed in the previous section. Not only would this argument not threaten Eleatic monism, but the premiss (1) is clearly paralleled by an assertion of Parmenides', that what-there-is all exists alike.[21]

There are three possible answers to the question of whether something is divisible. Something could be (i) divisible everywhere, or (ii) divisible just somewhere, while indivisible somewhere else, or (iii) divisible nowhere (that is, indivisible). The claim of (1) that what-there-is is homogeneous is intended to rule out (ii), by an indifference argument. The question Zeno is pushing is whether what-there-is is divisible: pluralists answer yes, monists answer no. If what-there-is is homogeneous, in that it is possible to describe it everywhere in the same way just as what-is, then it is impossible that it should be divisible here, while being indivisible there. Those differences would be incompatible with its being homogeneous. (2) gives the conclusion that finite divisibility, here but not there, is ruled out. The bulk of the argument is then aimed at ruling out (i), that it is divisible everywhere. If it were divisible everywhere then we could suppose it divided everywhere.[22] If it were divided everywhere then, as (4) and (5), the products of that division would be nothings. That inference is warranted by premiss (1) concerning homogeneity. Suppose something is everywhere divisible, and it is everywhere the same, insofar as it is everywhere describable as what-is. Then what results from its being divided everywhere cannot be something-that-is, since what-is can by hypothesis be divided. So what results from a division everywhere is nothing. That is taken to lead to absurdity. Whatever a thing is ultimately divided into is what it is composed out of, and what is composed out of nothings would itself be nothing. So it is impossible that a division of what is should issue in nothings. (i) is therefore ruled out, and Zeno is entitled to the conclusion that what there is is indivisible.[23]

Attention to that indifference argument allows sense to be made of another argument Simplicius mentions in the immediately preceding lines:[24]

(1) For if, he says, it were divisible let it have been divided apart, (2) and each of the parts divided apart, and this to have happened for ever (3) then it is clear, he says, that either some ultimate magnitudes will remain,

minimal and atomic, but infinite in number, (4) and then the whole will be composed of such minima, and it will be put together from an infinite number; (5) or it will vanish, and will be broken up into nothing, and put together from nothing; (6) which is absurd. (7) So it will not be divided, but will remain one.

This is a puzzling argument. The supposition of (1) and (2) is that what-there-is is divided as far as it can be. (3) and (5) are the two limbs of the dilemma that follows on that supposition. *Either* (3) atomic minimum magnitudes will remain, which will however be infinite in number; *or* (5) what remains will be nothings, presumably on the ground that they will have no magnitude. Yet those alternatives seem unfairly chosen. Why should (3) involve the thought that there are an *infinite* number of atomic minima? The more natural option would seem to be a *finite* number of atomic minima, especially since it is the claim about infinity that causes the trouble. The whole that is originally divided is plainly imagined to be finite in extent, since if it were not there would be no absurdity in the consequence that it is composed of an infinite number of magnitudes. Yet in that case it might seem obvious that a division of a finite magnitude into atomic magnitudes will be a division into a *finite* number of such magnitudes.

The argument makes sense only if we suppose that the alternative of a finite division is somewhere and somehow ruled out. One might say that it is simply assumed without argument that the division is infinite.[25] But that is a peculiar assumption to make once it is divorced from the assumption that every magnitude is by definition divisible; and that latter assumption *cannot* be supposed to feature in the argument. For if it did it would suffice to rule out the alternative given in (3), that any number of *magnitudes* remain after the division, without need for any mention of infinity.

The argument of 139.27–33 provides no grounds for ignoring the alternative of a finite division. But the indifference argument immediately following at 140.1–6, and discussed above, does: it is the homogeneity of what there is that rules out a finite division. Perhaps then the later indifference argument makes explicit what is *required* for the argument preceding it, in much the way that indifference reasoning was seen to be *required* for the arguments found in Zeno's B fragments.

Good sense can be made of the argument of 139.27–33, once it is allowed that the possibility of a merely finite division is ruled out by an indifference argument on the basis of an appeal to the homogeneity of what is to be divided. (2) specifies that the division is *complete*. We can infer quite a lot about the products of the division from that specification. They will be ultimate, minimal and atomic, since a division that is complete could hardly go further, and its products could hardly be further divisible. What is left open is whether the products of that complete division would have magnitude or not. (3) and (5) are the two alternative answers to that open question. If they do have magnitude, we have (3): ultimate, minimal and atomic magnitudes, which are infinite in number – it being assumed that the possibility of a *finite* division is ruled out on the basis of indifference reasoning. But then the fact that there are an infinite number of products of division which also have magnitude is claimed to lead to the contradiction in (4) – presumably as a consequence of the thought that any infinite number of magnitudes must sum to an infinite magnitude. Perhaps on the other hand the products of the complete division do not have magnitude, as (5) suggests. In that case the more direct implication is that they will be nothings, no doubt on the basis of Zeno's view that what has no magnitude is nothing,[26] which also leads to unacceptable consequences.

There are other reports of Zenonian arguments concerning plurality which can be better understood if supplemented by indifference reasoning.[27] That is in line with the conclusion of the previous section. Moreover we now have a report from Simplicius of a Zenonian argument in which indifference reasoning is well to the fore. But we do not have to rely on the comments of a sixth-century Neoplatonic commentator. The role of indifference reasoning in arguments against plurality suggested by Simplicius' report is in accord with the account given by Aristotle in *GC* 1.8 of the basis of Eleatic monism.

Aristotle describes this Eleatic argument against plurality:[28]

(1) And again there could not be a plurality without something to separate them. (2) And if someone thinks the universe is not continuous but consists of divided pieces in contact with each other, this is no different, they held, from saying that it is many, not one, and is void. (3) For if it is divisible everywhere, there is no unit, and therefore no many, and the whole is void. (4) If on the other hand it is divisible in one place and not another, this seems like a piece of fiction. (5) For how far is it divisible, and why is one part of the whole like this – full – and another part divided?

Aristotle has started his outline of the Eleatic position by retailing the argument that there is no motion if there is no void. The passage above follows after that. (1) gives an argument from continuity. If there is no void then the whole is continuous, and so there is nothing to differentiate the units required for a plurality, and so there is no plurality. (2) considers another model of what a plurality would consist in. Why should there not be a plurality of distinct things in contact with one another? That is just the model of plurality one might expect prior to the atomist introduction of a void. Now there is a familiar dilemma. The whole comprised of these distinct things in contact will be divisible either everywhere or just somewhere. (3) argues against divisibility everywhere: the *division* of such a whole could not be a division into the units of a plurality. (4) and (5) comprise an indifference argument against the whole's being divisible just somewhere. Since void is not admitted the whole is homogeneous, and so there is no reason why it should be divisible at some points but not at others.

So it is plausible to accept that Zeno used indifference reasoning in arguing against the existence of pluralities. The reasoning is intended to justify a move from homogeneity to indivisibility. It gains purchase because Zeno's opponents can be expected to admit that the collections they reckon to be pluralities are homogeneous. Zeno's arguments, thus understood, will not threaten Parmenides' monism. More positively than that, the connection between homogeneity and indivisibility *appears* to be anticipated in Parmenides' poem. It is worth considering now just how much Zenonian indifference reasoning owes to Parmenides.

2.3 Parmenides and Division

There is one place where indifference reasoning does appear in Parmenides. Parmenides gives the following argument against the possibility of something's being generated from what-is-not:[29]

> And what need would have driven it later rather than earlier, beginning from the nothing, to grow?

While that is clearly enough an indifference argument, it does not illustrate the sort of indifference reasoning which was required by the Zenonian arguments concerning plurality. Yet it is evidence that the indifference argument *form* is used by Parmenides. More germane to our concerns is a passage in which Parmenides concludes that there is no division, and where he seems to derive that conclusion from a claim about homogeneity:[30]

> Nor is it divided, since it all exists alike;
> nor is it more here, which would prevent it from holding together,
> and less there, but it is all full of being.
> So it is all continuous: for what is draws near to what is.

It is tempting to think that 8.22–5 contains an indifference argument from homogeneity to indivisibility, and so is a precursor of the Zenonian arguments considered above. Is that a reasonable way of taking this Parmenidean passage?

There are numerous questions which can be raised about 8.22–5, as about every other line of Parmenides' poem. Commentators disagree about the translation of the lines. Is Parmenides claiming that the subject of the discussion is *not divided* or that it is *indivisible*?[31] Does line 22b say something about the manner in which the subject of Parmenides' argument exists – that it all exists uniformly, to the same extent – or does it attribute some character to it – that it is all alike, the same, homogeneous?[32] There is disagreement about the internal structure of these four lines – as to which lines are premisses, which restatements and which conclusions. Commentators argue about the relation of these lines to the rest of the poem: it is unclear what in the preceding lines entitles Parmenides to the premisses he uses in ll.22–5, and how ll.22–5 relate to such later passages as 8.46–8. There is a basic disagreement about *what* Parmenides is trying to establish in ll.22–5: some say that he is concerned with temporal continuity, others that he has spatial continuity in mind, others that he intends continuity in a very general sense.[33] In addition to further questions specifically concerning ll.22–5, there are a host of more general relevant issues about the interpretation of Parmenides to take into account.

In consequence it is with some trepidation that one says anything at all about Parmenides. What follows is, however, fairly minimal. It is a reading of ll.22–5 on which there is some implicit appeal to indifference reasoning concerning division. The indifference arguments against the possibility of finite divisibility discussed earlier will thus be not only consistent with Parmenides' position, but a development of what is

suggested by Parmenides.[34] It should be possible to remain neutral on
at least some of the questions to which ll.22–5 give rise, and so what
I say about ll.22–5 should not be overly contentious. In what follows
I will talk of *regions* and *gaps*. If Parmenides' concern in ll.22–5 is with
temporal continuity, his conclusion is that what is thought about
contains no temporal gaps or interruptions, and that it undergoes no
changes which would mark out distinct temporal stages and differentiate
one temporal region (here) from another (there). On the other hand,
if it is spatial continuity which is at issue, these regions and gaps are
spatial: the conclusion is that what is thought about contains no gaps
at any places, and that it is no different from one place (here) to another
(there). In either case the argument proceeds along the same lines.

It appears reasonably clear that 'it all exists alike' (πᾶν ἐστιν ὁμοῖον)
is a premiss of the argument. How is Parmenides entitled to that as a
premiss? It is derived from an earlier and very basic position:[35]

> Come now, and I will tell you . . . the only ways of enquiry that are to
> be thought of. The one, that [it] is and that [it] is impossible for it not
> to be, is the path of Persuasion (for she attends upon Truth).

Parmenides' enquiry proceeds along a determinate path, from a single
starting point, that it is (8.2). A popular view of Parmenides is that he
is offering an account of whatever can be thought about or spoken of,
starting from the fact that it *can be* thought about or spoken of. What
that secures as a starting point is that whatever is thought about or
spoken of *is*, since it is impossible that one could speak or think about
what is not. It is a large question how the verb 'is' (ἐστι) should best be
understood. Is Parmenides making a point about the impossibility of
thinking about what does not exist, or the impossibility of thinking about
what has no properties, or are those two thoughts inextricably intertwined
for him? However, it is not necessary to offer an answer to that question
in order to agree that Parmenides' final account will only attribute those
characteristics to what can be thought about which can be deduced from
his starting point, that what can be thought about *is*.

So, given a single starting point, that *it is*, and given that the only
admissible characteristics of what is thought of are derived from that
single starting point by following 'the path of Persuasion (which) attends
upon Truth' (2.4), it follows that 'it all exists alike' (8.22b). The inference
here is one Parmenides is entitled to whether he is making a point

about the *manner* in which what is thought about is – that it all exists uniformly, in the same way – or making a claim about what it is like – that it is all the same everywhere. If his point is the former, it will subsequently follow from his assertion that the starting point applies in the same manner everywhere that any other characteristic which follows from that starting point applies equally everywhere, and so in consequence it exhibits no differences. If he intends rather to claim the latter he will be aiming more directly for the point that it is all alike.

What is of interest now is the move from homogeneity (22b) to being undivided (22a). ll.22–5 mainly concern an argument from 'not more here and less there' (23a, 24a) to 'it is all continuous' (25a). How does that relate to the move from homogeneity (22b) to being undivided (22a)? 'Not more here and less there' (23a, 24a) is offered as a gloss on 'homogeneous' (22b). It is a reasonable gloss because the assertions that it is not more here and less there and that it is homogeneous are equivalent. If what can be thought about is homogeneous, then it is the same everywhere and so cannot exhibit such differences as being more here and less there; on the other hand, if it is not more here and less there it does not exhibit differences and so is all the same and homogeneous. Further 'all continuous' (25a) is taken as equivalent to 'not divided'. Assuming those equivalences, the argument of ll.23–5 from 'not more here and less there' to 'all continuous' is intended to explicate the move in 1.22 from 'homogeneous' to 'not divided'.

The thought is this. If it *were* 'more here and less there' there would be differences. There would be some basic difference of *being*, the starting point 'it is' would apply more here and less there; and that would open the possibility of further derived differences in respect of characteristics which follow from the starting point 'it is'. Yet if one region is more than another there is a discontinuity marked between the region that is more and the region that is less. In that case it would not 'hold together': it would be separated into distinct regions. The alternative Parmenides gives to its being 'more here and less there' is that 'it is all full of being' (24b). Parmenides' talk of more and less will naturally suggest the comparison of what is deficient and less with what is complete and full. It is not surprising that the assertion that what can be thought of is deficient and less should be unacceptable to Parmenides, and that in consequence he should claim it to be complete and full. Talk of degrees, of more and less, involves talk of what-is-*not*. For example, an appealing explanation of A's being *less blue* than B would be that A contains more of what is *not blue* than does B; and an equally attractive way of putting the point that B cannot contain what is *not blue* is that B is all full of blue. For *blue* read *being*, and the characteristics derived from the starting point that *it is*, and one has Parmenides' line of thought. Finally (25) if something is 'all full of being' it will be continuous, and will not admit of gaps or differences.

Now if it is assumed that 'all continuous' at 1.25b restates the conclusion announced at 1.22a that makes it more likely that Parmenides is actually aiming for the conclusion that what is thought about is *not divided*, rather than the stronger conclusion that it is *indivisible*. Yet a sympathetic reader of Parmenides' reasoning might plausibly think that Parmenides should have aimed for, and would have the materials to attain, the stronger modal conclusion. That it is not divided is established by *a priori* argument, and so even the possibility that it should be divided is ruled out. Parmenides' starting point is modal, '[it] is and it is impossible for [it] not to be' (2.3); the argument of ll.22–5 is that if something were divided then it would not be full of being, and so, we might add, since that latter is *impossible* it should follow that it cannot be divided. Parmenides draws modal conclusions elsewhere in his poem. The subject of his deductions is immovable, held fixed by a strong necessity (8.29f); it is imperishable (8.3) and is not allowed to come into being or perish (8.13f); it is *unthinkable* that it should come into existence from what is not (8.7f). So reflection on Parmenides' position might well lead to the question of how one would get from homogeneity to *indivisibility*. The indifference reasoning attributed to Zeno answers just that question. That reasoning starts from a position enunciated by Parmenides; it imports the thought, to which Parmenides would presumably agree, that *infinite* divisibility is an impossibility; it is reasoning to a conclusion that Parmenides could and should have drawn. In sum, while that indifference reasoning is not to be found explicitly in ll.22–5 of Parmenides' deduction, it is not unreasonable to see it as supplementary to, and suggested by, his argument in that passage. Whether Parmenides' original aim here was to make a point about temporal continuity or not, if that passage did provide an impetus to the development of indifference reasoning in Zeno, the arguments as they were developed came to be applied to issues of spatial continuity and indivisibility.[36]

What conclusion emerges as regards Parmenides' use of indifference reasoning? While the indifference reasoning required by, and attributed to, Zeno in the previous section is not found explicitly in Parmenides, the materials for constructing such indifference arguments are to be found. The Zenonian reasoning, which is adapted by the atomists and provides an account of atomic indivisibility, can then be seen as a development of Parmenidean ways of thinking. Indifference reasoning as such is not foreign to Parmenides, but it is not explicitly used as it is in Zeno in order to prosecute an anti-pluralist case.

The heterodox conclusion that it was not a prime concern of Parmenides' to make an anti-pluralist case, that he did not argue for monism at all, should, however, be resisted.[37] For there is not for Parmenides a significant logical gap between undividedness/homogeneity and monism.[38] What does a monist require? Just that any apparent plurality of objects cannot really be taken as the discrete units of a plurality. Parmenides' discussion of homogeneity at 8.22–5 establishes just that. What-is is homogeneous in that it is a seamless whole: as Parmenides expresses it, what is draws near to what is. There could then be no grounds for picking anything out as a unit, and so no grounds for supposing that there is a plurality. It is not as if there could be gaps between units, or differentiations by which one unit is marked out from another. Now it might seem that Parmenides merely assumes that there is no logical gap between homogeneity and monism, and that assumption might well be challenged. The indifference reasoning we have been interested in is intended to meet just such a challenge, by supporting what it may be that Parmenides merely assumes. Since that reasoning can be seen as suggested by Parmenides' thought, and since it is consistent with Parmenidean views, it is reasonable to see a commitment to monism in Parmenides.

2.4 Indifference Reasoning in Melissus?

We might expect to find indifference reasoning against plurality developed also by Melissus. It is not disputed that Melissus aims for monism, and that he has a case to argue against pluralists: indifference arguments would therefore be conducive to his purposes. He asserts that what there is is homogeneous: that assertion could serve him as the premiss of an indifference argument. Some of his conclusions plainly *are* established by appeal to homogeneity: indifference reasoning would be a strong sort of reasoning to use, which would start from claims about homogeneity. He aims for a negative conclusion about division: indifference reasoning to such a conclusion should appear tempting. These expectations will not, however, survive a cursory look at Melissus' arguments. Still, Melissus is interesting, since he seems to appeal to something connected with indifference reasoning in a less obvious context.

Melissus argues for monism from a premiss about the unlimitedness of what there is:[39]

if it were not one, it would be limited by another.

For if it were [infinite] it would be one; for if it were two, the two could not be infinite, but would be limited by one another.

This rests on other arguments in Melissus for the conclusion that what there is is both temporally and spatially unlimited.[40] The argument for monism is essentially that there could not be more than one unlimited or infinite thing. This would be a fairly plausible argument, if by *infinite* Melissus meant what is *all inclusive*;[41] or equivalently if Melissus supposed that what is infinite in extent could not be of any greater extent. For in that case Melissus can avoid an obvious objection to his argument. Why should there not be one entity A which has always existed through an infinite past, and which is then replaced by another entity B which continues to exist through an infinite future; alternatively, why should there not be a line in the universe to the left of which a red thing stretches infinitely away, and to the right of which a distinct blue thing stretches infinitely.[42] In neither case, Melissus could reply, would we have *all-embracing* or *all-inclusive* entities, since in both cases the entities in question could be of greater extent. A could have existed, but does not exist, at times when B did; and the red thing imagined could have occupied, but does not occupy, places which the blue thing occupies. Hostility to *what is not* would give Melissus reason for refusing to countenance things which fail to be all embracing and all inclusive. Still, however Melissus' argument for monism goes, it is plain enough that it does not proceed *from* a premiss about homogeneity. Quite the contrary. Melissus moves from monism *to* the claim that what there is is homogeneous:[43]

Being one it is alike in every way; for if it were unlike, being plural it would no longer be one but many.

If something were not homogeneous it would vary in some respect. A difference of characteristics is sufficient to mark out different entities, and so introduce plurality. If plurality is already ruled out, what there is must be a single and homogeneous entity. Since this is not an argument *from* a claim about homogeneity, it is unsurprising that it is not an instance of indifference reasoning. Still, the conclusion Melissus comes to is precisely the premiss from which Zeno's indifference argument concerning division started.[44] Perhaps Melissus' own argument concerning division will start from the assertion of homogeneity as a premiss, to which Melissus is entitled, and will parallel the Zenonian argument. Melissus' argument proceeds quite differently, however, and makes no explicit appeal to homogeneity:[45]

> if what is has been divided, it is in motion; but it would not be in motion.

What position is Melissus arguing for here? Melissus takes it that if what there is has been divided, then it will move. Let us not concern ourselves at present with Melissus' grounds for that conditional. The fact that he accepts that conditional shows us how Melissus intends to take the supposition that something is divided. The argument mentioned earlier by which Melissus established homogeneity makes it plain that the existence of *any* variations is sufficient for the existence of a plurality. Imagine cubes of different sorts of wood crammed up against each other: that would be a heterogeneous plurality of different bits of wood. Yet Melissus would not think that those bits would move. His argument concerning motion crucially depends on the thought that motion requires something empty for the motion to be into:[46]

> Nor does it move. For it cannot give way at any point, but is full. For if there were such a thing as empty it would give way into what was empty; but since there is no such thing as empty, it has nowhere to give way.

A plurality of different bits crammed up against one another would not move. But Melissus thinks that something which has been divided *would* move. So when Melissus says that something has been divided he cannot mean simply that it is a plurality, but that it is a *divided* plurality, a plurality which has been *separated out* into bits.

In that case, though, the argument against division seems unusually weak. After all, Melissus has another argument which rules out there being *any* plurality, whether of bits which are crammed up against one another, or of bits divided and separated out from one another. What does his present argument about division add? It would be a more substantial argument if it concerned *divisibility*. For then Melissus would be reinforcing the conclusion that there is no plurality, by arguing that there is a single indivisible whole.

Unfortunately Melissus does not say that he is making a point about divisibility. Still, to later eyes it would appear that the argument could be extended along these lines. If something is divisible then no impossibility will result from supposing that it has been divided; but (Melissus thinks) if what there is has been divided, then it moves; yet motion is impossible;[47] so, what there is is not divisible. To philosophers more familiar with Aristotelian reflections on how to establish modal conclusions, that would seem on all fours with the argument Melissus actually offers.[48]

A neo-Melissan argument extended in that way is an advance over Zeno's arguments for indivisibility. For Zeno's indifference argument against divisibility needs the premiss that what there is is homogeneous, and the additional premiss that it is impossible that something should be infinitely divisible. The neo-Melissan argument needs neither of those claims. It could be applied just as well to a heterogeneous as to a homogeneous whole; and its power would not be diminished should an opponent succeed in making sense of infinite divisibility. However, if we consider the argument a little further we see that it does connect with Zenonian indifference reasoning at another point.

Why does Melissus say that if what there is has been divided then it is in motion? As we have seen it is plausible to think he supposes that what has been divided has to be separated into bits, that if the bits are separated there must be gaps between them, and that if there are gaps between them the bits could move into those gaps. Now while it is plain enough that Melissus *thinks* that the sort of division he is concerned to rule out involves a separation into bits, it is a further question whether he is *justified* in thinking that. An opponent could object that there appears to be a distinction between, for example, a large bronze cube and a lot of small bronze cubes packed into a crate and touching one another. The former is an undivided though divisible mass of bronze, while the latter is a mass of bronze both divisible and divided up, but with its bits remaining in contact. Melissus might just insist that the latter would *not* be bronze divided up, but it is unclear why an opponent should be at all impressed by mere insistence. A more substantial response by Melissus would bring in the indifference reasoning underlying Zeno's argument in his fragment B3 discussed earlier. Zeno's argument there rested on the thought that, unless there is a separator, there is no more reason to take something as a unit than as itself a further plurality; but if there are no determinate units there is no genuine plurality. Melissus could make a similar point about division. If something has been divided it must have been divided into bits; but unless the bits are separated from one another there is no more reason to take them as bits than to take them as further wholes divided into bits. In that case there would be no bits, and so no division (into bits).

Both the argument Melissus actually offers and the extended neo-Melissan argument involve the thought that, if there has been division, then there is motion. Following that thought through suggests that it would be natural to buttress Melissus' argument by appeal to indifference reasoning. Admittedly, though, that is digging below the surface and guess-work. If indifference reasoning is to be found more explicitly in Melissus, it will presumably be when he goes on to derive *other* conclusions from the assertion of homogeneity.

Homogeneity is appealed to in connection with the striking claim that what there is is not in pain. Melissus provides three different arguments for this conclusion, which is plainly important for him. First, something in pain could not exist for ever; second, something in pain would be deficient in power, relative to what was healthy. His third argument is this:[49]

> nor would it be alike if it were in pain, for it would be in pain in virtue of something's passing from it or being added to it, and it would no longer be alike.

This is a special case of a more general argument given earlier in the same passage:[50]

> And it will not lose anything nor become larger nor rearranged, nor does it suffer pain or anguish; for if it were affected by any of these it would no longer be one. For if it alters, it is necessary that what is should not be alike, but that what was earlier perishes and what is not comes into being.

The most charitable reading here is that by not-being-alike Melissus means being different over time. Imagine something that alters at an instant from being red everywhere to being blue everywhere. The sense in which it would most plausibly follow that it would be not alike is that one temporal phase of it would be different from another: it would be temporally heterogeneous.[51] Likewise, the most charitable way to take the claim that if something becomes larger it is no longer one is as the claim that since it will vary over time it will be a plurality of temporal phases. Melissus' subsequent argument then relies on connections he has made previously. Nothing can have temporal limits (B1); hence what there is is just one unlimited temporal phase (B6); hence it is temporally homogeneous (*MXG* 974a12–14, alike *in every way*); hence it does not alter, and in particular does not feel pain (B7). Indifference reasoning was not significant in those earlier arguments. Nor, then, contrary to our expectations, does it feature in the conclusions Melissus draws from the assertion that what there is is homogeneous.

It might seem that discussion of Melissus has been rather pointlessly negative. Apart from suggesting that Melissus would have been wise to use indifference reasoning to bolster his argument about division, expectations about the use of this sort of reasoning in Melissus have largely been disappointed. There is a final argument in Melissus, however, which seems to rely on considerations of indifference, and which points forward in an interesting way to the atomists.

The passage reproduced immediately above from Melissus continues in this way:[52]

Indeed, if it were to become different by a single hair in ten thousand years, it will all perish in the whole of time.

The antecedent of this conditional is a striking way of referring to an alteration as small or inconsequential as you like. If there is *any* alteration, however trivial and however rare, then eventually – in the whole of time – 'it will all perish'. What does Melissus mean by talk of 'perishing'? Melissus goes on to give an argument intended to rule out rearrangement, which rests on assimilating rearrangement to existential change. If something is rearranged one arrangement is succeeded by another, and that could as well be described as one arrangement perishing and another coming into existence. So also more generally in the case of an alteration. If A alters from being red to being blue that could as well be described as red-A perishing and blue-A coming into existence. Yet it is not quite that to which Melissus refers in this passage. Let us grant that it is true enough that if A undergoes an alteration, however trivial, then *something* perishes. In that case, though, what it is that perishes will perish completely as soon as the alteration occurs; whereas what we need to make sense of is Melissus' comment that *in the whole of time* it will *all* perish – and the implication of that remark, that as time goes on more and more parts perish. It is best to think of Melissus' point in terms of another possible way of redescribing alterations. If A alters from being red to being blue, that can also be equally well described as the perishing of A's *being red*. That would not unreasonably be thought of as the perishing of a part of A, so that if *every* property of A ceased to hold, A would have *all* perished.

If that is Melissus' thought, his claim is that if something perishes in *any* part – that is, undergoes *any* alteration – then given enough time it will perish completely – it will cease to be characterized in any way whatever. Why should Melissus believe that? If A undergoes *any* alteration, then alteration is possible. Consequently there is no reason why A should not alter in other respects too: no reason why, as it were, it should not perish in other parts. That thought is recommended by an indifference argument. Melissus has an idea of what would count as reasons why alteration would not be possible. These will be such general points as that coming-into-being is impossible, to which he adverts in his other arguments. Such general reasons do not discriminate between different alterations. Hence, so far as such reasons go, either no alterations are possible or any alteration you like is possible. But if you suppose that some alteration, however trivial, actually occurs clearly *some* alteration is possible, and so all alterations are possible.

Melissus' argument might appear to be more simple than this, and not to involve any claims about the *possibility* of alterations. Perhaps he is thinking that if something alters in one respect, then since there is no more reason for one alteration to occur than any other, it will alter in every respect, and so 'all perish' – every property F will be lost, 'perish', and be followed by being not-F. But that does not get over the force of his saying that what is guaranteed is that it will all perish *given enough time*, 'in the whole of time'. I suspect that Melissus is also tempted by the thought that if any alteration you like *can* occur eventually it *will*. There is no telling how slowly alterations will follow on one another – one could suppose as he says that only the most trivial property is lost in ten thousand years – but given enough time every property that can perish will perish.

If Melissus is to be read along anything like these lines his comment is an instance of an influential and more general principle concerning the relation of possibility and time. There is a distinction among possibilities between those that will remain possible forever and those that will at some time cease to be possible. If the human race were to survive forever it would remain forever a possibility that five babies of exactly the same weight should be born at exactly the same time; in contrast the possibility that I will learn to play the oboe will cease to be a possibility at my death. Suppose the question is raised whether there could be possibilities which are never actualized. There is an understandable temptation to be suspicious of such possibilities, since their lack of connection with the actual might seem to render them of tenuous status. There are two forms which suspicion of unactualized possibilities could take, corresponding to the two types of possibility mentioned above. The stronger form would hold that *every* possibility is actualized at some time, whether the possibility be temporally limited (like the possibility of my learning to play the oboe) or temporally unlimited (like the possibility of five babies of the same weight being born at the same time). That view has come to be known as the principle of plenitude.[53] It is the view that if something is possible now it is either actual now or will be actual. Consider something which *seems* possible now but which ceases to be possible without having been actual: for example, this freshly minted coin which it seems could show heads in its first five tosses, but which after five tosses has not done so. In that case, according to the strong principle of plenitude, it was not really possible that the coin would show heads in its first five tosses.

A weaker view will avoid that conclusion, and will admit temporally limited possibilities which are never actual. In common with the stronger principle of plenitude, this weaker principle rules out there being possibilities which remain forever, through an infinite future, mere unactualized possibilities. It does not follow from something's being possible now, however, that either it is actual or it will be actual: all that follows is that either it is actual or it will be actual or it will cease to be possible. This weaker view can be referred to as the principle of plenitude for eternal things. Consider something which is granted to remain eternally possible: this weaker principle asserts that it either is or will at some time be actual.

The stronger principle of plenitude and the weaker principle of plenitude for eternal things diverge just in the case of putative possibilities which cease to be possible before being actualized. The stronger principle denies there are any such possibilities, while the weaker principle admits them. The divergence of these two principles is not significant as regards the reasoning attributed to Melissus above. The suggestion is that Melissus is canvassing the possibility of an alteration, however trivial it may be, in order to rule out the possibility of alteration. The sort of possibility in question is the same sort of modality as the *im*possibility Melissus will come to claim for rearrangement.[54] In neither case are temporally limited changing modalities relevant. So only the weaker and more plausible principle of plenitude for eternal things is required in order to reveal the force of the intuition behind Melissus' argument: that if *any* alteration, however trivial, were to occur, all alterations would be equally possible, and so, given enough time, given a future stretching on and on, all possible alterations would at some time occur. As we shall see presently, this weaker view is both plausible and connected with atomist uses of indifference reasoning.[55]

2.5 Eleatic Indifference Reasoning

The result of the discussion of Eleatic thought is this. Some of Zeno's arguments against plurality require appeal to indifference reasoning. There are also passages in which an attribution of indifference reasoning to Zeno is more explicit. These arguments start from a Parmenidean claim about homogeneity, and they are for conclusions which are at least consistent with Parmenides' views. There is indifference reasoning in Parmenides. Since the materials from which Zeno could fashion indifference arguments against plurality are found in Parmenides, there is reason to think of Parmenides as the stimulus for this way of thinking. The arguments do not have the same importance in Melissus: because of the order in which he constructs his arguments, they would not be so useful to him. Yet considerations of indifference are operative below the surface in Melissus too. It is not that Parmenides was the first person ever to be impressed by indifference reasoning – in a later chapter we will have cause to talk about Anaximander's arguments. But what is of interest is the connection of indifference reasoning with questions about division and plurality, which is suggested by Parmenides' arguments, which is focused on by Zeno, and which reaches its fullest development in Democritus. It is to the atomic theory we should now turn.

NOTES

1   For example Sinnige (1971) prefers to see Democritus as reacting to the physical speculations of such as Anaxagoras, and providing a more economic physical theory.

2   For example, Booth (1957); Solmsen (1971); Barnes (1982, pp. 231–7).

3   The desire to rescue pluralism from Eleatic attack is common to the two characters distinguished in the previous chapter, the philosophical Democritus and the scientific Democritus. They differed, it will be recalled, not in their opposition to Eleatic monism, but in the motives for their opposition.

4   DK 29 B 2.19.

5   For example, Philoponus at *in Phys* 80.23–81.7, cited by Lee (1936, §3); Simplicius *in Phys* 139.19ff and Themistius *in Phys* 12.1–3, cited by Lee as §1.

6   That it is an infinite magnitude, DK, 30 B 3; that it is one, B 5, B 6 and possibly B 9; that it is not divided, B 10. I will say something later on the choice between 'undivided' and 'indivisible'.

7   DK 28 B 8.42ff.

8   It is denied, for example, by Coxon (1986, pp. 213–17).

9   B 2.17f, οὐδὲν ἔχει μέγεθος ἐκ τοῦ ἕκαστον τῶν πολλῶν ἑαυτῶι ταὐτὸν εἶναι καὶ ἕν.

10 Compare the argument of Melissus B9 'if, then, it were, it must be one; and being one it must not have body; but if it had solidity it would have parts, and be no longer one'.

11 B 2.6f: ὅτι οὐ μήτε μέγεθος μήτε πάχος μήτε ὄγκος μηθείς ἐστιν, οὐδ' ἂν εἴη τοῦτο Compare Aristotle *Met* 3.4 1001b7–13.

12 This form of argument is often attributed to Zeno. See Simplicius and Philoponus at DK 29 A 21, Eudemus at 29 A 16, Philoponus at *in Phys* 80.23–81.7 (Lee, §3). The same principle, that there is no plurality without a unit, appears in the arguments of the second part of Plato's *Parmenides*. At 144c it is said that there could not be a part of being which is not *one* part; see also 165e, 'But if none of them is one thing (ἕν), all of them are no thing (οὐδέν), so there is no many (πολλὰ)', and 159d. The same argument form is found in later philosophers: for example, Leibniz, *The Leibniz – Arnauld Correspondence*, trans. H. T. Manson (Manchester University

Press, Manchester, 1967), p.121, from Leibniz to Arnauld, 30 April 1687; Hume, *A Treatise of Human Nature*, 1.2.2.

13 Compare Aristotle's reaction to the Eleatics at *GC* 1.8 325a 18–23. Philoponus, *in Phys* 42.9 on (partly at DK 29 A 21), says that Zeno's opponents based their support for a plurality on its obviousness (ἐνάργεια).

14 B 1.4–12: εἰ δὲ ἔστιν, ἀνάγκη ἕκαστον μέγεθός τι ἔχειν καὶ πάχος καὶ ἀπέχειν αὐτοῦ τὸ ἕτερον ἀπὸ τοῦ ἑτέρου. καὶ περὶ τοῦ προύχοντος ὁ αὐτὸς λόγος. καὶ γὰρ ἐκεῖνο ἕξει μέγεθος καὶ προέξει αὐτοῦ τι. ὅμοιον δὴ τοῦτο ἅπαξ τε εἰπεῖν καὶ ἀεὶ λέγειν. οὐδὲν γὰρ αὐτοῦ τοιοῦτον ἔσχατον ἔσται οὔτε ἕτερον πρὸς ἕτερον οὐκ ἔσται. οὕτως εἰ πολλά ἐστιν, ἀνάγκη αὐτὰ μικρά τε εἶναι καὶ μεγάλα· μικρὰ μὲν ὥστε μὴ ἔχειν μέγεθος, μεγάλα δὲ ὥστε ἄπειρα εἶναι.

15 For a far fuller critical discussion of appeals to partlessness, see Makin (1989). Some revised material from that paper is included in this and the following chapter.

16 See Parmenides B 8.5f (it is now, all together, one, continuous, ὁμοῦ πᾶν, ἕν, συνεχές) and B 8.22 (since it all exists alike ἐπεὶ πᾶν ἐστιν ὁμοῖον).

17 B 3.5–10: εἰ πολλά ἐστιν, ἀνάγκη τοσαῦτα εἶναι ὅσα ἐστὶ καὶ οὔτε πλείονα αὐτῶν οὔτε ἐλάττονα. εἰ δὲ τοσαῦτά ἐστιν ὅσα ἐστί, πεπερασμένα ἂν εἴη. εἰ πολλά ἐστιν, ἄπειρα τὰ ὄντα ἐστίν. ἀεὶ γὰρ ἕτερα μεταξὺ τῶν ὄντων ἐστί, καὶ πάλιν ἐκείνων ἕτερα μεταξύ. καὶ οὕτως ἄπειρα τὰ ὄντα ἐστί.

18 This response is just as cogent on the more traditional understanding of void (as empty space) as it is on the interpretation of Sedley (1982), according to which void for the presocratic atomists is a negative space occupier. All the envisaged response requires is the truth of two claims: (i) there is void between atoms, and (ii) void is not homogeneous with the atomic stuff. Whether void is empty space or a negative space occupier, (i) is no more obscure than the claim that there *is* void – though that may, of course, leave it actually pretty obscure; (ii) will also be true on either interpretation, since neither empty space nor a negative space filler are homogeneous with the atomic stuff.

19 *in Phys* 140.1–6, = Lee (1936, §2): καὶ γὰρ δὴ (1) ἐπεὶ πάντηι ὅμοιόν ἐστιν, (2) εἴπερ διαιρετὸν ὑπάρχει, πάντηι ὁμοίως ἔσται διαιρετόν, ἀλλ' οὐ τῆι μέν, τῆι δὲ οὔ. (3) διηρήσθω δὴ πάντηι· (4) δῆλον οὖν πάλιν ὡς οὐδὲν ὑπομενεῖ, (5) ἀλλ' ἔσται φροῦδον, καὶ εἴπερ συστήσεται, πάλιν ἐκ τοῦ μηδενὸς συστήσεται. (6) εἰ γὰρ ὑπομενεῖ τι, οὐδέ πω γενήσεται πάντηι διηιρημένον. (7) ὥστε καὶ ἐκ τούτων φανερόν φησιν, ὡς ἀδιαίρετον τε καὶ ἀμερὲς καὶ ἓν ἔσται τὸ ὄν. The translation is mine.

20 Other commentators also attribute this argument to Zeno. See Simplicius himself at *in Phys* 140.21; Philoponus provides indirect support with the

attribution of a similar argument to Zeno at *in Phys* 80.23–81.7. Also Lee (1936, p. 22); Owen (1957, p. 48 n. 10), with weaker endorsement from Barnes (1982, pp. 246f and 619 n. 29).

21 B 8.22.

22 This is where Aristotle will later diagnose the fault of the argument. The atomist response to the Eleatics takes a different line, and so Aristotle's criticisms function as criticisms both of the Eleatics and the atomists. The status of this step is discussed in Forrester (1973).

23 In case that argument is so abstract as to be unconvincing, consider this parody. Imagine that what is water is homogeneously water, water through and through. Consider the question whether what is water is (insofar as it is water) divisible or not. If water is divisible it could not be divisible just at some places but not at others, for it is equally *water* at all places – that is the indifference argument. Nor could what is water be divisible everywhere. If it were divided everywhere, what results could not itself be water (because if it were it could be further divided), but what is homogeneously water cannot be composed out of what is not water. The remaining conclusion is that water is indivisible. That is an argument on all fours with Zeno's argument, with homogeneity in this case justified by reference to the characterization *water* rather than *being*.

24 *in Phys* 139.27–32 = Lee (1936, §2): (1) εἰ γὰρ εἴη, φησί, διαιρετόν, τετμήσθω δίχα, (2) κἄπειτα τῶν μερῶν ἑκάτερον δίχα, καὶ τούτου ἀεὶ γενομένου (3) δῆλόν φησιν, ὡς ἤτοι ὑπομενεῖ τινὰ ἔσχατα μεγέθη ἐλάχιστα καὶ ἄτομα, πλήθει δὲ ἄπειρα, (4) καὶ τὸ ὅλον ἐξ ἐλαχίστων, πλήθει δὲ ἀπείρων συστήσεται· (5) ἢ φροῦδον ἔσται καὶ εἰς οὐθὲν ἔτι διαλυθήσεται καὶ ἐκ τοῦ μηδενὸς συστήσεται· (6) ἅπερ ἄτοπα. (7) οὐκ ἄρα διαιρεθήσεται, ἀλλὰ μενεῖ ἕν. The translation is mine.

25 As Lee (1936, p. 23) suggests.

26 B2.6f and Aristotle *Met* 3.4 1001b7–13.

27 For example, the argument reported by Philoponus at *in Phys* 80.23–81.7 (Lee, §3). Philoponus remarks that the argument rests on 'the infinite divisibility of the continuum'. That is far more charitably taken as the claim that the argument has the conditional premiss, that *if* what is continuous is divisible *then* it is infinitely divisible. That premiss in its turn is most plausibly supported by indifference reasoning.

28 *GC* 1.8 325a5–12: οὐδ' αὖ πολλὰ εἶναι μὴ ὄντος τοῦ διείργοντος – τοῦτο δ'οὐδὲν διαφέρειν, εἴ τις οἴεται μὴ συνεχὲς εἶναι τὸ πᾶν ἀλλ' ἅπτεσθαι διηιρημένον, τοῦ φάναι πολλὰ καὶ μὴ ἓν εἶναι καὶ κενόν. εἰ μὲν γὰρ πάντηι διαιρετόν, οὐθὲν εἶναι ἕν, ὥστε οὐδὲ πολλά, ἀλλὰ κενὸν τὸ ὅλον· εἰ δὲ τῆι μὲν τῆι δὲ μή, πεπλασμένωι τινὶ τοῦτ' ἐοικέναι. μέχρι πόσου γάρ, καὶ διὰ τί τὸ μὲν οὕτως ἔχει τοῦ ὅλου καὶ πλῆρές ἐστι, τὸ δὲ διηιρημένον; Translation as KRS §545.

29 B 8.9f.

30 B 8.22–5: οὐδὲ διαιρετόν ἐστιν, ἐπεὶ πᾶν ἐστιν ὁμοῖον· οὐδέ τι τῆι
μᾶλλον, τό κεν εἴργοι μιν συνέχεσθαι, οὐδέ τι χειρότερον, πᾶν δ'
ἔμπλεόν ἐστιν ἐόντος. τῶι ξυνεχὲς πᾶν ἐστιν· ἐὸν γὰρ ἐόντι πελάζει. I have
slightly altered the order of the KRS translation, so as to bring it more
in line with the order of Parmenides' words, and ease reference to
individual lines. It will be necessary in what follows to give references to
Parmenides which are more fine grained than line references: 8.22a and
8.22b, for example, refer to the first and second halves respectively of
8.22.

31 KRS, Barnes (1982), Sorabji (1983, p. 130) prefer the translation *not divided;*
Tarán (1965), Mourelatos (1970), Coxon (1986) prefer *indivisible*. The KRS
translation is given in the text; however, see further below.

32 For the former adverbial alternative, Owen (1960), and compare Schofield
(1970, 116f and n. 20), and the KRS translation given; for the latter
adjectival reading, Tarán (1965), Mourelatos (1970), Barnes (1982), Coxon
(1986).

33 For example, on temporal continuity, Owen (1960), Barnes (1982), Sorabji
(1983); on spatial continuity, Schofield (1970); on a general sense of
continuity, Coxon (1986).

34 It is not too surprising then, as mentioned earlier, that the argument
reported by Simplicius *in Phys* 140.1–6 (Lee, 1936, §2), should have been
attributed by some ancient commentators to Parmenides.

35 B 2.1–4.

36 Parallels between ll.22–5 and ll.32f, 42–9 are often noted, and sometimes
taken to indicate that the former passage, unlike the latter, is concerned
with temporal matters. If that were so, then given the similarities between
the passages one might expect to find indifference reasoning implicitly in
ll.32f, 42–9 also. ll.32f, 42–9 make new points, however, even if ll.22–5
are taken to concern spatial characteristics. ll.42–9 expand on the claim
of l.32 ('it is right that what is should not be imperfect'), and explain
how the subject of Parmenides' poem is perfected: ll.42b–44a, 'it is
perfected, like the bulk of a ball well rounded on every side, equally
balanced in every direction from the centre', and l.49, 'being equal to itself
on every side, it lies uniformly within its limits'. Quite how those
explications are to be taken is a matter of controversy. It is plain enough,
however, that Parmenides could not have made his point directly following
ll.22–5. One premiss he relies on, at l.33a, that 'it is not deficient', *could*
have been fairly straightforwardly derived from ll.22–5; but there is a
further premiss, at l.42a, that 'there is a furthest limit', which follows on
the talk of bonds and limits at l.26 ('changeless within the limits of great
bonds it exists without beginning or ceasing') and ll.30b, 31 ('For strong

Necessity holds it within the bonds of a limit, which keeps it in on every side'). The idea that it is equally balanced and symmetrical, however it is to be taken, is clarified at ll.44b, 45 ('For it needs must not be somewhat more or somewhat less here or there'), and ll.46–8 provide a dilemmatic argument in support of ll.44b, 45. The two premisses of that argument are at l.46a ('neither is it non-existent', as KRS translate; οὔτε γὰρ οὐκ ἐὸν ἔστι) and l.48b ('it is all inviolate'). The premiss at l.48b is also additional to what is available at ll.22–5. So, even if ll.22–5 do establish a conclusion about spatial characteristics, ll.32f, 42–9 do not merely repeat reasoning about spatial continuity, and it should be unsurprising that the indifference reasoning implicit in ll.22–5 is not also suggested by ll.32f, 42–9.

37 See Barnes (1979), Curd (1991). Curd distinguishes material monism (that there is a single underlying stuff), numerical monism (that there is just one thing) and predicational monism (that whatever there is can admit only one predicate); she denies that Parmenides should be interpreted as a numerical monist, while allowing predicational monism.

38 On that logical gap, see Barnes (1979, pp. 10f and 12). Curd (1991) generally endorses Barnes's critical questioning as to whether the texts usually taken to reveal numerical monism in Parmenides achieve their purpose. She allows that Parmenides argues for indivisibility, homogeneity and continuity at B 8.22–5. Yet this is said to introduce not numerical but predicational monism: 'That it is of a single kind ensures the internal homogeneity of being and so its predicational monism' (Curd, 1991, p. 256). Whether or not one agrees with the thought in the body of my discussion that there is a plausible route available for Parmenides from homogeneity to numerical monism (via an argument for indivisibility), there surely does not seem to be any good inference from internal homogeneity to predicational monism. Imagine that all there is a spherical green warm solid: that will be internally homogeneous just so long as it is equally green throughout and equally warm throughout (so long as green draws near to green and warn draws near to warm, as Parmenides might put it). Yet predicational monism does not hold of it, since it admits descriptions as green and warm. On the other hand, it's hard to see what the sense would be in claiming this to be other than *numerically* one green warm thing.

39 DK 30 B 5, εἰ μὴ ἓν εἴη, περανεῖ πρὸς ἄλλο. B 6 εἰ γὰρ <ἄπειρον> εἴη, ἓν εἴη ἄν· εἰ γὰρ δύο εἴη, οὐκ ἂν δύναιτο ἄπειρα εἶναι, ἀλλ' ἔχοι ἂν πείρατα πρὸς ἄλληλα.

40 B 2, B 3, B 4.

41 Compare the view Aristotle mentions at *Phys* 3.6 206b34–207a2, and which he opposes, that the infinite is what has nothing outside it. This view

could be suggested by the final sentence of B 2 which reads: for what is not entire cannot be always, οὐ γὰρ ἀεὶ εἶναι ἀνυστόν, ὅ τι μὴ πᾶν ἔστι. That is to say, what is not entire and an all-embracing whole cannot be *always*, even if it were to stretch on and on in just one temporal direction. It is consistent too with B 4 (nothing that has both beginning and end is either eternal or unlimited, ἀρχήν τε καὶ τέλος ἔχον οὐδὲν οὔτε ἀίδιον οὔτε ἄπειρόν ἐστιν) which is just the claim that *if* something has *both* a beginning and an end *then* it is not unlimited.

42 For the temporal objection, see Simplicius on Eudemus at DK 30 B 5; for the difficulty as regards space, see pseudo Aristotle *MXG* 976a31ff.

43 DK 30 A 5, pseudo Aristotle *MXG* 974a12–14, ἓν δὲ ὂν ὅμοιον εἶναι πάντη· εἰ γὰρ ἀνόμοιον, πλείω ὄντα οὐκ ἂν ἔτι ἓν εἶναι, ἀλλὰ πολλά.

44 'It is alike in every way': compare ὅμοιον εἶναι πάντη at *MXG* 974a12, note 43 above, with the Zenonian πάντηι ὅμοιόν ἐστιν in Simplicius' report at *in Phys* 140.1, note 19 above.

45 DK 30 B 10, εἰ γὰρ διήιρηται τὸ ἐόν, κινεῖται· κινούμενον δὲ οὐκ ἂν εἴη. For KRS translation, see §547 at KRS p. 409 n. 4

46 B 7 (7), οὐδὲ κινεῖται· ὑποχωρῆσαι γὰρ οὐκ ἔχει οὐδαμῆι, ἀλλὰ πλέων ἐστίν. εἰ μὲν γὰρ κενεὸν ἦν, ὑπεχώρει ἂν εἰς τὸ κενόν· κενοῦ δὲ μὴ ἐόντος οὐκ ἔχει ὅκηι ὑποχωρήσει.

47 The *impossibility* of motion is established by Melissus' argument against motion at B 7 (7)–(10). There are three premisses: (i) if it is full it does not move (εἰ τοίνυν πλέων ἐστίν, οὐ κινεῖται); (ii) it *must* be full if there is no such thing as empty (ἀνάγκη τοίνυν πλέων εἶναι, εἰ κενὸν μὴ ἔστιν); (iii) there is no such thing as empty (κενοῦ μὴ ἐόντος).

48 So Simplicius prefaces his report of Melissus' argument by saying that Melissus shows that what there is is indivisible: at DK 30 B 10, αὐτὸς γὰρ ἀδιαίρετον τὸ ὂν δείκνοσιν.

49 B 7 (4), οὐδ' ἂν ὁμοῖον εἴη, εἰ ἀλγέοι· ἀπογινομένου γάρ τευ ἂν ἀλγέοι ἢ προσγινομένου, κοὐκ ἂν ἔτι ὁμοῖον εἴη.

50 B 7 (2), καὶ οὔτ' ἂν ἀπόλλυοι τι οὔτε μεῖζον γίνοιτο οὔτε μετακοσμέοιτο οὔτε ἀλγεῖ οὔτε ἀνιᾶται· εἰ γάρ τι τούτων πάσχοι, οὐκ ἂν ἔτι ἓν εἴη. εἰ γὰρ ἑτεροιοῦται, ἀνάγκη τὸ ἐὸν μὴ ὁμοῖον εἶναι, ἀλλὰ ἀπόλλυσθαι τὸ πρόσθεν ἐόν, τὸ δὲ οὐκ ἐὸν γίνεσθαι.

51 One way of interpreting the argument of Melissus' B 2 would suggest a different reading of 'if it alters, it is necessary that what is should not be alike'. Melissus might be arguing in B 2 *from* the lack of temporal limits *to* the lack of spatial limits, *via* an assumption that if something had temporal limits (started coming into being at some time) it would have spatial limits too (some bit of it would be the first bit to come into existence). If Melissus did think that he might also have held that if something alters it will start altering at some time, and so there will be some

bit which is the first bit to alter: in that case it would no longer be 'all alike' since the first bit to alter would be different from the other bits which had yet to alter. Anyone who argued in that way would not like the case imagined in the text, of something changing *at an instant* from being red everywhere to being blue everywhere. While that is a possible way of taking Melissus, the assumptions it involves are, to say the least, contentious. What is offered in the text is preferable, because it requires only the view that what alters is different at different times.

52 B 7 (2), εἰ τοίνυν τριχὶ μιῆι μυρίοις ἔτεσιν ἑτεροῖον γίνοιτο, ὀλεῖται πᾶν ἐν τῶι παντὶ χρόνωι.

53 The term is introduced by Lovejoy (1936), in connection with inferences 'from the assumption that no genuine potentiality of being can remain unfulfilled'.

54 B 7 (3): but neither is it possible (οὐδὲ ἀνυστόν.) for it to be rearranged.

55 Chapter 7 below.

3

The Atomists

$$\blacklozenge$$

It is with Democritus more than any other philosopher that we find indifference arguments used commonly and systematically. There are three areas of Democritean thought to which this sort of argument is relevant: the indivisibility of the atom, the variety exhibited among atoms, and epistemology. An account of how it is that atoms are indivisible, and how they differ from one another, comprises the *basic atomic theory*. It will emerge that the basic atomic theory is generated by a single type of reasoning: by repeated applications of indifference arguments. We have seen in the previous chapter the place of indifference reasoning in Eleatic thought. If the account of the basic atomic theory in the first two sections of this chapter is appealing, it will be plausible to see Democritus as seeking to make more cogent use of an Eleatic form of reasoning, in order to arrive at a less stultifying world view. That is the approach of the philosophical Democritus of the first chapter: someone not so much concerned to defend a theory of nature – an explanatory account of the commonsense world – against Eleatic attack, as aiming to get as much as possible out of indifference reasoning, while making the minimal adjustments necessary to avoid Eleatic monism.

3.1 Indifference and Indivisibility

Zenonian indifference reasoning proceeded from homogeneity to indivisibility. From the premiss that the whole of what there is is homogeneous, the conclusion is drawn that there is just one indivisible thing.

The minimal motivation for atomism is the desire to avoid monism. There are two aspects to the atomist response to the Eleatics. First, the atomists introduce a *void*. Given the existence of void, it need no longer be granted that every arbitrarily selected mass is homogeneous; there will be both the full (the atomic stuff) and the empty (the void).[1] Second, anything which contains no void will be homogeneous; hence any such thing can be shown to be indivisible by Zenonian reasoning; atoms contain no void, and so they will be indivisible in exactly the same way as Zeno showed the Eleatic One to be indivisible.

Any atom is homogeneous. As Aristotle puts it in his account of the roots of atomism in *GC* 1.8, what properly is is completely full.[2] A homogeneous atom could not be divisible everywhere, since then there could be nothing into which it is divided.[3] Nor could a homogeneous atom be divisible just somewhere, since there is no reason why it should be divisible just that far and no further. The sole remaining alternative is that a homogeneous atom is indivisible. That is the familiar indifference argument which Aristotle reports in Eleatic guise in the earlier part of *GC* 1.8.[4] On the other hand, some large-scale object which contains void will be just finitely divisible, divisible only somewhere. There *is* a reason why it is divisible just this far and no further: just this far and no further gets us to some void. So, Democritus can accept Zeno's claim that divisibility everywhere is impossible, without being forced into monism.

That is a pleasing account of Democritus' view of atoms. It is made more pleasing by two further facts. First, it displays a continuity between what Democritus says about the indivisibility of the atoms and the rest of the basic atomic theory. Second, it allows us to steer a way through long-running disputes about the way in which Democritus' atoms were indivisible. Some caution is called for, however. I have mentioned Aristotle's account of atomism in *GC* 1.8. Aristotle does not *say* there that Democritus offered this account of atomic indivisibility. Nor does he say it elsewhere. Aristotle's reticence about such a basic feature of Democritean thought might appear surprising.

It should not occasion surprise. Aristotle's prime concern in *GC* 1.8 is not with the question of atomic indivisibility, but with the account given by the atomists of action. He wants to show why someone would introduce atoms, and so take a particular view of the way in which one thing produces an effect on another. He is as interested in drawing comparisons between the atomists and Empedocles as he is in giving a comprehensive account of the thought of Leucippus and Democritus. So it need not be a matter of great concern that Aristotle does not explicitly mention the homogeneity argument in connection with the atomists in *GC* 1.8. It is, as we have seen, attributed to the Eleatics, to whom the atomists are said to make concessions. If the homogeneity account of atomic indivisibility is consistent with other Aristotelian reports concerning the origins of atomism, we should feel free to avail ourselves of its benefits.

In *Physics* 1.3 Aristotle speaks of those who adopted a very accomodating strategy in dealing with Eleatic argument:[5]

> Some gave in to both of these arguments – to the argument that all is one if what is signifies one thing, by saying that what is not exists, and to the argument from dichotomy, by positing atomic magnitudes.

Now while these people are not explicitly identified, I will take it that the atomists are intended.[6] It is not necessary here to go much into precisely how the first argument Aristotle mentions proceeds. The response that what-is-not nevertheless exists refers to the introduction of void. One way in which the introduction of void evades Eleatic arguments is by blocking the move from homogeneity to monism. Aristotle describes this response as a giving in, since it does not challenge the validity of the Eleatic argument. In this it contrasts with Aristotle's own reaction, that the Eleatic premiss is not true, and the conclusion does not follow from it anyway.[7]

The second reply Aristotle mentions focuses on atomic magnitudes, and so we would expect issues of divisibility to be well to the fore. Yet it might seem that it is not arguments concerning plurality, and *a fortiori* not indifference arguments concerning plurality, that are in view. Aristotle uses the term *dichotomy*, as the proper name of an argument sufficiently well known that he does not need even to outline it. That may suggest that attention should focus on the Zenonian argument against *motion*, which Aristotle elsewhere refers to as the Dichotomy.[8] That is the argument that no body can complete a journey, since in order to do so it would *per impossibile* first have to cross half the distance, then half the remainder, then half the remainder and so on *ad infinitum*. It is not clear, however, how the introduction of atomic magnitudes would of itself constitute an answer to that argument. If the dichotomy argument concerning motion were significant in the development of

Democritean atomism, that atomism would have to involve an atomic structure for space also, and be closer to the atomism of Diodorus Cronus.[9] That point applies regardless of the account to be given of the indivisibility *of the atom.* For even if, as seems unlikely, it were useful to suppose that Democritus intended his atoms to be partless, that would not touch the application of Zenonian dichotomy arguments concerning motion to the distances covered by atoms.[10] Zeno's argument could just as well be run to establish that no atom can move across any region since it would *per impossibile* first have to cross half that region, then half the remainder and so on *ad infinitum.* Indeed, only a spatial atomism *could* be relevant to opposing the dichotomy argument about motion. For we need be told nothing about the nature of the moving entity in order to appreciate the force of Zeno's argument against motion, and so it is hard to see how asserting that what moves is, in whatever sense, indivisible could be expected to touch the paradox. Yet there are no grounds for thinking that Democritus did offer a spatial atomism. What is more, the impression given by Aristotle in *GC* 1.8 is that the Eleatic argument about motion which worried the atomists was Melissus' argument that there could be no motion if there were no void.[11] The existence of motion is secured by denying the premiss of this argument, that there is no void, while conceding the argument's validity,[12] rather than by tackling Zeno's dichotomy argument against motion.[13]

Aristotle's use of the term *dichotomy* could as well be taken to refer to the Zenonian dividing argument against plurality reported by Simplicius and discussed in the previous chapter.[14] That argument is actually referred to in Simplicius' citation from Porphyry as one which attempts to establish monism by means of *dichotomy.* We can see clearly enough how the introduction of atomic magnitudes of itself avoids *that* argument. It makes it possible to deny Zeno's premiss that what there is is everywhere the same. If there are atomic magnitudes then some random object is not everywhere the same, and so it is not arbitrary why it should be divisible just this far and no further. Just this far and no further gets one to atomic magnitudes. If that response is to work, the atomic magnitudes must be introduced as separated from one another. If they were not separate, but were in contact, they would not constitute a cogent response to Zeno's argument, but would fall prey to the Eleatic argument reported by Aristotle at *GC* 1.8 325a6ff against the 'discrete things in contact' model of plurality, which was discussed earlier. Two putative atomic magnitudes in contact would form a homogeneous whole. Then there would be the question of why there is atomicity at just *this* point rather than some other.[15] What is introduced in response to the Zenonian argument are atomic *objects* rather than bare intervals or abstract magnitudes.[16] The account of atomic indivisibility offered earlier is an account consonant with atoms' being introduced to evade Zeno's dividing argument by blocking the assumption of homogeneity.

At *GC* 1.2 Aristotle gives a lengthy discussion of the introduction of atomic magnitudes, which is often cited as presenting Democritean reasoning.[17] That chapter does not even manifest the minimal interest shown in *GC* 1.8 in the notion of homogeneity: again one might wonder whether homogeneity could possibly be the critical notion for understanding what Democritus says about indivisibles.

The argument in *GC* 1.2 is a *reductio ad absurdum*. An absurdity is derived from an initial assumption, which in consequence is negated. The opening assumption is that there is a body with magnitude which is everywhere divisible.[18] Then a problem follows if we suppose that it is everywhere divided.[19] What could the products of such a division be? They could not be magnitudes (since *ex hypothesi* the initial magnitude has been divided across every magnitude), nor points nor nothings (since in neither case could they combine to give the original magnitude); nor could the original magnitude somehow drop away like sawdust during the division.[20] Hence the original assumption should be rejected. That gives the conclusion that there must be indivisible bodies and magnitudes.[21]

Now it would be surprising if this argument *did* tell us very much about the way in which Democritus' indivisibles are atomic. For the argument is extremely abstract. It could be run as regards the division of bare intervals, without any specification of what those intervals are: whether atoms, atoms plus adjoining regions of void, regions of void themselves, geometrical lines, or whatever. That is only to be expected, since at this stage Aristotle's interest is in a very general question: whether the primary things are indivisible magnitudes.[22] It is a further question what those things would be, if there were any: whether bodies (as the atomists claim) or planes (as Plato held).[23] While there are references to *bodies* (σώματα) throughout the argument[24] none of those references are essential to the argument, nor to Aristotle's diagnosis of it.

So all the *GC* 1.2 argument is likely to tell us about Democritus is that he thought there were indivisibles, since some contradiction would follow from supposing magnitudes to be everywhere divisible. Indeed, as it stands the argument presented in *GC* 1.2 need be no more an atomist than an Eleatic argument. The core point it rests on is the impossibility of dividing everywhere, which is urged also by the Zenonian arguments considered earlier.[25] As a result any account of atomic indivisibility which renders the atom indivisible in the same way that the Eleatic One is indivisible will be consistent with the argument presented by Aristotle in *GC* 1.2. Aristotle's presentation of atomism as a reaction to Eleatic arguments at *GC* 1.8 suggests a positive story about what the indivisibility of the Democritean atom consists in, which satisfies that condition.

An advantage of the homogeneity account of atomic indivisibility is that it provides Democritus with a cogent and engaging response to Eleatic argument. The failure of Aristotle explicitly to identify that account of atomic indivisibility should not be overly worrying. Previously I mentioned another advantage of this account, that it is substantially different from, and to be preferred to, either of the two views of atomic indivisibility which are usually offered. It is agreed on all sides that it is *impossible* that an atom be divided. Then a basic exegetical distinction can be introduced by asking about the type of impossibility that is posited. If it is impossible to divide an atom for physical reasons (say, because they are too hard, or because they are too small) then the atoms are taken to be physically indivisible. On the other hand, it might be that what prevents division are conceptual matters: for example, the atoms are partless, and it is conceptually impossible that what has no parts should be divided, since division is into parts. In that case the atoms are taken to be conceptually or theoretically indivisible.

Now there is considerable disagreement on the way in which the Democritean atom was indivisible.[26] The homogeneity account aims to steer between the more common alternatives, while at the same time accounting for a considerable amount of the evidence, which on any reckoning presents a confused picture.[27]

The homogeneity account is not to be assimilated to either physical or conceptual explanations. On the one hand, it makes reference to atomic *solidity* (that is, the absence of gaps within atoms). But given the Democritean view that there is a single type of atomic stuff,[28] a solid atom is homogeneous, and the further claim is that it can be shown by *argument* that something solid and homogeneous cannot be divided. On the other hand, while allowing that there are conceptual difficulties in supposing an atom to be divisible, there is no sympathy for the notion of partless atoms, or geometrical atomism, and no embarrassment about the variety of atomic sizes, or Democritus' seeming commitment to the existence of very large atoms. Indeed, as we shall see, the existence of very large atoms follows by the same sort of indifference reasoning as underlies the homogeneity account of atomic indivisibility. Since the homogeneity account shares something with each of the approaches more commonly offered, texts can be cited in its support which are more usually taken as the exclusive preserve of the commonly opposed accounts.

A number of doxographers refer to solidity (ναστότης) as the ground of atomic indivisibility.[29] To be solid is to be without gaps and homogeneous.[30] But that does not suggest physical indivisibility.[31] Solidity is a distinct property from hardness. To be solid is to be homogeneous, to be hard is to resist pressure. An atom which is homogeneous yet soft, no less than one homogeneous and hard, would be shown to be indivisible by a Zenonian indifference argument; there is nothing to suggest that such an atom could not be one of the atomic magnitudes required by the argument of *GC* 1.2. Democritus did, of course, think that his atoms actually were hard,[32] but that additional point can be derived from the claims that they are solid and that there is just one type of atomic stuff.[33] There are passages which cite *hardness* as a ground of indivisibility, but they should be taken as running together the notions of hardness and solidity in a way which understates the strength of Democritus' position. Proponents of a conceptual reading of Democritus make a good point in objecting that atoms which were simply too hard to be broken into pieces would not constitute any plausible reply to Zeno's arguments. As we shall see, appeal to atomic solidity or homogeneity is not vulnerable to the same objection.

Those passages which suggest that Democritean atoms have parts are also accommodated by the homogeneity account. There is no reason why an atom with parts should not be homogeneous. The point could be put more forcefully: homogeneity might most naturally be explained as a relation of similarity between parts.[34] Simplicius says explicitly that Democritus' atom had parts.[35] Other doxographers indirectly suggest the same view of Democritean atoms as having parts, in reporting that it was Diodorus who first spoke of atoms as partless.[36]

There are, however, other reports to the effect that Democritus' atoms were part*less*.[37] These can be accommodated by the homogeneity account at least as well as by any alternative. Proponents of a physical reading typically find such passages a considerable worry. Those who offer a conceptual reading should also be worried by them. Partless atoms do not seem consistent with the variety of atomic shape and size. The introduction of partless atoms does not suggest an account of atomic indivisibility that would enable us to see why the possibility of extremely large atoms should appeal to Democritus.[38] It might of course be claimed that the reports concerning large atoms are unreliable. Yet even so problems remain, since it is no easier to see why talk of atomic partlessness should be connected with the claim that the atoms are *small*, as they are by Simplicius[39] – who elsewhere, however, links smallness and *solidity* together.[40] The reports that the atoms were partless do not in themselves inspire confidence. One is due to Simplicius, who also writes to exactly the opposite effect. Another is due to Aëtius, who is one of those who speaks of very large atoms. It will not do merely to put these reports to one side, though. In order to disarm the case for partless or conceptually indivisible atoms, it is necessary first to give some explanation of how there could come to be a misattribution of partless atoms to Democritus, and second to show that appeal to homogeneity provides an account of atomic indivisibility sufficiently strong to answer Zeno.

The prime reason for partlessness entering the atomist tradition was not Eleatic reasoning, but the arguments of Aristotle in *Phys* 6 concerning partless entities. For example, there is the argument there that if any of space, time or magnitude were partless then all would have to be. Many accept that Diodorus Cronus and Epicurus were influenced by these Aristotelian arguments.[41] If Democritus was not Aristotle's target in those arguments, then it is an innovation of Epicurus' to combine two quite different types of theory: the Democritean theory and whatever theory *was* Aristotle's target in *Phys* 6.1. As Epicurean atomism came to be of greater importance, commentators and doxographers came to read the interest of that tradition in partlessness back into Democritus. Further, there is little reason to think that Democritus was Aristotle's target. Aristotle's stated aim is to show that it is impossible that something continuous should come from indivisibles. The example offered is lines and points.[42] It does not seem likely that Democritean atoms would combine to form continuous entities.[43] The example does not sound particularly Democritean, especially since at *GC* 1.2 Aristotle explicitly contrasts Democritus' theory of indivisible bodies with the Platonic theory of indivisible planes. Elsewhere[44] Aristotle says that this Platonic view would require for consistency that planes be composed of lines and lines of points, which brings us to the target of *Phys* 6.1. That target is thus more plausibly taken to be a Platonic than a Democritean theory.

That is consistent with the difficulties Aristotle raises in *de Caelo* 3.1 for the Platonic theory of the *Timaeus*.[45] Aristotle distinguishes the mathematical and physical applications of a theory which reduces bodies to planes. By parity of reasoning, planes should be reduced to lines and lines to points, and those reductions will create mathematical problems. In addition there will be distinct problems if this is taken as an account of the constitution of physical bodies. For example, since points have no weight, neither will lines nor planes, and so bodies will have no weight, which is absurd.[46] There are similar problems to be raised about density, rareness, hardness and softness. Talk of a series of reductions of planes to lines and lines to points is reminiscent of *Phys* 6.1 (which seems likely to be the reference intended by Aristotle at 299a11) rather than of the sort of objections levelled against Democritus at *GC* 1.8 325b33 on.

All this makes it likely that Aristotle's concern in *Phys* 6.1, and thus the source of the reaction which introduces partlessness into the later atomist tradition, is not Democritean atomism, but a Platonic theory. Hence it will be reasonable to discount doxographies which attribute partless atoms to Democritus. So the fact that the homogeneity account has no room for partless atoms should not tell against it.

The second requirement mentioned above was that the homogeneity story should provide Democritus with as good a reply to Zeno as does the appeal to partlessness.

As seen earlier, Zeno's B1 argument draws unacceptable consequences from the assumption that there is a plurality. So it might seem a sufficient response to that argument to point out that the atom is *not* a plurality, and that it is a unity in the very same way as Parmenides' One. The worry that underpins the conceptual account of atomic indivisibility is, of course, that if it is allowed that an atom has parts, then it *will* be a plurality, namely *of those parts*.[47]

Consider this argument:

(i) If a particular atom has parts it has infinitely many parts;

(ii) an atom cannot have infinitely many parts;

therefore

  (iii) it cannot have parts;

therefore

  (iv) it is partless.

That is an argument sufficiently familiar to worry anyone worried by Zeno's arguments in the first place. (i) could be generated by the indifference argument which underlies Zeno's B1: 'it is the same thing to say [it has parts] once and to go on saying it always, for no such part of it will be last.'[48] Both atomists and Zeno agree to (ii), on the (dubious) grounds that each part would have magnitude, and thus taken together would sum to an infinite magnitude.

  There is room for an atomist response to this argument, consistent with offering a homogeneity account of atomic indivisibility. Democritus could *deny* (i); he could then allow that (ii) is true, although given the falsity of (i) it will be irrelevant to an argument for (iv). This response would need to be bolstered with an account of why (i) should *seem* true. (i) seems true because it is supposed that the only alternative to (i) is

  (v) if a particular atom has parts it has finitely many parts,

and (v) in its turn is read as

  (vi) if that atom has parts, then for some finite number N, it has exactly N parts.

Now there is every reason to think Democritus would deny (vi). (vi) runs straight into an indifference argument: why N rather than N+1 parts? Further there is no reason to suppose Democritus holds the (Epicurean) minimum parts account which (vi) entails.[49] If a particular atom did contain just N parts, each one of those N parts would itself be partless, though it would have magnitude, since N of them together compose that atom. In that case, *if* (v) and (vi) are equivalent, and if (i) and (v) are the only alternatives available to Democritus, it will follow that denying (vi) commits him to accepting (i).

There is a way ahead for Democritus, if it could be plausible to see him as disputing the equivalence of (v) and (vi). (v) and (vi) are equivalent so long as having a finite number of parts is having a *determinate* number of parts – exactly N. Democritus could, however, be struck by an alternative way of taking (v). Something might contain a finite though indeterminate number of parts. If I say it contains N parts and you say it contains M parts then we are both correct: it does not contain determinately just N nor determinately just M. So long as the parts in question are *not* parts from which the whole is composed, that might seem a reasonable supposition. Democritus could even offer as an illustration Aristotle's raindrop example.[50] A raindrop contains however (finitely) many parts you like; given *any* finite number it will be true to say that a raindrop contains that many parts. In that case there is no determinate number of parts contained by a raindrop, no finite N such that a raindrop contains exactly N parts, neither more nor less. There is, however, a gap between saying that and saying that a raindrop contains infinitely many parts. Democritus is worried by the Zenonian thought that admitting a raindrop contains an infinite number of parts is admitting that it is infinitely large. Saying that for any finite N you like it contains N parts will not have that consequence.

This strategy should appeal to Democritus if he is impressed by the homogeneity account of atomic indivisibility. If it is reasonable to say that something contains a finite though indeterminate number of parts, those parts cannot be units from which the whole is built up. The assumption of Zeno's argument was that if there is a plurality there must be some unit which is not itself a further plurality of which it is composed. Democritus' view of an atom as a homogeneous mass of stuff is precisely the thought that there are no bits from which an atom is composed. Again the point can be illustrated by the example of a raindrop: if a raindrop were homogeneously water, water through and through, then there would be no unitary or minimal bits of water, a determinate and finite number of which constitute this raindrop.

Democritus can now replace (i) by

(vii) if a particular atom contains parts, it contains a finite though indeterminate number of parts.

(ii) is then irrelevant as part of an argument for (iv); while the corresponding

(viii) an atom cannot contain a finite though indeterminate number of parts

does not share the support that (ii) had, since it is not true that a finite though indeterminate number of parts will sum to an infinite whole.

All this may, however, seem an unrealistically subtle position to attribute to Democritus. There are two worries. The first is that it might seem as if Democritus achieved as sophisticated a position concerning continuity as Aristotle later struggled to;[51] the second is that is it now unclear why Democritus should have been impressed by the argument for atomic magnitudes mentioned earlier, which Aristotle criticizes in *GC* 1.2. 315a15–317a2.

Neither worry is conclusive. The position offered to Democritus is substantially less sophisticated than that achieved by Aristotle. It is not the view that the atom contains an infinite number of parts of ever-decreasing magnitude. Nor is it really a stable or complete view, since something would need to be said, in completion of the position, about the *status* of parts in the atom. An answer to that question would be on the way to the notion of a potential infinity of parts, and that would be a substantial move towards allowing that what is continuous is infinitely divisible. The view offered here to Democritus, however, is not that a continuum is infinitely divisible. For that reason, as we shall see, Democritus is still impressed by the argument reported at *GC* 1.2. The view offered is rather a hybrid, which combines the conviction that infinite divisibility would be problematic with the thought that an atom is not *composed out of* parts. By allowing that there are parts of an atom, while denying that they are parts which stand to the atom as atoms stand to macroscopic compound objects, the view seeks to avoid Zeno's B1 argument, since the atom is not seen as a plurality compounded out of parts.

Now, however, the second worry looms, concerning the argument of *GC* 1.2. According to that argument, atomists, in common with Eleatics, saw difficulties in allowing that a magnitude could be everywhere divisible. But, if Democritus allows that there are an indefinite number of parts in an atom, that suggests that a part can be picked out anywhere you like, and surely picking out a part is a sort of dividing off of parts from one another. Again this is not powerful. *GC* 1.2 concerns *dividing*, and it is of course not Democritus' view that an atom can be *divided* into as many parts as you like. It cannot be divided at all, since if it could it could be divided everywhere (since it is homogeneous), and that is impossible. That is just the argument of *GC* 1.2, which Democritus endorses.

Trouble seems to arise because an atom's having parts is assimilated to parts being picked out in an atom, and then the latter is assimilated to an atom's being divided *in thought* into those parts. While talk of picking out parts is figurative, the problem could be put more concretely in terms of the variety of atomic sizes. Imagine some atom A. It will follow by the sort of indifference argument which Democritus uses that there should not be *any* size such that there are no atoms less than that size, since there is no reason why one size rather than another should be such a size. Each of the atoms smaller than A will be the same size as some part of A. If I imagine each of those parts being picked out in A – say, by one of these smaller atoms standing in front of different parts of A – then I am imagining a division of A *ad infinitum*. It looks as if Democritus should see no problem in that. On the other hand, if Democritus endorses the argument of *GC* 1.2, he should think it impossible.

What should really worry Democritus, given that he is as hostile as Zeno to infinite divisibility, is the thought of an infinite number of atoms of different sizes all standing together within the bounds of A. Perhaps Democritus would just have insisted that that would not be an infinite *division* of A. But that will not help us much. There is an obvious further point. Division to one side, if Democritus can make sense of an infinite number of non-overlapping atoms of different shapes standing within a finite area, he should not be worried about infinite divisibility: but he *is* worried about infinite divisibility. Perhaps Democritus did not realize the fruitfulness of his own position. Perhaps he did not think that the claim that there are atoms smaller than any size you mention (established by an indifference argument) was equivalent to the claim that an infinite number of non-overlapping atoms of different sizes could be fitted within the spatial boundaries of an atom A (which invites consideration of an infinite number of distinct atomic sizes constructed in Zenonian fashion, each half as large as the one before).[52]

We should not lose sight of what is at issue here. Whatever we say about Democritus' account of atomic indivisibility there will be some inconsistencies. Atoms which are merely hard do not seem to offer any response to Zeno, and are inconsistent with one set of doxographies.

Partless atoms do not seem consistent with varieties of shape and size, and do not fit with another set of doxographies. The claim here is that the introduction of atoms whose indivisibility follows by argument from their homogeneity involves fewer inconsistencies, and gives Democritus a more interesting and acceptable view than the alternatives.[53]

3.2 Indifference and Variety

A further advantage of the homogeneity account of atomic indivisibility is that it renders indivisibility independent of questions of magnitude. That is pleasing from the point of view of the attempt to accommodate evidence about the variety found in Democritean atoms. More positively the same sort of argument that underpins the account of atomic indivisibility will also generate conclusions about atomic variety.

Simplicius reports that the atomists used an indifference argument in connection with the variety of atomic shapes:[54]

Leucippus ... held ... that the number of shapes in the elements was infinite because nothing is rather thus than thus ... [Leucippus and Democritus] say that the number of shapes in the atoms is infinite because nothing is rather thus than thus.

An argument of the same form, for the conclusion that there are an infinite number of worlds, is reported by Philoponus:[55]

Democritus also holds that there are infinite worlds, holding that the void is infinite; for why would this part of the void be filled by a world, but that part not? So, if there is a world in one part of the void, so too in all the void. So, since the void is infinite, worlds will be infinite too.

The same argument form will generate many of the basic features of the atomic theory. That there should be an infinite void is recommended on these grounds: why should it stop here rather than there? The infinite number of atoms will follow by the same reasoning: if there were a limited number, why should there be this many rather than more or less? This far we are on safe exegetical ground.

Use of indifference arguments in those contexts creates a presupposition that they would also be applicable in cases which are sufficiently similar. Hence, it would be hard to see why Democritus should not also argue that there will be an infinite variety of *sizes* in the atoms: that there will be no least and no greatest atomic size, because there is no reason why one size rather than another should be the least, and no reason why any size should be the greatest. Here, however, the issue is not so clear. There is evidence that Democritus did hold just that view. Diogenes Laertius is explicit that 'the atoms are infinite in size and number'.[56] According to Dionysius, 'Democritus held that some atoms are very large'.[57] Aëtius reports that 'Democritus held that it is possible for there to be an atom the size of the cosmos'.[58] If anything a claim about *possibility* seems somewhat understated: one should expect that there *will* be an atom as big as the cosmos, and that there should be *no* upper bound on actual atomic size. Epicurus' later emphasis that atoms must be imperceptibly small, so that in consequence not every size is instantiated in the atoms, reads most naturally as setting up an explicit contrast with Democritus.[59]

On the other hand, some commentators say that the atoms are all very small. In some cases that is offered as a ground of the indivisibility of atoms.[60] Even if we ignore that point, others mention the smallness of atoms in other connections. At *GC* 1.8 325a30 Aristotle says that the reason the atoms are invisible is that they are so small, and the claim that they are small is repeated in his lost work on Democritus.[61]

If disagreement between doxographers were all there was to the matter we might well prefer the testimony of Aristotle, and others who follow him, to that of Diogenes, Dionysius and Aëtius, none of whom are particularly reliable. Aëtius, for example, elsewhere contradicts himself, and says that the atoms are partless. But in rejecting their testimony we would have to attribute some considerable blindness to Democritus, in supposing that he did not notice that arguments he did use would justify claims about large atoms. Since Democritus comes out a better philosopher if Diogenes, Dionysius and Aëtius are trusted here, charity requires that we should rather try to explain why Aristotle could have said that all atoms are small when in fact they are not.[62]

In *GC* 1.8 325a24f Aristotle contrasts the atomists favourably with the Eleatics as offering a theory which is consonant with perception, rather than being unreasonably seduced by contentious argument. However, one can imagine that it might be objected to Aristotle that the elements the atomists introduce are not accessible to perception, and that they give an ontology which sounds almost as odd as that of the Eleatics. *Any* explanation from within the atomic theory of why the atoms are not perceived will enable Aristotle to maintain his contrast between atomists and Eleatics. Aristotle offers the explanation that all the atoms are very small. That will suffice for his purpose, which is to show that the atomists are concerned with consistency with perception. The account Aristotle gives in both *GC* 1.8 and the fragment from the lost *On Democritus* is of the scientific Democritus. Aristotle is interested in the atomic theory primarily as an account of change in the perceptible world, and it is a matter of experience that no atoms relevant to the explanation of such changes are very large. They must all at least be smaller than the finest dust into which we can grind the macroscopic objects we come upon. There are other explanations which an atomist could provide of our not finding individual atoms in experience. Since vision involves atomic complexes being given off by what is perceived, a single atom, of whatever size, could not be perceived. Alternatively, since larger atoms will tend during the formation of worlds towards the centre of atomic whirls, it is unsurprising that they will not be perceptually accessible to beings living on the surfaces of those worlds. Since, then, we can see why Aristotle said what he said, while allowing that there can be large atoms, and rendering that consistent with atoms being perceptually inaccessible to us, charity recommends that we should take the attributions of large atoms to Democritus seriously.

Indifference arguments for an infinite variety of shapes and sizes in the atoms apply also to worlds, and give the conclusion that worlds will come in as many various shapes and sizes as are consistent with other principles of the atomic theory. There will be reasons why there are no worlds shaped like snakes, concerning the behaviour of atoms in the whirl in which worlds are formed.[63] But if atoms, due to the action of the whirl, form tambourine- shaped worlds, then there is no reason why the variety of these worlds should be limited to those of one radius rather than another.[64] Given such an infinite array of worlds, there seems no reason why there should be just one like this rather than more than one. Democritus draws that conclusion: there will be other worlds just like this one.[65]

Once set in train this sort of indifference argument will tend to spread. How many worlds just like this will there be? Presumably an infinite number, since there seems no reason why there should be this many rather than that many.[66] If there are an infinite number of atoms, how many atoms of some particular size will there be? Again, an infinite number. That is just the conclusion one should draw, although some ancient commentators saw it as a source of difficulty for Democritus. Philoponus pointed out as a criticism that there would have to be *more of an infinity* of atoms than of atomic shapes,[67] following Aristotle in his hostility to the idea of one actual infinity including other actual infinities.[68]

Quite how these indifference arguments are to be most charitably interpreted is a matter for a later chapter. The point to note here, with some admiration, is that Democritus seems to have been fully aware of the power of the argument form, and to have embraced, rather than been worried by, conclusions which to many of his successors seemed either ridiculous or incoherent. That is as we would expect of a philosopher concerned to derive as much as possible from indifference reasoning.

3.3   Indifference and Epistemology

Indifference arguments are connected not only with Democritus' atomist ontology, but also with what he says about our knowledge of the world. In *Met* 4.5 Aristotle discusses the view that all appearances are true. One motivation for that view is the thought that perceptions which are apparently of the same thing vary between different sorts of perceiver (humans and other animals perceive the same world differently), and also vary between perceivers in different states (the healthy and the ill taste the same wine as different, the mad hear voices where the sane hear nothing). Among those who considered this, according to Aristotle, was Democritus:[69]

> Which, then, of these sense perceptions are true or false is unclear, for these are no more true than those, but of equal standing (ποῖα οὖν τούτων ἀληθῆ ἢ ψευδῆ, ἄδηλον. οὐθὲν γὰρ μᾶλλον τάδε ἢ τάδε ἀληθῆ, ἀλλ' ὁμοίως). This is why Democritus, at any rate, says that either nothing is true, or it is unclear to us.

This small indifference argument is very fruitful. Discussion of it will take us quite a long way into Democritus' account of what our senses can tell us about the world. The argument as Aristotle gives it must be somewhat compressed. It cannot really be a *premiss* of the argument that the one set of perceptions is *no more true* than the other. That would contradict the second disjunct of the conclusion which Aristotle says Democritus drew, since what is unclear to us is *which* of the opposed perceptions is true. Whichever is (non evidently) true is more true than the other. What the indifference premiss is about is not the truth of perceptions, but our inability to adjudicate between conflicting perceptions.

Given conflicting perceptions, there is no more reason to endorse one as true than the other.[70] There are two possible conclusions which could be drawn from that. One is that we should endorse all the conflicting perceptions as true, the other is that we should endorse none. That is not the disjunction which Aristotle mentions. The first alternative gives Protagoras' strategy, in relativizing perceptions and endorsing each for the perceiver whose perception it is. Democritus is said to have offered arguments against Protagoras, and his response is just the opposite of Protagoras'.[71] Democritus concludes that we should not endorse *any* of the conflicting perceptions as true.

A further question now arises. Given that we should not *endorse* any perception as true, what follows about whether any of the perceptions *are* true? Again there are two possibilities, each consistent with our refraining from endorsing any of the conflicting perceptions. One possibility is that none of them are true, the other is that some are true, but that it is not clear to us which the true ones are. That is the disjunctive conclusion which Aristotle gives.

It is possible to give quite a deflationary account of why a disjunctive conclusion is attributed to Democritus. Democritus might have intended only to register the fact that a conclusion about what is true could not *follow* from an indifference premiss about what we have reason to endorse. That would be a perfectly correct point to make. If two people who appear equally trustworthy give different reports about who won the vote in Parliament then I have no more reason to endorse the one report than the other, but plainly I am in no position to conclude that both their reports are false. However, if Democritus were merely registering an intrinsic limitation of this type of indifference argument, it is hard to see why he would use the argument at all. For it would not be a type of argument which served him well in establishing the conclusion he would actually *want* about our perceptions (that none are true); and, what is more, he would *know* that it did not serve him well, since otherwise he could hardly have registered its limitations. Charity tells against attributing to someone an argument which they know to be wanting, and which fails to give the conclusion for which they are supposed to be arguing.

It would be more charitable to take it that each disjunct gives part of what Democritus wants to say about our perceptions. It might be that he thinks that in one sort of case none of our perceptions are true, while in another there can be true perceptions although we cannot know which perceptions they are. In both cases Democritus would be pessimistic about the possibility of our perceptions providing knowledge. In the first case, though, his pessimism would have what we might (anachronistically) call a metaphysical basis: there is something about the way the world is and the way we are that makes it impossible for perceptions to be true. In the second sort of case his pessimism is epistemological: our senses can tell us truths, although we do not recognize when they are doing so.

It is natural to read some ancient sources as saying that the first sort of case was the only sort admitted by Democritus, and to suppose that Democritus' scepticism was metaphysically based. For example, Sextus reports Democritus as holding that we are separated from reality,[72] and that in reality we do not grasp what sort of thing each thing is.[73] Sextus says that according to Democritus no perceptibles really exist.[74] Elsewhere Sextus says that Democritus abolishes all the phenomena, and according to Aëtius Democritus held that all perceptions are false.[75] Diogenes quotes a remark of Democritus that in reality we know nothing, since truth is in the depths.[76] According to Cicero, Democritus denied that truth existed, and said that the senses were full of darkness.[77] On the other hand, this impression, that our senses cannot deliver truths, will be misleading, if Democritus' view turns out to be that, while there can be cases in which perceptions are true, we nevertheless will not recognize them. In that case Democritus' view would be more accurately stated as being that our senses cannot deliver knowledge, rather than that they cannot provide truths. While that account of the atomist position would not augur any greater Democritean confidence in the senses, the significance of it will become clear later.

How we interpret Democritus' position as regards the senses goes along with the way we understand a distinction he draws between what is in reality (what is ἐτεῆι) and what is conventional (what is νόμωι). Different sources report this distinction in slightly different forms, but the following two citations include all the examples given on the side of convention:

> By convention sweet, by convention bitter, by convention hot, by convention cold, by convention colour; but in reality atoms and void.[78]

> by convention' colour, by convention sweet, by convention combination but in reality atoms and void.[79]

It is unsurprising that the question of Democritus' position as regards the senses should be closely bound up with the question of how this distinction is to be understood. To say of some perception that it is true is just to say that things really are as that perception presents them as being. If perception can give no access to real features of the world, can tell nothing about what is in reality, then perception will be unable to deliver truths. Indeed Sextus quotes the distinction precisely in order to support that view of Democritus:[80]

> Democritus in some places abolishes what appears to the senses, and says that none of them appears in truth (κατ' ἀλήθειαν) but only in opinion (κατὰ δόξαν), the truth in what there is being atoms and void. For, he says 'by convention sweet...'. That is to say, sensibles are taken conventionally and believed to exist, while in truth they do not, but only atoms and void do.

Most of the further remarks which Sextus goes on immediately to quote from Democritus concerning the status of perception involve use of the terms 'real' and 'in reality'. We are separated *from reality*;[81] *in reality* we know nothing;[82] to know *in reality* what each thing is in character is baffling;[83] *in reality* we do not grasp what sort of thing each thing is.[84] If perception *does* sometimes present real features of objects, perception *will* deliver truths. Nevertheless, if we do not recognize those perceptions which deliver truths, we will not know anything. That position is *consistent* with the passages quoted by Sextus: in reality we *know* nothing, it is impossible to *know* what sort of thing each thing is in reality, in reality we do not *grasp* what sort of thing each thing is.[85] It is a further question whether there are any positive grounds for attributing that position to Democritus.

The examples which illustrate Democritus' distinction between the real and the conventional are interestingly incomplete. On the conventional side are sensible properties which characterize only compound objects (colour, hot, sweet, etc.), along with the property of being a compound object. On the real side are not properties at all, but atoms and void. There are two other types of property, which are not mentioned, and whose status as real or conventional may be less clear.

First, a property such as being sticky or being fluid. These properties are not instantiated at the atomic level. No individual atom could be sticky or fluid. So one might group being fluid along with being hot and being bitter, as a conventional property. On the other hand, being fluid is a very different sort of property from being hot or being bitter. Whether or not some compound mass is fluid depends on the nature of the atoms composing it, and their relation to one another.[86] There is no reason to suppose that whether some mass is fluid depends on how it appears to an *observer*. Yet a number of commentators, ancient and modern, take it that what is characteristic of conventional properties is that they are *mind dependent*.[87] If that approach impresses, the temptation will be to place such properties as being fluid on the real side of the distinction.

This first sort of example might not seem, on reflection, overly perplexing. The fact that properties such as fluidity could not characterize atoms will weigh heavily. Following Plutarch's lead one could take compounds themselves as of conventional status, and conclude that properties which could only characterize the conventional are *ipso facto* conventional.[88]

The second sort of property which does not feature on the lists of what is real and conventional is what is found at both the atomic and the compound level: for example, being spherical or being shaped. There are a couple of reasons to think of being spherical as a real property of compound objects, such as bronze globes. One is that a bronze globe's being spherical is a matter of the spatial configuration of its atoms relative to one another, and not a matter of how those atoms are related to anything else, including an observer. If something is spherical it would be spherical whether or not other atoms existed. Another reason concerns the thought that real properties are those which are more explanatorily significant. Democritus appears to have had sympathy for that thought. Some reports have him citing the behaviour of compound objects as a model for occurrences at the atomic level, and the sort of behaviour at the compound level which is cited – of seeds in sieves and pebbles on the beach – would be explained in terms of the shape and size of the compound bodies concerned.[89] On the other hand, the thought that every compound entity is itself conventional is some reason to take the sphericity of a bronze globe as a conventional property. One point is that from an atomist perspective the bronze globe will be not properly *spherical*, but some other irregular shape, composed as it is of atoms. That is not what is important here, however. For since every shape is instantiated at the atomic level, if the globe has *any* shape at all there will be some shape found at both the atomic and the compound level. The important point is rather that the globe will not have any shape since there is not genuinely a globe to *have* a shape: there is instead some void along with an ever-shifting plurality of individual atoms, more or less loosely connected with one another.

There is then some unclarity about the status of properties which are not found on lists of the real and the conventional. Now we do not know how to take the fact that only a limited range of properties are explicitly cited in connection with the distinction. On the one hand, it might be that Democritus could just as well have said 'by convention round, by convention fast, by convention three cubits long', but that he just did not happen to do so; or perhaps he did so elsewhere, and no quotation has survived. It is equally possible that Democritus' non-inclusion of properties such as round, fast and three cubits long is deliberate and significant. There is one other possibility that is unattractive, just because it is so uncharitable. That is that Democritus was neither aware of nor interested in the fact that it is unclear how the distinction between the real and the conventional is to be applied. Since that is such an unattractive suggestion, it is important to clarify Democritus' distinction between the real and the conventional.

How should the status of a property such as sphericity be decided? First it is necessary to be clear on what Democritus' purpose was in drawing the distinction between the real and the conventional. The dichotomy between nature (φύσις) and convention (νόμος) was common, and various philosophical positions could be and were cast in terms of it. Yet we have very little idea what Democritus' purpose was in applying the distinction in connection with the atomic theory. Those ancient writers who cite the distinction invariably cite pretty much the same set of examples. We do not know how accurately that reproduces Democritus' own words. Nor do we know the original context of the remark about the real and the conventional in Democritus. We have no idea whether Democritus said other things about the distinction, and whether he offered other examples to illustrate it. One might, however, reasonably think that it would be surprising if a writer as prolific as Democritus seems to have been said nothing else about this distinction.[90] Ancient writers who cite Democritus' use of the distinction generally do so for a purpose of their own, to illustrate a point about the lowly status ascribed to 'perceptibles'. We cannot just assume that that was Democritus' purpose, nor that the distinction between the real and the conventional occurred in connection with other remarks about knowledge such as Sextus quotes at *M* 7.135–140. The connection of all those remarks together is intended to further Sextus' own purpose, which is to present the view of an earlier philosopher on the question Sextus is concerned with, that of the criterion of truth.[91]

A suggestion about the purpose of the real/conventional distinction is this. Recall the type described in chapter 1 as the philosophical Democritus, someone impressed by and aiming to make more cogent use of Eleatic forms of (indifference) reasoning. The basic atomic theory – the metaphysics, to use a later term – of the philosophical Democritus is as much a revisionary theory as the Eleatic outlook, and presents as much of a challenge to pretheoretical views of the world. One way in which the philosophical Democritus could offer something more cogent than the Eleatics would be to say something more detailed and substantial about how the claims that are to be revised (non-atomist claims) fare when looked at from the revisionary standpoint (the standpoint of the atomic theory). To do that would be an advance. Zeno so far as we know said nothing about how to deal with unreflective thought. Melissus and Parmenides attacked and condemned as false the common man's outlook, but went no further than that.[92]

Now saying something more detailed about how non-atomist claims should be treated by the atomic theory involves doing three things. It involves, first, providing a way of translating pretheoretical claims into an atomistically respectable form; second, having a view on what is required for those atomistically respectable forms to be true or false; third, adjudicating on whether some particular claim which has been rendered atomistically respectable *is* true or false. If Democritus could do all those things, he would have quite a sophisticated way of dealing with the revisions of world view required by the basic atomic theory.

The distinction between the real and the conventional is a contribution to the first stage of this project. I will illustrate with an uncontentious example: the claim that this olive is green. How does a claim like that look from an atomist perspective? First it is to be put in a way which is atomistically respectable: this olive is conventionally green. Then something is to be said about what has to obtain for the olive to be *conventionally* green: for example, that, given the way most perceivers are constituted, the common human agreement about this olive is that it is green.[93] Finally, it is to be decided whether the olive *is* conventionally green: presumably, given the way human perceivers actually are, the decision is that it is.[94] The upshot is that, from the atomist perspective, the claim that this olive is green can be endorsed so long as it is taken as the claim that it is conventionally green. To be able to take that position is an advance on simply rejecting the pretheoretical claim outright.

We can now return to the question of how to place certain properties on the real/conventional divide, which do not appear in passages presenting that distinction. There is indecision about that question because there are two possible ways of extending the real/conventional distinction, and those two possible extensions correspond to two possible ways of reformulating non-atomist claims from an atomist perspective.

One way of generalizing Democritus' distinction between the real and the conventional is this. It is not properties *simpliciter* that are real or conventional. The more basic notion is of a type of entity having a property really or conventionally. In summary form we have:

(1) An object is conventional if and only if it is a compound of atoms.
(2) An object has a property conventionally if and only if the object which has that property is conventional.
(3) An object has a property really if and only if the object which has the property is an atom or some void.
(4) A property is conventional if and only if anything which has the property has it conventionally.
(5) A property is real if and only if anything which has the property has it really.
(6) A property is neutral if and only if it is neither conventional nor real.

According to (1)–(6) the distinction between the real and the conventional is primarily a distinction between the fundamental and the compound. For the sake of brevity in what follows I will refer to (1)–(6) as FUND (for *fundamental*).

The use of *object* is non-committal, meaning just what can be described in some way. It may sound odd in (3) to speak of some void as an object, but to do so is simply a way of expressing the point that one could say of some void that it is empty, or that it is completely yielding.

(1) and (2) explain an object's having a property conventionally in terms of the status of the object which has that property. Take a non-atomist claim that an object has some property: for example, that this olive is green. What (2) recommends is that, in order to get an atomistically respectable reading of that claim, one should see whether the object said to be green is a conventional object; that is, whether it is a compound of atoms. In this case it is: the non-atomist claim goes over into the claim that the olive is conventionally green.

The passages cited earlier which give examples of the real/conventional distinction present an incomplete picture. The examples most usually given on the side of convention – sweet, hot, colour, and so on – are of conventional properties, as defined by (4). In giving combination as an example Plutarch brings (1) into view. Shapes and sizes will be neutral properties. Olives are merely conventionally oval, while some atoms are really oval. It is a fine question whether any properties are real.[95]

FUND is one possible way of generalizing the real/conventional distinction. Another possible extension reflects the temptation to see such properties as the shape of a bronze globe as real rather than conventional. This reading would make the distinction primarily one between the intrinsic and the relational. In place of FUND, consider INT (for *intrinsic*):

(7) An object is conventional if and only if it exists only in virtue of its relations to other objects.

(8) An object has a property conventionally if and only if the object which has that property could have it only in virtue of its relations to some other objects.

(9) An object has a property really if and only if the object which has that property has it independently of its relations to other objects.

(10) A property is conventional if and only if anything which has the property has it conventionally (= (4) above).

(11) A property is real if and only if anything which has that property has it really (= (5) above).

(12) A property is neutral if and only if it is neither conventional nor real (= (6) above).

(10)–(12) are the same as (4)–(6) above. The same properties will be conventional on this extension as on the previous one. Colours, for example, will only ever be possessed conventionally according to (8), since Democritus thinks of these as found only at the level of the compound, and as the result of an interaction between some feature of a perceived object and a perceiver.[96] So colour will be a conventional property on either extension. Shapes and sizes will count as real properties by the lights of INT, whereas from the point of view of FUND they were neutral.

Consider three claims with which an atomist will want to deal, and contrast how they fare on each of the accounts offered:

(a) this olive is green
(b) this olive is oval
(c) this olive is an indivisible unity.

On either account (a) will be reformulated as 'this olive is conventionally green'. From the atomist perspective an olive is a compound of atoms, and it has whatever colour it does in virtue of being related to perceivers of a certain constitution: it would be true that this olive is conventionally green so long as perceivers were so constituted that there was general agreement that this olive is green. Hence it is true from an atomist perspective that this olive is green, so long as that is understood as the claim that it is *conventionally* green.

How (b) and (c) are reformulated depends on which account is preferred. Since this olive is a compound of atoms, FUND will recommend reformulating (b) and (c) as 'this olive is conventionally oval' and 'this olive is conventionally an indivisible unity'. Whether those reformulated claims are true from an atomist standpoint depends on what the general agreement of perceivers and inquirers is. No doubt, from an atomist perspective, 'this olive is conventionally oval' will turn out true, 'this olive is conventionally an indivisible unity' false.

INT will diverge from FUND in its treatment of (b) and (c). Something is not oval or an indivisible unity in virtue of its relations to other objects, but in virtue of the relations which hold between the atoms from which it is compounded. Hence (b) and (c) will be rephrased as 'this olive is really oval' and 'this olive is really an indivisible unity'. The latter will be true just so long as the atoms from which this olive is compounded could not be separated from each other. Since they *could* be separated from one another, from an atomist perspective it will be just plain false to say that this atom is really an indivisible unit. 'This olive is really oval' will be true so long as the atoms from which the olive is compounded are so spatially related to one another as to occupy an area that is oval.[97] It *could* be the case that they are so related to one another, in which case it would be true that the olive is really oval. However, from an atomist perspective, perception of the olive could not tell me whether the atoms *are* so related – the same compound of atoms can look different shapes to different perceivers.[98] Hence from the atomist perspective Democritus will neither endorse nor deny the claim that this olive is really oval: we simply do not know.

So Democritus' view, given INT, will be that, if the atoms which constitute this olive are appropriately related to one another, it will be true that this olive is really oval. That view seems more reasonable once it is distinguished from two other views which would be very implausible for an atomist to hold. The first is that the atoms which now compose this olive *always* occupy an oval-shaped area. No doubt Democritus held that they do not, since they are constantly moving. All that follows from this for an atomist, though, is that if this olive is really oval now it might not have been really oval a short while ago, and it might not be really oval a while hence. The second view which it would be implausible to suppose that Democritus holds is that the atoms which now compose this olive *completely* fill an oval-shaped area, or that they compose a *solid* oval. For an atomist, of course, neither of those will be true, since there will be gaps between atoms, and irregularities. That should incline us against INT, however, only if we suppose it is part of an *atomist* outlook that the only objects which can be oval are perfect oval solids. There is no reason to suppose that. There is no reason why an atomist cannot make sense of soldiers standing in rectangular formations, piles of leaves being conical or paint marks on the wall being oval. What is at issue is what to say about unreflective claims about the world. INT recommends that the crucial question to ask is whether the property that is attributed to a compound object could, from an atomist perspective, be redescribed in terms of the relations between the atoms which compose the object, or whether any redescription would involve reference to something external to the compound.

It could be reasonable for an atomist to agree that that is the crucial question, without supposing that what it is to be oval is to be solidly or continuously oval.

Which of these alternative ways of expanding the real/conventional distinction should be preferred? There are three reasons for choosing INT rather than FUND.

The first is that the main ground for opting for FUND is not as strong as it might seem. Plutarch's inclusion of compounds on the conventional side tends to favour FUND over INT. Further it is not so much the mere fact of Plutarch's report that carries weight. More important is that we can see good philosophical reasons for Democritus' framing a distinction between the real and the conventional in terms of FUND. By downgrading compound objects Democritus can face up to Eleatic arguments to which he otherwise seems to have no response. Parmenides and Melissus argued that coming into being, destruction and even alteration are impossible. It would be a response to these arguments to hold that collections of atoms are nothing more than *relations* between individual atoms, and so are not something extra in the world, independent of, over and above, the individual atoms.[99] Since someone who holds that there are not really any olives (that olives are not real) will not be threatened by arguments that olives cannot be generated, destroyed or ripen, there is reason for Democritus to offer FUND as an account of the real/conventional distinction.

We should not overestimate how far that thought will carry us. Nothing in INT requires Democritus to endorse any claims about the metaphysical status of compound objects like olives. Suppose a farmer reports that an olive has changed shape from being spherical to being oval. (9) allows Democritus to endorse, from an atomist perspective, the claims that it is really oval and that it was really spherical. Need it follow that there is really an olive, or that there is a real shape which has come into existence? I do not see that it does. If the olive is to be downgraded to the status of a shifting set of relations between independent atoms, a farmer's talk of olives will be from an atomist perspective merely a convenient way of talking about atoms and their inter-relations. Let all that be granted. What (9) recommends is that the farmer's claim that the olive is oval should be replaced by the atomistically respectable 'the olive is really oval'. That latter will be true just so long as the property which the farmer attributes to (what is from the standpoint of the atomic theory) a shifting set of relations between atoms, when he says unreflectively that the olive is oval, holds just in virtue of the (no doubt merely shifting) relations between the atoms. Conversely, it will be false if the property attributed by the farmer holds only in virtue of the relation of those atoms to something else – if that were so all that would be true would be that the olive is conventionally oval. Democritus will of course think that the farmer is wrong if he supposes this olive to be an indivisible unitary object. He might even think that farmers have implicit views about the ontological status of olives – though it is not clear why he should have to think that about farmers – and that those views could not be true. But none of that comes into the picture when considering the claim that the olive is oval. If what is, after all, merely a shifting pattern of relations between atoms occupies an oval-shaped area, then that will be an intrinsic feature of that shifting pattern of relations between atoms, and thus by the lights of (9) a property really possessed by those atoms related together. Likewise with the claim that the olive was round.[100]

Does INT force Democritus into saying that there is really a shape which comes into existence? Not in any sense that should lead to problems from Melissan and Parmenidean arguments. Democritus can allow that what the farmer picks out as the shape of the olive is something wholly determined by and dependent on the shifting relations between independent atoms. According to INT, what is crucial as regards assessment of the claim about the shape of the olive is just that whether or not those independent atoms, shiftingly related to one another, occupy an oval area is wholly determined by and dependent on the relations *between those atoms*, and is not reliant on the relations between those atoms and anything else. Democritus can allow that collections of atoms have real properties without supposing that those collections are anything other than relations between the atoms, since according to INT whether the properties are real depends on what the relations which constitute them hold *between*. Admitting real features of collections of atoms along the lines of INT is quite consistent with supposing that change in respect of those features is nothing more than relational change of atoms *to one another*.

It is not necessary to agree that Democritus *did* downgrade the status of compound objects to that of relations between independent atoms as part of a response to Eleatic arguments. The point is that, whether he did or not, INT could be a reasonable way of extending the real/ conventional distinction for Democritus. In that case, Plutarch's inclusion of compounds as an example of what is conventional, and the philosophical motivation which lies behind that example, will not be sufficient to rule out INT as an account of Democritus' distinction.

The second reason for opting for INT rather than FUND is more positive. What is at issue between INT and FUND is a question about how non-atomist claims should be rendered respectable from an atomist point of view. There is no further disagreement between INT and FUND on the question of how a claim that something has a property conventionally is to be decided. From the atomist point of view whether or not it is true that something has a property conventionally is a matter of whether or not it is the consensus among perceivers that that thing has that property. It is only to be expected that INT and FUND will not diverge on the question of how claims about the conventional possession of properties are to be assessed. For the notion of the conventional has a sense outside Democritus' use of it. INT and FUND diverge just on what it is about certain properties which leads Democritus to count them as conventional. It now becomes clear, though, that FUND involves ignoring a distinction between large-scale properties that should have been obvious to and significant for Democritus, while INT gives proper weight to that distinction. Charity then should incline us to INT rather than to FUND.

Let us go back to the claim that this olive is oval. According to FUND it is to be rephrased as 'this olive is conventionally oval', and so it will be on a par with the claim that this olive is green. Whether either of those are true is a matter of whether the consensus is that the olive is oval and the olive is green. Now it is very plausible from an atomist perspective to suppose that whether or not an olive is conventionally green *is* a matter of whether the general consensus is that it is green. After all, it is allowed that its being green is a matter of the structuring of atoms composing it producing a certain effect in perceivers. If enough perceivers came to be sufficiently different the consensus could as well be that the olive is yellow. In that case there would be as much reason to agree that the olive is conventionally yellow as there is now to agree that it is conventionally green. Indeed, in that case the olive would *be* conventionally yellow.[101] It will be reasonable for Democritus to accept that as an account of the conditions under which something is conventionally green. For he will agree that whether or not some collection of atoms compose something green depends on the relation of that collection to something else (to a perceiver), and that it is impossible that they should be green just in virtue of their relations to one another.

It would be surprising, however, if Democritus treated the question of whether something is oval in the same way. When he says that worlds are formed by an atomic *whirl*,[102] or that the earth is *flat*[103] he appears to be saying something about how the atoms which compose the vortices in which worlds are formed are arranged relative to one another, and how the atoms which form the earth are related. Being whirl shaped is a property of large-scale collections of atoms which is respectable from an atomic point of view, and whether or not that property holds does not seem in any way to depend on convention, or on a decision of the majority about atomic vortices. What goes for very large collections such as atomic vortices or the earth should also go for smaller collections of atoms such as this olive. Yet according to FUND that would not be so. If the atomistically respectable claim is that this olive is conventionally oval, whether or not an atomist would agree that it *is* conventionally oval would depend on what the reaction of the majority is. INT does not have that consequence. Being oval would be an intrinsic property of the collection of atoms that this olive really is, just as being flat would be an intrinsic property of the collection of atoms that the earth really is. Since INT marks a difference between this olive's being green and this olive's being oval which it would seem should be of significance to an atomist, INT is to be preferred to FUND.

My final reason for recommending INT over FUND takes us back to the indifference argument from which we started. Recall the disjunctive conclusion which Aristotle reports Democritus as drawing:

Democritus at any rate says that either nothing is true, or it is unclear to us.

INT allows Democritus to offer cases to which the second of these disjuncts applies, in which some perception *is* true, although it is not evident to us *that* it is true. What could such cases be? While Democritus supposes that a conventional property such as being green is the result of a relation between an olive and a perceiver, he will of course allow that there are some real properties of the olive which contribute to that olive's being green in relation to this perceiver. They will be real underlying atomic structures. Is it possible that it should be those atomic structures of which Democritus holds that there is a truth which is not evident to us?[104]

It would be better not to take Democritus' conclusion in that way. The indifference argument starts from the premiss that in cases of conflict there is no more reason to endorse one perceptual report than another. The argument should issue in a conclusion about conflicting perceptions: that either none of them are true or it is unclear to us which of the conflicting perceptions are true. It would not be to the point to conclude that there is *something else* about which there is a truth, and which is unclear to us, something distinct from the conflicting perceptual reports from which the argument started – namely, the atomic structure of the object perceived. Underlying atomic structures are not presented in perception. On the other hand, properties such as size, shape and weight of compound objects are presented in perception; and there is perceptual disagreement about such properties. What seems large from one position seems small from a distance.[105] According to INT a claim about something's having a size or shape can be reformulated in atomistically respectable terms as a claim that it really has that size or shape. Hence there can be true perceptions. A perception which presents an object as of a size or a shape which is really possessed by it, in the way in which INT explains what it is really to possess a property, will be a true perception. Nevertheless there will be perceptual disagreement about such properties. The one farmer sees the olive as spherical, the other as oval. The perception of one of them will be true, so long as the olive is really (say) oval: that is to say, so long as the collection of atoms that is the olive occupies an oval area. Yet that does not suggest that it should be apparent to these two farmers, or to the atomist offering a respectable version of their claims, *which* of their conflicting perceptions is the true one. The position is exactly as *Met* 4.5 puts it: one of the perceptions is true, although it is unclear to us which.

While INT allows us to take both disjuncts of Democritus' conclusion as having application, FUND does not. For according to FUND there is no case in which a compound object possesses any property really; perception does not give access to individual atoms or to void; and so perception could never give access to any object which possesses a property really. Therefore no perception could be true, since no perception could present properties as possessed by an object which really has those properties. That is another reason to prefer INT to FUND as an account of the real/conventional distinction.[106]

What more general conclusions can be drawn about Democritus' epistemology from the choice of INT in preference to FUND? Democritus will be sceptical about the senses. For the senses cannot provide *knowledge*. Even in the sort of case which is most favourable from the atomist perspective we are never able to distinguish among conflicting perceptions between those which do and those which do not present real features of objects in the world. On the other hand, it should not be too misleading to express Democritus' view as the claim that the senses can provide *true belief*. What is attributed to Democritus thereby is really very minimal. It is the view that there can be true perceptions, and that perceptions give us beliefs. Previous discussion of the choice between INT and FUND was aimed at supporting the view that Democritus thought there could be true perceptions. Anyone who gets so far as reflecting upon questions about knowledge – as Democritus indubitably did – will presumably recognize that there are beliefs based on perception.

Now I do not mean to suggest that Democritus had any sophisticated account of what the difference *is* between true belief and knowledge, nor that he would have had any explicit views about whether or how true belief could be converted into knowledge. I do not mean to suggest, for example, that Democritus thought that true perceptual beliefs could not be knowledge because someone can have true perceptual beliefs and yet be deceived about whether they are true, whereas no one could have knowledge without knowing that they had knowledge. Nor do I mean to suggest that Democritus held that true perceptual beliefs could not be knowledge because knowledge requires rational justification, and that rational justification would necessarily involve some confidence about my perceptual state, which I could not have. It is not necessary either to suppose or deny that Democritus had got so far in reflecting upon knowledge to formulate any such thoughts explicitly.[107] It would be reasonable to describe Democritus' position in terms of a difference between knowledge and true belief so long as he accepted the following two points: first, that it is impossible for conflicting perceptions both to constitute knowledge; and, second, that one among conflicting beliefs can be true, without there being any reason to endorse that belief rather than any other. The fact that Democritus criticizes Protagoras suggests that he is alive to the first point. The fact that he concludes as he does in the indifference argument reported in *Met* 4.5 suggests that he endorses the second.

Is it reasonable to attribute to Democritus the view that we can have some true perceptual beliefs about objects, given what doxographers say about Democritus' position concerning the senses? The interpretation

is consistent with all those doxographical reports according to which
the senses do not provide *knowledge*. Further, since Democritus can hold
that we have no idea which among our perceptions are true ('it is unclear
to us'), he will not think even that we are entitled to some lesser degree
of confidence in our perceptions than would be appropriate if they
provided knowledge. Thus it is that some reports present Democritus'
view as a general pessimism about the senses.[108] In addition, the view
being attributed to Democritus is so epistemically weak that it is
unsurprising that it is not mentioned by doxographers, whose interest
is in whether our senses can give us any contact with reality that is
epistemically worth having; nor is it surprising that it should be
consistent with most of the doxography.[109]

There are two passages about which something should be said. The
first is this:[110]

> Of knowledge (γνώμη, cognition or cognitive state) there are two forms,
> one legitimate, one bastard. To the bastard belong all this group: sight,
> hearing, smell, taste, touch. The other is legitimate and separate from
> that ... When the bastard can no longer see any smaller, or hear, or smell,
> or taste, or perceive by touch, but finer ...

The point here is that the senses are deficient. They make a pretence
to being a source of knowledge: the unreflective will often say, on the
basis of perception, that they know this or that. What they actually
provide, however, compares to knowledge as the bastard compares to
the legitimate. The natural conclusion is that what the senses provide is
belief. The image of the bastard as opposed to the legitimate is a nice
expression of the relation of belief to knowledge. Our perceptual beliefs
make a pretence of presenting features of the world to us in a way that
only knowledge genuinely presents them. There is a question to raise
about Democritus' image of the bastard as opposed to the legitimate. Is
it part of the senses' pretence that they offer things as being true which
never are true? If Democritus' image were taken in that way, that would
tell against its being his view that there can be true perceptions.

We should not take Democritus' image so. There will be some
extremely general truths which the senses do tell us: that there is motion,
that there is more than one thing, that there is extended body. I have
taken that for granted so far; what has been discussed and what is
contentious is whether the senses tell truths about objects any more

specific than those. Still, mention of those very general truths indicates that the illegitimacy of the senses does not reside simply in their presenting as true what is not true. There is another way to take the thought that the senses lay fraudulent claim to a status which is the rightful possession only of the intellect. Legitimate knowledge has a power of conviction: to continue Democritus' metaphor, the conviction earned by rational argument can be *passed along* chains of argument, and *inherited* by a conclusion from premises. The senses pretend to have that power of conviction – the unreflective will accept and be convinced of things just on the basis of their perceptions, and will draw conclusions from what perception tells them – but it is merely a pretence, as indicated by the fact that the senses produce conflicting reports. Even when the senses deliver very general truths, it is not because they are delivered by the senses that they carry conviction. What entitles Democritus to the *knowledge* that there is motion and plurality is that the basic atomic theory shows how there *can be*. Appeal to the senses alone would not get one beyond the unreflective position of those Plato reports as making fun of Parmenides' views as absurd.[111] There is nothing in the image of the senses as an illegitimate or bastard source of conviction, then, to indicate that we could not have *true* perceptions.

A second passage calls for a similar response:[112]

> In reality we know nothing; for truth is in the depths.

Here is one way to take this. Truth is to be found only at the atomic level; our senses do not give us access to the atomic depths; hence our senses can deliver us no truths; hence we know nothing. For a number of reasons, though, it is hard to make clear sense of the passage in that way. If for Democritus we have reasoned access to facts about atoms – for example, by means of indifference arguments about atomic shapes and sizes, which give us 'legitimate' knowledge – we cannot take literally the remark that we know nothing in reality. The reference might rather be to the inability of our *senses* to provide knowledge of features of reality. We cannot tell much from the nine words Diogenes cites, and it would not be incredible to suppose they were excerpted from a series of Democritean arguments about the senses. The argument of these words could then be: our senses can provide no knowledge of what is in reality, for the only truths *we can know* are in the depths (that is, they concern the atomic level), to which our senses do not give access. In that case there is no longer the implication that we can have no true perceptions.

There is a final matter to raise. One might wonder what the *point* would be of Democritus' holding the view attributed to him. Extremely general truths would be available to perception; but there is nothing very exciting in saying that about Democritus. The other sorts of perception which are true are those which are of properties of collections of atoms which hold just in virtue of the relations of the atoms among themselves. Yet those true perceptions would not generate knowledge, nor anything approaching it. To allow from an atomist perspective that there are such perceptions is to allow something that is not worth very much.

In a way this is correct. It is not epistemological considerations which lie behind the view attributed to Democritus. What recommends this view of the senses is consistency with a metaphysical position. Once it is allowed that some features of collections of atoms are to be counted as *real* features of those collections, it follows straight away that since there can be perceptual access to those features it is possible for some perceptions to be true. Further there is considerable point in an atomist admitting some features of collections of atoms to be real – as it was put earlier, in adopting INT rather than FUND. For doing so allows for an atomistically respectable way of talking about what occurs on the macroscopic level, and a way that is consistent with greatly downgrading the status of objects on that level. We need not think of the motivations of the atomic theory as being those of the scientific Democritus in order to see this as an advance over the Eleatic position.

The promise at the start of this section was that thinking about the indifference argument attributed to Democritus by Aristotle in *Met* 4.5 would be fruitful. Such has turned out to be the case. The discussion has raised general matters about Democritus' epistemology and his view of the non-atomic world. In the previous two sections the central importance of indifference reasoning for Democritus' basic atomic theory was made clear. In the next chapter we will look at instances of indifference reasoning in contexts other than ancient atomism.

NOTES

1 For this way of putting the atomic theory, see Aristotle, *Met* 1.4 985b5ff; DK 67A6; Luria §173.

2 325a28f, τὸ κυρίως ὂν παμπλῆρες ὄν. Aristotle's fuller account runs from 325a23–325b5, and presents the picture of atomism as a response to the Eleatics from which chapter 2 started.

3 This part of the argument is what is expanded by Aristotle at *GC* 1.2 316a14–317a2, in his account of the introduction of atomic magnitudes. I will say more about this passage below.

4 *GC* 1.8 325a5–12, discussed above in chapter 2.2.

5 *Phys* 1.3 187a1–3: translation as KRS §546.

6 Though ancient commentators did not always agree on this identification. See Ross (1936, p. 479ff) on ancient claims that Plato and Xenocrates are one or both of those referred to, and Ross's own arguments for preferring the atomists; also Sorabji (1983, p. 342f).

7 *Phys* 1.3 186a23.

8 *Phys* 6.9 239b19, 22.

9 On Diodorus, see Sedley (1977), Denyer (1981), Sorabji (1983, ch. 24) and White (1985, ch. 3).

10 On the more traditional interpretation of the void as empty space, the Zenonian argument would apply to the division of the void through which atoms move. If the void is thought of as a negative space occupier, as in Sedley (1982), then the argument will apply to the division of the distances traversed by atoms. Either way, Democritus gains nothing simply by introducing indivisible *atoms*. It would be particularly hard to suppose that Democritus should not have seen this, if one hoped to accept the method that Furley (1987, p. 129ff) mentions, without endorsement, for reconciling a Democritean commitment to partless atoms with a continuist geometry: that geometry does not apply to the atoms but to the void.

11 *GC* 1.8 325a4f. For Melissus' argument, see DK 30B7 (7), and chapter 2.4 above.

12 *GC* 1.8 325a27f.

13 Both this point, and the account to be offered below of the indivisibility of the atom, leave it unclear how the atomists would have responded to Zeno's argument against motion. There are some (pure) conjectures one might make; but, given the possibility of applying the argument to void intervals, this question remains a problem for any exegesis of Democritus' account of the atoms.

14 *in Phys* 139.27–140.6 (Lee, 1936, §2).

15 This will cause problems for Democritus, since he wants to say that atoms can collide, hook on to one another, and so on. See note 43 below, and chapter 1.2.

16 As Aristotle expresses it, Democritus makes his atomic magnitudes substances: *Met* 7.13 1039a11, DK 68A42, Luria §211.

17 *GC* 1.2 316a14–317a2. See, for example, the comments in Williams (1982).

18   316a15f.

19   In setting out the argument, Aristotle is willing to pass over difficulties
     involved in the move to something's actually being everywhere divided.
     Hence we should not worry whether the division takes place all at the
     same time or not (316a18). The phrase 'and this is possible' (καὶ τοῦτο
     δυνατόν) at 316a17 is likewise an allowance for the sake of the argument
     that the division of what is everywhere divisible could be actually achieved.
     To allow that flies in the face of Aristotle's own view. One upshot of
     Aristotle's (obscure) diagnosis of the fallacy in this argument, at 317a2–17,
     is that it is not possible to bring about an actual division everywhere of
     what is everywhere divisible. The addition of the same words in the
     opening supposition, at 316a15f, is either to the same effect, or perhaps
     an error resulting from confusion with the succeeding occurrence.

20   316a24–316b8.

21   316b15f.

22   315b26ff.

23   315b28ff.

24   For example, in the statement of the initial supposition at 316a15f, and
     in the conclusion at 316b15f.

25   Compare the Eleatic argument summarized at *GC* 1.8 325a8f: for if it is
     divisible everywhere, there is no unit, and therefore no many, and the
     whole is void.

26   For discussions, see Guthrie (1969, pp. 503–7); Barnes (1982, pp. 346–60);
     Sorabji (1983, pp. 354–7); Furley (1987, pp. 125–31).

27   While most commentators defend one or another of the two alternatives
     mentioned, Sorabji (1983; prefigured in Sorabji 1982), claims that Demo-
     critus did not distinguish between theoretical and physical indivisibility,
     and takes the apparent confusion in the evidence as some confirmation
     of that. I argued for a position related to, though stronger than, that of
     Sorabji (in Makin 1989), which it may be useful to summarize here. The
     distinction between physical and theoretical divisibility is not usually clearly
     drawn. As in Sorabji, there is no such clear distinction to be found in
     Democritus; further, much of the use of these terms in exegesis by
     commentators does not succeed in making any cogent point. The most
     obvious way to explain the notion of what conceptual or theoretical
     indivisibility comes to is by appeal to partlessness. Since there is nothing
     in the texts and doxographies to *force* an explication of atomic indivisibility
     in terms of partlessness, reference to it would further the purposes of
     exegesis only if it made the content of Democritean atomism clearer to
     us. But it could not do that, since the notion of partless atoms which
     vary in shape and size does not in fact make sense. Hence it is unclear
     what view a commentator would be claiming that Democritus held in

attributing partless atoms to him. So it could not be good exegetical practice to attribute partless atoms to Democritus. The account of atoms as extended bodies with parts, whose indivisibility follows by an indifference argument from their homogeneity, recommends itself as the only account that makes good philosophical sense.

28 On Democritus' view that there is just one kind of atomic stuff, see Aristotle *Phys* 1.2 184b21, Luria §223; and *de Caelo* 1.7 275b31ff, DK 67A19, Luria §261.

29 Aristotle *Met* 1.4 985b6f, DK 67A6, Luria §173, one of the elements is the full, in conjunction with *GC* 1.8 325a28f, what properly is is a plenum; from Aristotle's lost *On Democritus*, Simplicius *in de Caelo* 295.5, DK 68A37, Luria §172; Simplicius *in Phys* 81.34 on, Luria §212; Simplicius *in de Caelo* 609.17, Luria §212; Simplicius *in de Caelo* 242.18ff, DK 67A14, Luria §214 (divisibility comes about as a result of the void in bodies, while the atoms contain no void and are solid); Alexander *in Met* 35.24ff, Luria §214; passages from Aëtius at Luria §214, DK 68A125, tell us that Democritus *called* the atoms 'the solids' (τὰ ναστὰ); Cicero *de Fin* 1.6, Luria §301; Lactantius *Inst* III 17.22, Luria §218; Theodoret at Luria §113.

30 A number of the doxographers gloss solidity in just this way: Simplicius *in de Caelo* 242.18ff, DK 67A14, Luria §214, refers to the atoms' being solid and having no part of the void (τὸ ναστὰς εἶναι καὶ ἀμοίρους τοῦ κενοῦ), for division comes about through the presence of void in bodies; Alexander *in Met* 35.24, Luria §214, mentions the atoms' being solid and having no share in void (διὰ ναστότητά τε καὶ ἀμιξίαν τοῦ κενοῦ).

31 Thus Simplicius' mention of the solidity (ναστότητα) and hardness (στερρότητα) of Democritus' atoms at *in Phys* 82.1ff, Luria §212, is to be taken more strongly than it generally is. For an example of the more typical reading, see O'Brien (1981, p. 274), who glosses Simplicius' remark as the claim that the atoms have parts but are 'indivisible *in practice*' (my emphasis).

32 On the atom as hard (στερεόν), and on hardness (στερρότητα): Aristotle *Met* 985b6f, DK 67A6, Luria §173; Dionysius at DK 68A43, Luria §219; Simplicius *in Phys* 82.1, Luria §212; Diogenes *Lives* 9.44, DK 68A1, Luria §215.

33 For more on that derivation, see Makin (1989).

34 Thus Parmenides B8.22–5 on the relation of indivisibility, homogeneity and continuity suggests that it would be hard to suppose the Parmenidean One to be partless.

35 *in Phys* 82.1, Luria §212.

36 See the passages collected by Luria at §124, from Aëtius, Sextus, Alexander, Galen, Dionysius, Clement.

37 Aëtius and Stobaeus, DK 68A48, Luria §106; Simplicius *in Phys* 925.10, DK 67A13, Luria §113.

38   Dionysius at DK 68A43, Luria §207; Aëtius at DK 68A47, Luria §207:
     Diogenes at DK 68A1 §44, Luria §184. See chapter 3.2.

39   *in Phys* 925.15, DK 67A13, Luria §113.

40   *in de Caelo* 609.17, Luria §212.

41   Furley (1967, Study I, chs 8, 9); Sedley (1977).

42   *Phys* 6.1 231a24–6.

43   If continuous, these would be homogeneous, and thus it should seem
     indivisible; Aristotle signals this problem at *GC* 1.8 325a32–4 and in his
     lost work on Democritus, Simplicius *in de Caelo* 295.12–14, Luria §293,
     DK 68A37; later at *GC* 1.8 326a32–4 he uses it to make trouble for the
     Democriteans, when he asks why atoms do not coalesce when they come
     in contact, like drops of water running together. That would indeed be a
     problem, if the atoms were indivisible due to their homogeneity, but there
     seems no reason why it should be thought a difficulty if Aristotle takes
     them to be partless objects. Philoponus says that the atoms do not really
     ever come in contact, *in de Gen et Corr* 158.26, 160.10, DK 67A7, Luria
     §236, though that is a hard solution to understand. Perhaps Democritus'
     position was that atoms are so shaped that they only ever come into
     point-to-point contact, and across a point-to-point contact there would
     not be a continuous body of atomic stuff. That in its turn may not seem
     a happy position: since there are atoms of every shape there will be
     flat-faced atoms; *they* at least could fit together surface-to-surface, in which
     case they would *per impossibile* become one. Democritus could try the
     following reply. There could not be any such congruent atoms now since
     if there were they would eventually (through an infinite future) come into
     contact and become one, which is impossible; nor could there ever have
     been such congruent atoms in the past, since they would by now have
     been moving for an infinite time and so would already have come into
     contact and become one, which is impossible. Hence there are no
     congruent atoms, and the point-to- point reply survives. Democritus' reply
     rests on the view that what can happen will happen given enough time;
     on the atomist credentials of that principle, see chapter 7.1 and 7.2. There
     will be no clash with the indifference argument concerning atomic shapes,
     on which see chapter 3.2; that argument concerns shapes as regards which
     there is no more reason for one than another to be instantiated in the
     atoms, whereas there *is* reason for there not to be congruently shaped
     atoms. But all this is conjecture, and problems remain. Of course charity
     does not require that philosophers are not vulnerable to problems, but
     just that coherence weighs very heavily in exegesis.

44   *de Caelo* 3.1 299a6f.

45   Cited explicitly at 300a1.

46   *de Caelo* 299a26 on.

47 This is the thought behind Melissus B9. Makin (1989) did not go far enough in considering the force of that thought, that what has parts is thereby many (viz. many *parts*).

48 Zeno B1.7–9.

49 The only report which suggests this, Alexander *in Met* 36.25–7, Luria §123, is insufficient to render it a reliable interpretation.

50 Offered in the course of a criticism by Aristotle, *GC* 1.8 326a32–4, note 43 above.

51 The temptation to think this is manifest in Simplicius' comment at *in Phys* 82.4 on. After saying that the Democritean atom has parts and is indivisible due to its solidity (precisely the homogeneity account) he adds that it is continuous and infinitely divisible, and for that reason potentially many: συνεχὴς καὶ διαιρετὴ ἐπ' ἄπειρον καὶ διὰ τοῦτο δυμάνει πολλά

52 It might seem to clash with recommendations of charity to ascribe such confusions to Democritus in exegesis. Yet the positions ascribed are far more plausible than those required by one who would attribute partless atoms to Democritus. In that case we should have to suppose that Democritus thought that (a) B is smaller than A, and (b) B is the same size as part of A, were non-equivalent.

53 I have not said anything about the claim that some of Aristotle's criticisms of Democritus suggest that *Aristotle* thought of the atoms as more than merely physically indivisible. See Furley (1967, pp. 86–90); Furley (1987, p. 129f). The most noteworthy passage is *de Caelo* 3.7 306a26–306b2. That could as well be taken as showing that Aristotle thought that Democritus would have had to deny some mathematical theorem in order to introduce indivisible atoms. It is hard to see why Aristotle should have thought that, if the atoms were just hard bits of matter. But if Democritus did offer a stronger homogeneity account, while not denying any mathematical theorem, all Aristotle's objection would show is that *he* took Democritus' position to be inconsistent – which of course he did.

54 *in Phys* 28.4 on, DK 67A8, 68A38, Luria §2: Λεύκιππος...ὑπέθετο...τῶν ἐν αὐτοῖς [ἐν τοῖς στοιχείοις] σχημάτων ἄπειρον τὸ πλῆθος διὰ τὸ μηδὲν μᾶλλον τοιοῦτον ἢ τοιοῦτον εἶναι...[Λεύκιππος καὶ Δημόκριτος] τῶν ἐν ταῖς ἀτόμοις σχημάτων ἄπειρον τὸ πλῆθός φασι διὰ τὸ μηδὲν μᾶλλον τοιοῦτον ἢ τοιοῦτον εἶναι. Compare Aristotle's report that Democritus made the shapes infinite in order to account for the infinite variety of the phenomena, *GC* 1.1 315b9ff, DK 67A9, Luria §240.

55 *in Phys* 405.23 on, Luria §1: ἔνθεν γὰρ καὶ ὁ Δημόκριτος ἀπείρους εἶναι κόσμους ὑπετίθετο, ὑποτιθέμενος κενὸν εἶναι ἄπειρον· τίς γὰρ ἡ ἀποκλήρωσις τόδε μὲν τὸ τοῦ κενοῦ μέρος ὑπὸ κόσμου πληρωθῆναι, ἄλλα δὲ μή; ὥστε εἰ ἔν τινι μέρει τοῦ κενοῦ κόσμος ἐστί, καὶ ἐν παντὶ ἄρα τῶι κενῶι. ἀπείρου οὖν ὄντος τοῦ κενοῦ, ἄπειροι ἔσονται καὶ οἱ κόσμοι.

Compare the argument of Metrodorus of Chios, DK 70A6, reported by Aëtius, which moves from an infinity of causes (αἴτια), identified as atoms, to an infinite variety of worlds. Though indifference reasoning is not explicitly given there, the argument should be expanded in those terms.

56 *Lives* 9.44, DK 68A1, Luria §184: καὶ τὰς ἀτόμους δὲ ἀπείρους εἶναι κατὰ μέγεθος καὶ πλῆθος.

57 DK 68A43, Luria §207: ὁ δὲ καὶ μεγίστας εἶναί τινας ἀτόμους, ὁ Δημόκριτος ὑπέλαβεν.

58 DK 68A47, Luria §207: Δημόκριτος...δυνατὸν εἶναι κοσμιαίαν ὑπάρχειν ἄτομον.

59 For Epicurus' claim, *Ep. Her* 55f, LS 12A; Dionysius is contrasting Epicurus and Democritus in the passage cited at note 57 above.

60 Simplicius *in Phys* 925.10, DK 67A13, Luria §113, where it is connected (mysteriously) with partlessness, on which see the discussion of the previous section; in Simplicius *in de Caelo* 609.17, Luria §212, smallness is connected (equally mysteriously) with solidity; Galen *de Elem Sec Hipp* 1.2, DK 68A49, Luria §112; Lactantius *de Ira Dei* 10.5, *Inst* III 17.22, Luria §218.

61 Quoted by Simplicius *in de Gen et Corr* 294.33 on, DK 68A37, Luria §204; also Philoponus *in de Caelo* 39.4 on, Luria §206.

62 Unless the application of charity to Democritus is supplemented with some explanation of Aristotle's testimony, one could as well take the fact that Democritus' arguments *should* have led him to posit large atoms as an explanation of how error crept into the later doxographies. This is the approach of O'Brien (1981, ch. 10, §4) who thinks that such as Aëtius and Diogenes got matters so wrong because they were misled by an argument in Lucretius to the effect that infinite variations in shape would entail (*per impossibile*) infinite variations in size, *de Rer. Nat* 2.478–99, LS 12C 1–2. My appeal to charity on behalf of Democritus is independent of that (dubious) Lucretian argument from variety of shape to variety of size. It is rather that the very same sort of argument which establishes an infinite variety of atomic shapes would just as well establish an infinite variety of atomic sizes.

63 Diogenes gives a full report of Leucippus' account of world formation, *Lives* 9.31f, DK 67A1 and 68A1, Luria §382; according to Diogenes (*Lives* 9.45, DK 68A1, Luria §23) and Sextus (*M* 9.113, DK 68A83, Luria §23), Democritus held that what was due to the atomic whirl was *necessary*; and so some shapes for worlds will be *impossible*.

64 Hippolytus *Ref* 1.13.2, DK 68A40, Luria §349, says that there are infinitely many words which differ in size (*shape* as one might expect is not mentioned).

65 Cicero *Acad* 2.55, DK 68A81, Luria §6.

66 For this conclusion, see Cicero *Acad* 2.125, Luria §6: there will be *innumerable* other groups of people with our names, looking like us, writing and reading books like this.

67 *in de Gen et Corr* 12.2, Luria §141.

68 *Phys* 3.5 204a20–6.

69 *Met* 4.5 1009b9–12, DK 68A112, Luria §3. See also Theophrastus, *de Sens* §69, DK 68A135, also at Luria §3: no one grasps the truth more than another, τὸ μηθὲν μᾶλλον ἕτερον ἑτέρου τυγκάνειν τῆς ἀληθείας.

70 The support for that indifference premiss is an underlying assumption that we cannot adjudicate on conflicting perceptions in terms of numbers, *Met* 1009b2. Nor therefore are we entitled, for example, to choose the perceptions of the healthy over the sick, since if more people tasted the honey water as bitter, they would be accounted the healthy perceivers (*Met* 1009b4ff).

71 Sextus *M* 7.389f, DK 68A114, Luria §76: Democritus, like Plato, used self-refutation against Protagoras, in order to combat the view that whatever appears so is so. Plutarch *adv Col* 1109A, DK 68B156, Luria §78: Democritus offered many cogent arguments against Protagoras' view.

72 *M* 7.137, DK 68B6, Luria §48.

73 *M* 7.136, DK 68B10, Luria §55.

74 *M* 8.184, Luria §57.

75 Sextus *M* 7.369, DK 68A110; Aëtius IV.9.1, DK 59A96; both at Luria §54.

76 *Lives* 9.72, DK 68B117, Luria §51.

77 *Acad* 2.73, DK 68B165, Luria §58.

78 Sextus *M* 7.135, DK 68B9, Luria §55.

79 Plutarch *adv Col* 1110E, Luria §61.

80 *M* 7.135.

81 DK 68B6, Luria §48.

82 DK 68B7, Luria §49.

83 DK 68B8, Luria §50.

84 DK 68B10, Luria §55.

85 From the same passage in Sextus: but we in actuality *grasp* nothing for certain (οὐδὲν ἀτρεκὲς συνίεμεν), but what shifts in accordance with the condition of the body and of the things which enter it and press upon it (*M* 7.136, DK 68B9, Luria §55).

86 Compare Theophrastus *de Sens* §62, DK 68A135, Luria §369, on Democritus' distinction between the hard and the soft in terms of the compact or loose packing of atoms.

87 Among ancient commentators, Aëtius IV.9.8, DK 67A32, Luria §95; Galen *de Elem sec Hipp* I.2, DK 68A49, Luria §90; Simplicius *in Phys* 512.28, Luria §59, *in de An* 193.27, Luria §60. Among moderns, Barnes (1982,

p. 376, who cites some of these passages in support), Fowler (1984, p. 267). Being fluid would come out as a *real* property on Barnes's account of what it is to be real (1982, p. 372f): Q is real if and only if Q is either a primary (essential) property of bodies, or a proper quality (that is, a determinant of a primary quality) of bodies. For being fluid is a determinant, along with being rigid, of some more general property (having a shape under pressure), which latter is a primary quality of bodies. There is evidence of the same response in Theophrastus' comment at *de Sens* §71, DK 68A135, Luria §441, that Democritus attributes some substantial status (ποιεῖ τιν' οὐσίαν) to hard, soft, heavy and light. Theophrastus makes this point, however, in critical spirit, going on to say that they are also counted as relative to us (λέγεσθαι πρὸς ἡμᾶς).

88 Although Plutarch is alone in offering combination as an example in reporting Democritus' distinction, others make similar points. Diogenes *Lives* 9.44, DK 68A1, Luria §93, says that Democritus' view was that the principles of everything are atoms and void, and that everything else has been laid down conventionally (τὰ δ' ἄλλα πάντα νενομίσθαι). Aëtius IV.9.8, DK 67A32, Luria §95, says that according to Democritus and Leucippus only atoms and void are natural (φύσει).

89 For these examples, see Sextus *M* 7.117f, DK 68B164, Luria §§11, 316.

90 Even given healthy scepticism about the works that are attributed to Democritus, it is unlikely that there would be nothing more about the real/conventional distinction somewhere in books such as *On Nature or On the Nature of the Universe, On Mind, On Perception, On Tastes, On Colours, On the Different Forms, On Changes of Form*, and various books on causes (for example, of fire, sounds, seeds, animals). For these titles, see DK 68B5c, 5e–i, 8a, 11b–i.

91 *M* 7.140. The discussion of Democritus is preceded by an account of Heraclitus' position on the same question (*M* 7.126–34) and followed by accounts of the views of Plato (*M* 7.141–4), Speusippus (*M* 7.145f), Xenocrates (*M* 7.147–9), and so on. On Sextus' discussion, see Sedley (1992).

92 Melissus DK 30B8; Parmenides DK 28B1.30, 6.4ff, 8.38b–41.

93 To decide on whether something is conventionally green in this way is quite consistent with the assumption behind the indifference argument reported in *Met* 4.5, that we are not to decide between conflicting perceptions by counting heads. The point there is that the fact that most perceivers agree that this olive is green does not give reason to endorse the claim that it is *really* green, that the *truth* of the matter is that is green (in reality).

94 Characterizing something as conventional does not involve supposing that every claim about how it *is* conventionally is equally true. Olives *are*

conventionally green, and they are not (as things stand) conventionally blue; honey water is conventionally sweet, and cactus juice is not. McKim (1984) emphasizes this, and points out that it is just the position we would expect someone concerned to oppose a Protagorean position to take.

95 Perhaps properties such as being solid, being indivisible and being completely empty would count as real. But the general agreement of the unreflective might be that this diamond is absolutely solid and indivisible (as opposed to that sandstone), and that this bucket is completely empty (as opposed to that one which contains a few grains of sand). In that case these would be conventionally (although not really) solid and empty respectively. It is beside the point that *when pressed* people could be brought to recognize, for example, that the former bucket is full of air. We are after all considering what the consensus of unreflective opinion would be. From Aristotle's remark at *Phys* 4.6 213a24f, it appears that even people engaged in the question of whether there is void could confuse what contains only air and what is empty and void – and they will not be the most unreflective speakers. Compare too *Phys* 4.7 214a6f, where Aristotle gives as one sense of void what contains no tangible body.

96 Theophrastus *de Sens* §§61, 63f, 67, 69f. At §63, DK 68A135, Luria §71, Theophrastus gives as a ground for saying that a sensible quality does not have an independent nature (ὡς οὐκ εἰσὶ φύσει) that it varies according to the condition of the perceiver.

97 Talk of these atoms occupying an *oval-shaped area* is intended just as a shorthand way of saying that the atoms stand in the appropriate spatial relations to one another. I do not mean to suggest that Democritus is explaining what it is for complex entities to have shapes by reference to the shapes of spatial areas. The reader might be tempted to say that atoms never *could* stand in the appropriate relations to compose something really oval, because there will always be gaps and irregularities. I will say something to answer that worry below.

98 There are two slight complexities to note. Perception for Democritus is somehow mediated by atoms which pass from the object perceived to the perceiver, and one reason why, for example, oval things can look round is that the atoms are buffeted in their passage: hence Aristotle reports Democritus as holding that if the intervening distance were empty one could see an ant on the vault of the sky, *de An* 2.7 419a15f, DK 68A122, Luria §468 – presumably because in that case atoms passing from the ant to the eye would have as free a passage as one could wish. It might seem that in consequence Democritus should deny that perceivers ever do disagree about the shape of what they perceive, for two reasons: (i) no two people ever do see the same thing (that is, the same atoms never do arrive at the eyes of different perceivers), and (ii) once the atoms get to the eye

there will be no further error about shape. However, there is no indication that Democritus *does* hold (i), and no reason why he would have to conflate what mediates perception with what we perceive. As regards (ii) it is just uncharitable to suppose that Democritus could not have been aware that factors internal to the perceiver, such as illness, pressure on the eye and drugs, could affect perception of shape and size.

99 Wardy (1988) emphasizes this line, and the requirement of charity that Democritus should be seen as taking Eleatic argument seriously, rather than ignoring it. For Melissus' argument, which was mentioned earlier in chapter 2.4, see DK 30B7.6–8 ('For if it alters, it is necessary that what is should not be alike, but that what was earlier perishes and what is not comes into being'), and B7.10–12 ('But neither is it possible for it to be rearranged. For the order which was earlier does not perish, nor does an order which is not come into being').

100 A claim such as 'this is an olive' is harder to make out. One reason it is hard to make out is that Democritus might want to retain room for the thought that whether or not something is an olive will depend partially on its *conventional* properties: say its colour. Aristotle makes this remark about Democritus at *Part An* 1.1 640b29ff, DK 68B165, Luria §65: 'But now if each animal and part exists by shape *and colour*, Democritus might be right; for this seems to be his assumption. At any rate he says it is clear to everybody what sort of thing man is in conformation, suggesting that he is known by shape *and colour*' (translation Balme (1972), my emphases). If we take that as fair comment, Democritus will have noticed that conventional properties such as colour play quite a role in people's *identifying* collections of atoms as a man (rather than, say, a statue) or an olive (rather than, say, a wooden bead). The salient point, however, is that even if 'this is an olive' is reformulated in line with INT as 'this is really an olive', there is nothing in INT to suggest that it should be further taken as a claim that this olive is a metaphysical unity over and above the atoms that compose it. So whether or not 'this is an olive' *is* reformulated as 'this is really an olive', Democritus might hope to avoid the Eleatic arguments we have mentioned.

101 The underlying atomic structure would be the same, of course. So, if Democritus did go in for giving accounts of colours by reference to underlying atomic structures, as Theophrastus *de Sens* §73 on suggests, then under conditions where enough perceivers were different enough, the underlying structure which is now associated with green would then be associated with (say) yellow. Perhaps that is why Democritus says that in reality we do not grasp what sort of thing each thing is (Sextus *M* 7.136, DK 68B10, Luria §55). When particular connections between atomic structures and conventional properties are attributed to Demo-

critus they seem to be guided by the way things with those conventional properties look. For example, Theophrastus says that what is black is composed of atoms which are rough, irregularly shaped and different from one another (*de Sens* §74, DK 68A135, Luria §484). That seems appealing because things which are composed of bodies like that will cast many shadows, and so will look dark – imagine a rough and irregularly undulating surface in comparison with one which is smooth. But Democritus will also allow that things which are black can look different colours to perceivers in different states. Hence Democritus will have no confidence that things which look dark to us – coal, oil and thunderclouds – are in fact composed of atoms which are rough, irregularly shaped and different from one another.

102 Diogenes *Lives* 9.31f, DK 67A1, Luria §382.
103 Aëtius III.10.5, DK 68A94, Luria §405.
104 Compare Furley (1987, p. 134f).
105 Compare the variations between perceivers which *Met* 4.5 1010b4ff mentions: things appearing different sizes from different distances, and different weights to the sick and the healthy.
106 There is another less substantial point which could be made. The models in terms of which early commentators report Democritus' account of what goes on in perception suggest that he should be sympathetic to the possibility of perceivers being in states in which their perceptions are more accurate. According to Aristotle, Democritus explains seeing as involving a kind of mirroring, which occurs because the eye is smooth (*de Sensu* 2, 438a5 on, DK68A121, Luria §477; compare Alexander *in de Sensu* 24.14 on, DK 67A29, also at Luria §477). Theophrastus draws the conclusion that eyes which are in the right physical state for reflecting – moist, yet not too dense or oily – will be possessed of better visual powers (*de Sens* §50, DK 68A135, Luria §478). We need not pass judgement on whether Aristotle and Theophrastus provide accurate reports of what Democritus said about perception. So long as Democritus said *something* about what becomes of perception within the atomist perspective, and so long as it is along materialist lines (as it inevitably will be), there should be sympathy for the idea that there are better perceptual states, and that might incline one to suppose that there are perceptual states in which something is correctly perceived.
107 It is not necessary to attribute any sophisticated view to Democritus about the rational requirements for knowledge, and their being incompatible with a materialist outlook, in order to understand the argument reported by Sextus, *M* 7.137, DK 68B7, Luria §49: 'this argument too shows that in reality we know nothing; but that for each of us there is a reshaping – belief' (δηλοῖ μὲν δὴ καὶ οὗτος ὁ λόγος, ὅτι ἐτεῆι οὐδὲν

ἴσμεν περὶ οὐδενός, ἀλλ' ἐπιρρυσμίη ἡ δόξις). We do not know the context from which Sextus takes this, and in particular we do not know whether 'the argument which shows that in reality we know nothing' *is* just 'that for each of us there is a reshaping – belief'. All Sextus wants is a quotation to support his contention that according to Democritus there is no perceptual knowledge. It is as likely that the argument Democritus speaks of should have *preceded* the quoted sentence, that Sextus was not much interested in reproducing the argument, and that he cited only the conclusion and Democritus' comment on that. Democritus' point will be that, while we do not have knowledge, we do have belief – and, from an atomist perspective, belief is some sort of atomic restructuring. If the argument did go from the premiss that a belief is a reshaping to the conclusion that there is no knowledge, then it would show just as plausibly that *thought* could generate no knowledge as that there is no *perceptual* knowledge. But that would be at odds with Democritus' claim that there is a *legitimate* form of knowledge (Sextus *M* 7.138f, DK 68B11, Luria §83), and his repeated statements about what there is in reality. Rather than suppose that Democritus is driven to scepticism about the whole atomic theory, it would be preferable to see the 'reshaping' passage as giving the conclusion of an argument critical of the senses, without giving the argument itself. Galen cites a response of the senses to the mind (DK 68B125, Luria §§79–80): 'Having slandered the phenomena by saying "by convention colour, by convention sweet, by convention bitter, but in reality atoms and void" [Democritus] makes the senses speak thus to the mind: "Wretched mind, do you take your assurances from us and then overthrow us? Our overthrow is your downfall".' That suggests that Democritus' discussions included arguments specifically directed at sense perception (attacks by the mind on the senses), any one of which could generate the conclusion of the 'reshaping' passage.

108 For example, Cicero *Acad* 2.73, DK 68B165, Luria §58: the senses are full of darkness. Sextus *M* 7.137, DK 68B6, Luria §48: a man must know by this yardstick that he is separated from reality (γιγνώσκειν τε χρή ἄνθρωπον τῶιδε τῶι κανόνι, ὅτι ἐτεῆς ἀπήλλακται). I am separated or cut off from reality if I do not know which of my perceptions are true, and if I have no method of finding out.

109 There are well-known reports of Democritus' views on knowledge which appear to conflict with the general sceptical position. Most significant are various comments by Aristotle. Immediately following the indifference argument we have been discussing, Aristotle groups Democritus with Empedocles and almost all the ancients as holding that whatever appears is true, *Met* 4.5 1009b13ff, Luria §73. According to Aristotle,

Democritus holds that truth lies in the appearance (*GC* 1.2 315b9f, DK 67A9, Luria §70); he identifies soul (ψυχή) and mind (νοῦς) since he identifies what appears with what is true (*de An* 1.2 404a27f, DK 68A101, Luria §67). See also *de An* 3.3 427a25–427b5, and Philoponus at *in de An* 71.19, DK 68A113, Luria §69, *in de Gen et Corr* 23.2, Luria §96. This is not the place to discuss what to say about those passages. I do not think the issues they raise will be closely connected with the view of Democritus I have given.

110 Sextus *M* 7.139, DK 68B11, Luria §83: γνώμης δὲ δύο εἰσὶν ἰδέαι, ἡ μὲν γνησίη, ἡ δὲ σκοτίη· καὶ σκοτίης μὲν τάδε σύμπαντα, ὄψις, ἀκοή, ὀδμή, γεῦσις, ψαῦσις. ἡ δὲ γνησίη, ἀποκεκριμένη δὲ ταύτης…ὅταν ἡ σκοτίη μηκέτι δύνηται μήτε ὁρῆν ἐπ' ἔλαττον μήτε ἀκούειν μήτε ὀδμᾶσθαι μήτε γεύσθαι μήτε ἐν τῆι ψαύσει αἰσθάνεσθαι, ἀλλ' ἐπὶ λεπτότερον…The quotation as given by Sextus tails off. It is not clear whether that is due to Sextus, or whether Democritus' original remark tailed off – perhaps as a striking reflection of the way in which the senses tail off as we move progressively from the compound to the atomic levels.

111 *Parm* 128d.

112 Diogenes *Lives* 9.72, DK 68B117, Luria §51: ἐτεῆι δὲ οὐδὲν ἴδμεν. ἐν βυθῶι γὰρ ἡ ἀλήθεια. Diogenes reproduces these words in the course of his life of Pyrrho, as part of a review of founders or precursors of scepticism.

4

Some Other Indifference Arguments

◆

4.1 Preamble

The previous two chapters have concentrated on indifference arguments as related to presocratic atomism. The same sort of arguments are also found in other philosophers. In this chapter I will say something about some of those arguments as encountered in other presocratics, in Plato and in Aristotle.[1]

It is not uncommon to find the conclusion of an argument stated in a way which suggests indifference reasoning. The expression *ou mallon* ...*ê*..., meaning 'not rather... than...' or 'no more... than...' occurs for example in the statement of Democritean views on the status of atoms and void: what-is no more is than what-is-not.[2] Since atoms are what is, and void is what is not, both atoms and void exist. Use of the expression *ou mallon* functions here as a vivid way of expressing the Democritean position and endorsing the existence of atoms and of void. The same point is illustrated by some uses in Plato. At *Theaetetus* 182e, the argument against the Heraclitean view that everything is constantly changing in every respect concludes with a *ou mallon* claim. If everything were constantly changing in every respect one could not call a particular perception seeing *rather than* not seeing, nor any one perception *rather than* any other;[3] the associated account of knowledge as perception has turned out to provide something which is no more knowledge than not.[4] At *Charmides* 160b, c, a refutation of the suggestion that temperance might be quietness culminates in a claim of the same sort. Given that a temperate life is a good life, temperance is no more acting quietly than acting hastily (since of actions agreed to be better at least as many are hasty as are quiet). Nor is a quiet life any the more temperate than a hasty and impetuous life (since hasty and impetuous actions are no less good than quiet actions).

In some cases context makes it perfectly plain that an *ou mallon* statement is to be read with the force of an endorsement of the assertions which *ou mallon* relates. For example, the Democritean claim is that atoms exist and so does void. Equally clear is *Meno* 74d, e, where, in the course of clarification of the generality required of a Socratic definition, the thought that straight is a shape and round is a shape too is glossed as: round is no more shape than straight and *vice versa.*[5] In other cases the opposite holds, and *ou mallon . . . ê . . .* is to be taken with the force of a pair of denials. Again from Plato: at *Meno* 78e the remark that the possession of such goods as wealth is no more virtue than the lack of them is intended as the claim that being wealthy is not virtue, and nor is being poor.[6]

What is added to a bare assertion of p and q, or a straightforward denial of p and q, by the indifference claim 'p no more than q'? A claim in that form involves implicit reference to an underlying indifference argument. It is an indication that indifference reasoning could be provided to show that *either* both p and q should be endorsed *or* both p and q should be denied. There is rhetorical force in the indifference assertion in such cases because it is plain which of those conclusions should be drawn. For example, Plato's saying that round is no more shape than straight indicates an indifference argument: whatever reason there could be for identifying the more general kind *shape* with *round* could be matched by reason for the identification of *shape* with *straight*. Furthermore, since it is plain that those identifications are incompatible, it is clear that neither should be endorsed.

In other cases a conclusion can be expressed in *ou mallon* form in order to mark the possibility that choice between endorsement and denial should wait on further distinctions. Consider, for example, Plato's use of *ou mallon* in explication of the distinction between those perceptions that do and those that do not stimulate thought, at *Republic* 7, 523b on. Those stimulate thought which no more present one thing than its opposite.[7] *Ou mallon* is a particularly apt phrase to use here, since there is both something correct and something misleading in saying, for example, either that sight presents a finger as both large and not large, or that sight presents the finger as neither large nor not large. In one way it is correct to say that sight presents a finger as both large and not large. I am not making a visual error when I agree both that this finger is large and that it is not large. No further visual information would lead me to revise either of those claims. At the same time there is also something correct in saying that sight does *not* present a particular to me as large, at least not in the way that it presents it to me as a finger. This is why Plato raises the question as to whether sight sees largeness and smallness adequately, and talks of the sense as deficient or defective.[8] The puzzle raised is that it does not seem possible to think of something presented by sense in a stable way as being (say) large, or small, or both large and small, or neither large nor small.[9] The way forward offered by Plato, as is well known, is a way of locating certain things *between* being and not-being. Use of the *ou mallon* locution in saying that sight presents something as no more large than not large reflects exactly the position required, distinct on the one hand from endorsing and on the other from simply repudiating these deliverances of sense.

There is further implicit reference to indifference reasoning when there is appeal to considerations of parity of reasoning. In some cases appeal to parity of reasoning is a constructive move. At *Phaedo* 75 c, d, Plato generalizes an argument initially run with reference to equality, that perceptual experience reminds us of knowledge gained before we were born. The argument *no more* concerns the equal itself than it does the beautiful, the good, the just and the holy.[10] That is to say, there is no more reason to apply the argument to the one case than to the others. In other cases considerations of parity are cited for critical purpose, the intention being to show that an opponent holding one position *may as well say* something else which is agreed to be ludicrous. For example, Aristotle at *de Caelo* 3.8 307a24–30 ridicules the atomists' account of fire in just this way. If it is allowed that when something is burnt it is turned into fire by the action of fire, that must be explained on atomist principles as a body being broken up *by* fire atoms *into* fire atoms; but even if it is granted that bodies can be broken up *by* spheres or pyramids, it is ludicrous to suppose that they should break them *into* spheres or pyramids. One might as well think, Aristotle says, that knives cut things into knives and saws into saws.

It is indifference reasoning that underlies such cases. Appeal to parity of reasoning forces an opponent to a case with which he is uncomfortable because there is reference to a structure common to the cases. An argument can give reason to accept a conclusion only so long as it is valid, and validity is a feature of the structure of arguments, which is shareable. Hence if the argument I offer you really is on all fours with the argument you use, you have *no more reason* to accept the conclusion you want than to accept the conclusion I seek to force on you. As in the case of *ou mallon* conclusions mentioned above, the appeal to indifference arguments here is implicit. It will be of greater interest now to look at examples of arguments where an indifference claim is explicitly offered as a premiss, and where indifference reasoning is closer to the surface.

4.2 Anaximander's Earth

One of the earliest easily identifiable indifference arguments is that attributed to Anaximander by Aristotle, as an account of the position of the earth:[11]

> There are some who say, like Anaximander among the ancients, that it [the earth] stays still because of its equilibrium. For it behoves that which is established at the centre, and is equally related to the extremes, not to be borne one whit more either up or down or to the sides; and it is impossible for it to move simultaneously in opposite directions, so that it stays fixed by necessity.

There is reference to the same account in Plato;[12] it is also, it seems, misattributed to both Democritus and Parmenides.[13] While it has been doubted by some that Anaximander could ever have used such an argument, it is of more interest here to consider just what would be required for the argument to succeed.[14]

Aristotle's report mentions two conditions concerning the earth: first, that the earth is at the centre (τὸ ἐπὶ τοῦ μέσου ἱδρυμένον), and second that it is equally related to the extremes (ὁμοίως πρὸς τὰ ἔσχατα). The second of these adds something to the first, in that it makes explicit what the first requires. The centre of the cosmos, it might be supposed, is a position that could be picked out without saying anything about what is at that position. Anaximander's argument requires not merely that the earth be at that position, but also that it be so shaped that it can be equally related to the edges. While I can place an irregularly shaped rock in the middle of a circus ring, it may be that I cannot so place it that it is equally related to the edges.

The version of the argument found in Plato's *Phaedo* suggests further conditions:[15]

> if [the earth] is round and in the centre of the heaven, it needs neither air nor any other such force to prevent its falling, but the uniformity of the heaven in every direction with itself is enough to support it, together with the equilibrium of the earth itself; because a thing in equilibrium placed in the middle of something uniform will be unable to incline either more or less in any direction, but being in a uniform state it will remain without incline.

There are two distinct conditions to note: the uniformity of the heaven in every direction with itself[16] and the equilibrium of the earth itself.[17] The former is not equivalent to either of the conditions mentioned above in Aristotle's report of Anaximander's argument. It is the condition that the cosmos should be so shaped and structured that an appropriately shaped body at the centre *could* be equally related to the extremes. If the circumference of the cosmos were of irregular shape there might be no point at which a suitably shaped body could be at the midpoint of every straight line going through it from one edge to the opposite; if one part of the circumference exercised a particular influence on the earth – an unusual attraction or repulsion – then a body at the centre would not be equally *related* to the extremes.[18]

The argument can now be put more generally. In order to show by an indifference argument that the earth will not move to the edges of the cosmos, but will remain still, the following conditions need to be fulfilled:

(a) the earth is at the centre of the cosmos;
(b) the earth is so shaped,
(c) and the cosmos is so shaped and structured that . . .
(d) the earth *can* be equally related to the extremes of the cosmos.

Consider now what can be said more generally about conditions (b) and (c). Plato's argument in the *Phaedo* specifies that the earth is spherical, and the sphere is indeed a shape which satisfies (b). But it is not the only shape which does so. Anaximander did not take the earth to be circular, but to be a cylinder, with a depth one third of its width: an earth of that shape satisfies (b) just as well as a spherical earth.[19] In the case of Anaximander (c) is satisfied by reference to circles of fire, from which the earth is equidistant;[20] those details are also inessential to the core of the argument.

Given conditions (a)–(c), a minimal version of the indifference argument can be stated as follows. Suppose the cosmos is of such a shape that there is at least one line through it about which it exhibits reflective symmetry: what is on one side of that line is the mirror image of what is on the other. Suppose the earth likewise exhibits reflective symmetry around at least one line. Then that is enough for an indifference argument on all fours with Anaximander's to proceed. Imagine a set-up as in figure 4.1. AB is the line round which the universe exhibits reflective symmetry; the earth is somewhere on AB, and also reflectively symmetrical with respect to it. If Anaximander's argument is granted, the earth will have no tendency to move off the line AB, since there is no reason why it should move to one side rather than to the other, each side being a mirror image of the other. It might, however, move along the line AB. Now there are positions at one end of AB such that if the earth were placed in those positions it would move towards A, and positions at the other end such that if placed there it would move towards B.[21] As we go from A to B we pass continuously from positions of the first sort to positions of the second sort. Hence there will be some point along AB at which the tendency to move towards A is balanced by the tendency to move towards B. At that point the earth will remain still, with no reason to move off the line AB, and no reason to move in either direction along AB.

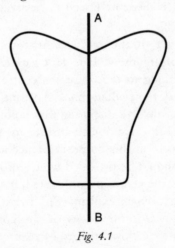

Fig. 4.1

An indifference argument along the lines of Anaximander's could then be run for any body and any container such that at some positions within the container the body tends towards one position on the edge of the container, so long as both body and container were reflectively symmetrical about at least one plane. An example would be a ball-bearing within a wire magnetized either so as to attract it or so as to repel it. In the argument as given by Plato, and as attributed to Anaximander by Aristotle, both the earth and the cosmos exhibit reflective symmetry around far more planes than one. Yet the various versions of the argument taken together manifest an awareness of the general conditions required for any set-up in regard to which the argument is to be run. How Anaximander arrived at the particular claims about the shapes of the earth and the cosmos involved in his use of the argument is not our concern here; nor is the fact that Anaximander's cosmology was false. The argument is interesting precisely because it admits of the more general formulation.

The response of Aristotle to Anaximander's type of argument is surprisingly hard to judge.[22] Aristotle offers examples of arguments comparable to Anaximander's which seem at first blush intended to reduce Anaximander's argument to absurdity, since the conclusions to which they lead appear ludicrous.[23] Aristotle mentions

> the analogy of the hair which, it is said, however great the tension, will not break under it, if it be evenly distributed, or... the man who, though exceedingly hungry and thirsty, and both equally, yet being equidistant from food and drink, is therefore bound to stay where he is.

Yet in the same chapter of the *de Caelo* Aristotle appears to endorse Anaximander's form of argument. It is as it happens true, he says, that it is necessary for anything to remain at the centre which has no more reason to move this way rather than that.[24] Aristotle's detailed objections to Anaximander do not involve disputing that point, or objecting to the indifference argument form. He objects instead to Anaximander's use of an argument of that form in this context. An account of why the earth remains at the centre should be provided which also explains why pieces of earth should *move* to the centre if unhindered; it should be an account of the same sort as that which explains why fire is at the edges of the cosmos, and moves towards the edges of the cosmos if unhindered. On these grounds Aristotle's own theory of natural places is preferable to what Anaximander says. Anaximander's approach could as well be used, Aristotle says, to show why fire, if it were at the centre of the cosmos, should remain there.

That last point makes it plain that Aristotle's apparent endorsement of Anaximander's argument form has to be taken with a pinch of salt. Not *everything* which has no more reason to move this way rather than that is bound to remain at the centre. In the case of the earth Anaximander added the premiss that it is impossible for it to move in opposite ways at the same time. That does not apply in the case of what is not rigid but fluid, such as fire.[25] So one would expect an indifference argument to give the conclusion that fire at the centre will separate and move equally to different points at the edges; and that is just the conclusion Aristotle accepts.[26]

4.3 Aristotle against the Void

Aristotle himself uses indifference arguments in *Phys* 4.8, in the course of denying the existence of void. *Phys* 4.8 contains arguments of different types aimed to show that it is impossible that there should be a void. In a number of them Aristotle's strategy is to argue that, far from void being *required* in order that motion should occur, the existence of void rather makes the occurrence of motion impossible.[27]

While the atomists are Aristotle's most obvious target, the arguments of *Phys* 4.8 are not simply *ad hominem* arguments intended to show that the historical atomic theory did not have the materials to explain how motion could occur in a void. They are aimed to show rather that *as a matter of fact* there could be no void and that motion in a void would be impossible. So there is no need in discussion of these arguments to limit ourselves to points that historical atomists might have been able or motivated to make for themselves. If Aristotle's arguments are good arguments they should not be vulnerable to more sophisticated responses.

Aristotle's criticisms are not all aimed at the same features of the void. Three characteristics which he sees as giving rise to trouble are the *emptiness* of void, the *uniformity* of void and the *infinity* of void. These are characteristics which differ in status. The first two are essential features of void, whereas the third is significant rather for historical reasons: the atomists who posited a void did in fact posit an infinite void. Aristotle's hostility is not limited to an infinite void, however.

He will also want to show that there could not be a finite void: for example, that there could not be an enclosed cosmos with particles of stuff moving round within it in a limited void. Arguments which rest on the *infinity* of a void are unlikely to be indifference arguments. Aristotle's indifference arguments about the void gain purchase because what is void is uniform. Yet there is no reason why an *infinite* medium for motion would have to be uniform: there could as well be an infinite heterogeneous medium. The first two characteristics, emptiness and uniformity, while both essential to void, also differ significantly. Emptiness is both an essential and a defining characteristic of void, while there could be media other than a void which were uniform. Given that a void is empty it *follows* that it will be uniform. As Aristotle puts it, as there are no differences in what is nothing, so there are no differences in a void.[28]

The indifference arguments Aristotle uses in *Phys* 4.8 are, as one might expect, directed primarily at the uniformity of the void. There are a couple of general points concerning Aristotle's arguments which follow from that.

First, since not everything uniform is void it should always be possible to reformulate these indifference arguments so as to raise problems about the possibility of motion through a uniform though non-void medium. It will typically be important to Aristotle that his own conception of motion should not be vulnerable to such reformulated arguments. In consequence Aristotle's use of indifference arguments to establish conclusions about void will leave him open to a dilemma. *Either* the arguments will apply equally well to models of motion which Aristotle would prefer to endorse, *or* the moves by which they are shown not to threaten Aristotle's preferred account of motion could be taken up by one who would evade the arguments and defend the possibility of motion in a void. This will be illustrated in what follows at some length as regards one of Aristotle's arguments, and then far more briefly as regards others. Later responses to Aristotle's arguments can often be viewed in terms of that dilemma, as features of Aristotle's own account of motion were adapted for accounts which admitted the existence of void.[29]

Second, it also follows that the arguments must apply no more and no less appropriately to the possibility of intra-cosmic void – there being void regions within the cosmos – than to the possibility of extra-cosmic void – there being void surrounding a cosmos which does not contain any void within its own boundaries. For since Aristotle's indifference arguments concern a feature of void shareable by non-void media they could be run equally appropriately as regards any uniform medium whether non-void, or a void. Consider one of these arguments applied to the case of a body moving through a homogeneous non-void medium. Plainly that argument would concern motion within a cosmos, since the stuff constituting that non-void medium would itself be part of a cosmos. Since what would be essential to the argument would be the uniformity rather than the non-emptiness of the medium, that argument would then apply equally well if the body were taken to be moving through void within a cosmos. This is a point about the logic of the indifference arguments concerning void, and does not necessarily establish anything straight off about the targets Aristotle had in mind in offering them. Still, given that the indifference arguments would be equally good in either case, it should not be surprising that Aristotle does not specify that their application is limited either to extra-cosmic or to intra-cosmic void.[30]

Of course, if the *indifference* arguments Aristotle uses turn out not to be good arguments, then while that will be interesting for our purposes it may show very little about whether Aristotle's rejection of the existence of void was a reasonable position for him to adopt. It may be that those of his arguments which are not indifference arguments are better arguments, or that those other arguments would be considered by Aristotle to be the more central arguments. None of that will be to the point here, however, since our main concern is with a type of argument rather than with Aristotle's views about void.

One of the arguments Aristotle uses mentions the indifference account of earth's position explicitly:[31]

Just as some say that the earth is at rest because of symmetry (διὰ τὸ ὅμοιον), so in the void too [a body] must be at rest, there being nowhere for it to move to more or less [than anywhere else], since the void, as such, admits no differences.

Another argument is that it is impossible that a body moving in a void should ever stop left to itself:[32]

Again, no one could say why something moved will come to rest somewhere; why should it do so here rather than there? Hence it will either remain at rest or must move on to infinity unless something stronger hinders it.

A third argument follows immediately, aimed at the reasons offered for supposing that a void should be required for motion. Melissus' argument was that without void there could be no motion, since a body would always run up against other bodies in its way.[33] The introduction of void provides something which yields to bodies:[34]

> Again, as things are it is thought that a body moves into a void because the void yields to it; but in the void this property is everywhere alike, so that it will move in every way.

The first argument will be considered first, and at greater length. Why should the fact that there are no differences in a void pose a threat to the possibility of motion? Aristotle's attack is aimed at the possibility of *differential* motion: motions of different types of things in different directions. For Aristotle himself differential motion is manifest *par excellence* in the basic natural motions of the elemental bodies. Even without reference to such a peculiarly Aristotelian example, it is a plain fact of experience, for which his opponents need to make room, that there are differential motions – for example, that olives fall down from trees while smoke rises up chimneys. If Aristotle can show that the existence of void renders differential motion impossible, void cannot be a necessary condition of motion.

It might seem at first sight as if the argument rests on the view that void *makes* bodies move. Since a void is uniform it could no more *make* a body move in one direction than it could *make* it move in another. Thus the existence of void would not allow for differential motion. That is the impression given by Aristotle's comparison with the indifference argument concerning the earth's position, and the examples Aristotle offered in *de Caelo* 2.13 to illustrate that argument structure. In the starving man example there, the unfortunate victim is trapped because food and drink *pull* him equally in opposite ways. Similarly it seems Anaximander's earth remains still as a result of balanced and opposed, yet unspecified, attractions. The third indifference argument mentioned above, used at 215a22–4, also seems vulnerable to the charge that it runs together the thought that void *allows* bodies to move and the thought that void *makes* bodies move. The argument was that, since a void yields in every direction equally, a body should *per impossibile* move in every direction at once in a void. But there is an obvious response to that. What is required to answer Melissus is that a void should *allow* bodies to move: since it is quite different to say that void *makes* bodies move into it the conclusion Aristotle alleges will not follow. Similarly, if the argument of 214b31–215a1 had proceeded in this way, then it would be a very poor argument. Even if atomists had in fact conflated the thoughts that void allows motion and that void makes motion occur – though it is uncharitable to suppose they did – still the argument is not aimed just at what historical atomists actually said. It should have been easy enough for someone else on hearing Aristotle's argument to distinguish what the atomists conflated. This first response to Aristotle's argument would, however, be too quick. The argument is far more interesting than that first reaction would allow, and it aims to show just what Aristotle says: that there *is* nowhere for a body in a void to move to more or less than anywhere else.[35]

The argument that follows at 215a1–14 brings the concept of natural change into the picture. It is against that background, of which Aristotle is convinced on the basis of other arguments, that we should understand his claim that a proponent of void would be unable to account for differential motion.[36] He attacks two aspects of the atomist account of motion: that it occurs in a *void* and that void is *infinite* in extent. As one might expect, given my earlier remarks, the arguments he uses are separable. First Aristotle claims that in an infinite cosmos there could be no natural places because there could be no distinction between up, down and middle.[37] That argument is independent of any considerations of indifference and the uniformity of a void. The same argument could be run for an infinite cosmos full of an infinite number of various-sized patches of different kinds of stuff, in contact with one another. Indeed earlier Aristotle did run much the same argument concerning the infinite with no reference to void, at *Phys* 3.5 205b31–206a1.[38]

What is of greater interest here is the other line of argument Aristotle cites at 215a1–14. The problem in holding that there is a *void* in which motion occurs is not so much that there would be no up or down, but, as he says, that there would be no *difference* between them.[39] This is not mere repetition of the problems raised concerning infinity. The focus is on the uniformity of a void, and it is here that we get an indifference argument. Suppose one could make out in geometrical terms an absolute distinction between up and down, in a uniform void, as one could if that void were finite in extent. Still, that would not be sufficient to legitimize an explanation of differential motion as, for example, motion up rather than down. For in a wholly uniform void what was up and what was down would be insufficiently distinct to count as genuinely different regions. We should expect that this argument could be run as regards a finite enclosed void, since it involves no appeal to infinity. Further, since the argument does not essentially concern the emptiness of void, except insofar as void's being empty shows it to be uniform, it should apply similarly to any uniform homogeneous medium for motion.

Imagine a cosmos that was finite yet wholly homogeneous: say a sphere of water beyond the edges of which there was just nothing.[40] One could make out a distinction in that cosmos between the edges and the centre, and so there would be room for drawing an absolute distinction between up and down. Up would be towards the edges, down towards the centre. If the argument of 214b31–215a1 from the uniformity of a void to the impossibility of differential motion is a good argument, it should also tend to show that differential motion would be impossible in this completely uniform medium. Yet that consequence should be unwelcome to Aristotle.

At *de Caelo* 4.3 310b3–5 Aristotle runs a thought experiment in order to illustrate the strength of explanatory appeal to natural places. If the whole earth were to be moved elsewhere in the cosmos and held there, bits of earth whose motion was unhindered would still move to where the earth actually is now (to the centre), rather than to where it is imaginatively specified to be (say, to the lunar sphere). We do not go much beyond what Aristotle imagines if we expand that counterfactual set-up a little. Suppose the area presently occupied by the earth and the area round it is imagined to be occupied by a watery sphere, and imagine further a bit of earth displaced from the centre somewhere in that watery mass. The reaction in this case consonant with Aristotle's response to his own thought experiment is that that bit of earth would move if unhindered to where the earth actually is now, to the centre. Why, however, should not a parody of the indifference argument of *Phys* 214b31–215a1 be effective?

> Just as some say that the earth is at rest because of symmetry, so too in that watery sphere a body must be at rest, there being nowhere for it to move to more or less than anywhere else, since the watery sphere, as such, admits no differences.

In order to say something about an Aristotelian response to that parody, it is necessary first to say something about Aristotle's more general notion of place.

Aristotle's account of place is primarily an account of what it is for something to have a place. A main ground for supposing that there is such a thing as place is that one body comes to be where another used to be.[41] The place of something is defined by Aristotle as the inner surface of what surrounds it.[42] What has a place is something with something else outside it.[43] What is of interest for our purposes here is that Aristotle draws consequences from this as regards places in a homogeneous medium. If A surrounds B but B is continuous with and not divided from A, then A is not the place in which B is, but a whole of which B is a part.[44] The parts of a continuous homogeneous mass do not have a place actually but only potentially.[45] That illustrates a point both about the lack of identity of such parts, and about the concept of place. A mass of water such as constitutes a lake has an identity and a place relative to some heterogeneous boundaries. Its place is, say, the surface of the earthy hollow in which it is collected. Its having a place marked out in that way goes along with its having some status as a particular mass of water. Parts of that mass of water do not have any such status as particular bits unless they are divided out in some way. Suppose I immerse a lobster pot in that water. Then there is the water within that pot which comes to have an identity and a place relative to the heterogeneous boundaries of the pot. All I can now say of the water within that pot prior to the immersion of the pot in the lake is that then it was only potentially marked out, and had a place only potentially.[46]

If the water now within this lobster pot had no actual identity prior to the immersion of the lobster pot in the lake, then the place now actually constituted by the boundaries of the lobster pot, which is now the place of that water, was not an actual place prior to the immersion of that pot. We will find this surprising only if we think of place as being marked out by reference to a wider set of coordinates. For in that case there could be in principle no objection to describing some volume of water as that which is so many feet from the bottom and so many feet from each bank of the lake, and the volume of water so described being just the water which will come to be enclosed by the lobster pot when it is immersed. But Aristotle's concept of place is precisely not made out in terms of wider sets of coordinates, but in terms of one body exactly surrounding another. In that case the consequence about place is only to be expected. If place is defined as the inner surface of a surrounding body at which it touches what it surrounds, then if there is not actually anything to be surrounded there is not actually any surrounding body, and so in that case there is not actually any place.

Suppose we now apply all this to the case of natural places. Aristotle's typical appeal to natural places in explanation of motion involves attributing some power to place.[47] As things in the cosmos actually are, the natural place to which appeal is made in explaining the natural motion of, say, a piece of earth is an actual place. It is the place of a mass of earthy stuff, and is the boundary of the surrounding stuff at which it touches that earthy stuff. The motion of a piece of earth to its natural place is, Aristotle says, a sort of actualization.[48] What it is to be heavy is to move towards the centre. The activity (ἐνέργεια) of what is heavy is its being at its natural place.[49] Something's being heavy is most fully expressed in its being at its natural place.

Something needs to be added if Aristotle is to give an account of the natural motion of a piece of earth in the counterfactual set up imagined earlier. In that case, it will be remembered, there is no actual place to which a fragment of earth is naturally moving. There is, however, a potential place. The upshot of the unhindered motion of the fragment of earth is now a dual actualization. Here the imagined example provides a nice illustration of how place can exercise a power (δύναμις) in natural motion: that is, teleologically. There is an actualization of a potentiality of the fragment of earth, as in the more normal case described in the paragraph above. In addition there is the actualization of the place that the fragment of earth naturally moves to. Once that fragment is there, there is an actual place which is the boundary of the surrounding watery stuff at which it is in contact with the piece of earth. In this case the natural motion terminates in a natural place becoming actualized, in its becoming the actual place of something whose nature is most fully actualized in its being at rest just there.

Recall now the indifference argument from which this discussion started. The argument will not apply to the Aristotelian cosmos as it in fact is, since that is a heterogeneous cosmos and the places to be appealed to in explanation of differential motion are constituted by actual boundaries between different elements. However, if we consider some counterfactual set-ups in which there are no longer actual boundaries to constitute natural places, the dilemma mentioned earlier comes to the fore. One possibility is that the adapted indifference argument might succeed in raising a problem about the Aristotelian account of natural motions and natural places. The charge would be that it is unclear why in the imagined set-up something *should* move back to a place which can be picked out only as a geometrical point in a homogeneous mass. The allegation will be that nothing said earlier about actualizations made anything any clearer. If that is the case, the indifference argument no more makes problems for the proponent of void than it does for Aristotle himself. The other possibility is that the adapted indifference argument generates no genuine difficulty for Aristotle, and that he can reasonably appeal to potential places actualized in unhindered natural motion in the way outlined above. In that case, however, a sufficiently sophisticated proponent of void should be able to adapt Aristotle's response, and say something along similar lines, in order to escape the charge that there could be no account of differential motion in a void.

The same sort of dilemma is manifest in the case of the other indifference arguments Aristotle offers in connection with void. The argument of 215a19–22 was that a body will not stop left to itself in a void, since there is no reason for it to stop at one place rather than another. Suppose someone were to ask a similar question about a body left to itself moving through air or water. One possibility is that this question should pose a real problem. Insofar as the air or water is a uniform medium a body in motion has no more reason to stop at one place rather than another. Plainly Aristotle will not be at all inclined to be worried about that possibility. The alternative is that whatever account Aristotle offers of why a body should stop at one place rather than another in, say, homogeneous air could as well be adapted to account for the cessation of motion in a void.

That possibility might not seem terribly plausible, though. There is a crucial difference between motion through a void and motion through air, and it is one that Aristotle can exploit in explaining why a body should slow down in a non-void medium. A body is slowed down by the resistance of what it passes through as it moves in the medium. That sort of explanation is indicated by the arguments Aristotle offers which aim to derive unacceptable conclusions about the velocity of bodies moving in a void.[50] Aristotle's claim is that the density of a medium and the weight of a body both make a difference to the velocity with which bodies move through media. A heavier body moves faster *ceteris paribus* than a lighter because the heavier body divides the medium more easily. Bodies of equal weight move more quickly in proportion as the medium through which they move is less dense because the less dense medium resists less. In that case the velocity of a body in motion across a void could not stand in any proportion to the velocity of a body moving across any other medium, since a void has no density at all. The velocity would be infinite. Further, since differences of density of medium give rise to differences of velocity, bodies in motion in a void would all have to move equally fast.

I have nothing to say here about whether those are good arguments or not. The point to notice is rather that what they identify as being problematic about void is not that it is uniform but that it is empty. It may be that Aristotle would have thought such arguments to be the most weighty. The consequence of that as regards the indifference argument at 215a19–22, though, is that it is not appeal to the *uniformity* of the void which causes trouble. *If* someone were to offer an account of why bodies slow down which had as a consequence that bodies would also slow down in a void, there would not be a further question of why a body should stop here rather than here in a uniform void to cause additional embarrassment.[51] Suppose, to put it crudely, I think that bodies slow down because they 'run out of steam', and that they would 'run out of steam' in a void no less than in a filled medium: then I will not be worried by the question of why a body should stop at one place rather than another in a uniform void, any more than I will be by the question of why it should stop here rather than there in a homogeneous mass of air. In effect I would avoid the problem Aristotle raises about the emptiness of void, and then apply the account of why bodies stop at one place rather than another in homogeneous non-void media to the case of void.

Finally, there is the argument that a void will yield equally in every direction. Of course the reason why atomists introduced a void in reaction to Eleatic arguments was that a void was *empty*. But the crux of Aristotle's argument at 215a22–4 is that emptiness is found in the void *everywhere alike*. It is properly the uniformity of void that is taken to cause the problems: and if that is the source of the difficulty the argument could be applied more widely. Suppose someone, such as Aristotle himself, believes that it is not necessary to introduce something empty in order to avoid Eleatic arguments. Still, motion obviously requires a medium that yields. That is why rocks move through fluids but not through solids. Media that yield typically do so in every direction alike. In that case there is a dilemma. One option is that it follows that a body moving through *any* homogeneous medium should *per impossibile* move in every direction at once. If that is the case Aristotle should be worried, no less than the proponent of void. The other option is that the conclusion does not follow, and that some account of motion can be provided to show why it does not. In that case the proponent of void might hope to adapt that account himself to explain motion in a void.

4.4 Agents and Patients

In *GC* 1.7 Aristotle discusses the account to be offered of action and passion, and of what it is for one thing to act on another. The views of his predecessors are given by reference to a dichotomy. Agent and patient will be either dissimilar or similar. The majority view was that agent and patient would have to be dissimilar, and Aristotle provides an indifference argument to render that plausible:[52]

Like is in every case incapable of being affected by like, since one is no more active or passive than the other, for all the same things belong equally to like things.

After reporting Democritus' peculiar view, that agent and patient are similar, Aristotle endorses the argument previously cited:[53]

That which is like, in the sense of being altogether and in every respect indiscernible, might well be argued not to be in any way affected by its like. Why, the argument might go, should one be active rather than the other?

The same type of argument, restricted to the case of one thing giving rise to another, is found in the pseudo-Aristotelian *Melissus, Xenophanes, Gorgias* in support of the first limb of an argument by dilemma, to show that god could not have come into being either from what is similar or from what is different. Something could no more have been begotten by than have begotten what is similar to it.[54] Nothing here rests on whether Xenophanes actually used that form of reasoning. That is perhaps no more likely than that *GC* 323b3–6 preserves reasoning actually employed by non-atomist presocratics as opposed to Aristotelian explication. The indifference argument itself, though, is an interesting one, and calls for some comment.

The argument used by Aristotle seems at first sight reasonably clear. Aristotle's target is the claim that what explains why one thing acts on another is their similarity to one another.[55] Similarity is a symmetrical relation: if A is similar to B then B is in just the same respects similar to A. Yet at least in many cases particular actions are asymmetrical: if a fire heats up some water the water does not also heat up the fire, though it will give rise to some other change in the fire. Whatever explains why one thing acts in a certain way on another should explain the asymmetry in such a case. Now Aristotle takes the notion of similarity that is at issue as a very strong notion.[56] Those things are counted as similar which are similar in every respect. As we shall see below, it is important to say how the notion of similarity involved should be taken. What is clear enough at present, though, is that such a strong relation of similarity is taken by Aristotle to rule out any asymmetries between A and B that could possibly explain why A should act as it does on B but not *vice versa*. The underlying thought here is that the asymmetries manifest in some type of action cannot be explained by appeal to symmetries between the objects involved.

That principle is sufficiently general and appealing to generate a *prima facie* plausible argument.[57] The passages cited from *GC*, however, suggest that a stronger and more contentious argument is on offer. What Aristotle attributes to his non-atomist predecessors is the bare claim that something will not be affected by what is similar to it. This is offered as completely general, with no limitation to cases of action in which there are asymmetries requiring explanation. Insofar as the argument is aimed against an atomist conception of action it is obviously preferable that there should not be such limitations. For an atomist the most basic vehicle of action is atomic collision, and the particular action of one atom on another in collision is apt to be a symmetrical *inter*action. While it would be fair for Aristotle to demand some account of how basic atomic collisions give rise to observed action at the macroscopic level, it would not be much of an argument against the basic atomic model of action to assume that there is a significant distinction which requires explanation between agent and patient.

The stronger argument is offered immediately following the passage previously quoted:[58]

Again, if something is capable of being affected by what is like it, it will also be capable of being affected by itself; and if this were the case there would be nothing imperishable or immovable, given that like *qua* like is capable of acting, for everything would move itself.

This argument starts from a conditional which encapsulates an indifference argument: if it were possible for something to be affected by what is similar to it, it would be possible for it to be affected by itself. Suppose A and B are sufficiently similar that there is as much reason for A to bring about a change in B as there is for B to bring about that very change in A. If A and B are that similar then, as Aristotle puts it, why should one be active rather than the other? So far this is the argument mentioned earlier. A further conclusion will now follow, since by parity of reasoning essentially the same argument will apply as regards anything which is at least as similar to A as B is. A itself is bound to be such an object. In that case there would be as much reason for A to bring about a change in itself as there is for B to bring about a change in A. Then if it is not possible that A should bring about a change in itself it is not possible that a change should be brought about in A by anything which is as similar to it as B: that is, by anything such that there is as much reason for it to produce a change in A as there is for A to produce that change in it.

To come to a view on this argument it is necessary to say something about the notion of similarity involved. It is necessary to ask what sort of similarity between A and B *is* sufficient for there to be as much reason for A to act on B as for B to act on A. In pursuing that question it becomes apparent that whether or not the argument is good depends on further views concerning the account that is to be given of some particular types of action. Those views are in themselves of considerable interest.

Mention was made earlier of similarity in *every* respect, as a gloss on Aristotle's expression 'what is like, in the sense of being altogether and in every way indiscernible' (323b18f).[59] The structure of the indifference argument is more perspicuous if that notion is clarified, along these lines. Let us say that A and B are *strongly similar* if and only if every shareable property of A that is generally characterizable is a property of B, and *vice versa*. There is good reason for the inclusion of these two qualifications here. A property of A is shareable if it is possible that it be possessed by A and something else besides. The point of that qualification is to guarantee that A and B's being strongly similar will be consistent with their being numerically distinct. Aristotle clearly does not have in mind similarities between objects of the sort we might take to imply identity – as, for example, similarity of spatial position. A property of A is generally characterizable if and only if it is not necessary to mention some other particular object in order to say what the property is. It is necessary to add that qualification in order that there can be two objects which are strongly similar. That would not be possible if the qualification were not added, and strong similarity required common possession of *every* shareable property. Being-to-the-left-of-B is a shareable property of A (since things other than A can be to the left of B), but it is not a property that it is possible for B to have.

The conditional from which Aristotle's argument starts can now be put as follows:

(1) if A and B are strongly similar and B can produce an effect on A, then A can produce that effect on itself.

Is that conditional true?[60] If it is true that must be as a consequence of what is involved in one thing producing an effect on another. A more abstract version of (1), which did not mention the production of effects, would not be at all plausible: if A and B are strongly similar, then if B can stand in some relation to A, A can stand in that relation to itself. A counter-example would be the relation 'is five feet away from'. So what would one have to hold about one thing's producing an effect on another in order that (1) should be true?

As expounded above the indifference argument which lies behind (1) involves claims about *reasons* for one thing's producing an effect on another. Undifferentiated talk of such reasons is unhelpfully broad. In giving the reasons why something produces an effect on something else, one thing it is appropriate to cite are those properties reckoned to be *efficacious* in the production of the change in question. To say that the reason the cup marked my table is that it was hot rather than that it was red is to identify temperature rather than colour as *efficacious* in the production of that mark. There are other features which can be cited as reasons *relevant* to a change's being produced in one thing by another, but which one might balk at identifying as causally efficacious. It is equally true to say that the reason the cup marked my table is that it was placed upon it without a mat. In general some appropriate contact between A and B will be required if B is to bring about a change in

A, and, depending on what a questioner wishes to be explained, that contact could be cited as a reason why the change was produced. The distinction between causal efficacy on the one hand and a weaker notion of causal relevance on the other is significant. What is causally efficacious as regards a particular change is what explains why that change occurred as it did, why it took the direction it did, why it was a change from *this* set-up to *that* set-up. What is causally efficacious is what a good scientific explanation of a change would aim to cite.[61] What is merely causally relevant will include background conditions, conditions which enable the change to occur but do not explain why it occurred as it did.[62] What is merely causally relevant is what would be offered in other less strict sorts of explanation. To the extent that the distinction between a good scientific explanation and a less strict sort of explanation is clear, the distinction between efficacy and relevance will be clear also.

There is a specific claim about what is involved in the bringing about of a change which is sufficient to render (1) true. That claim is the view that all properties which are efficacious are both shareable and generally characterizable. A consequence of that claim is that further properties which are relevant to the occurrence of a change, but which are not both shareable and generally characterizable, will not be efficacious properties. They will rather be background conditions: they will be necessary for, or enabling conditions of, the change. Given that view, (1) is defensible. Suppose A and B are strongly similar, and suppose that B can bring about some particular change in A. Does it follow that A can bring about that change in itself? Given that B *can* produce the relevant change in A, any background conditions required for the change to occur are fulfilled. If they were not then the change would not even be possible. An obvious and significant example of such a condition is that A and B should be in the appropriate contact. While B's being in contact with A is a shareable property it is not generally characterizable: it is a property reference to which requires reference to *A*. Given the view that efficacious properties are shareable and generally characterizable, it follows that contact between A and B will not be counted an efficacious property, but a background enabling condition. The properties that are efficacious in the change are those that would be appealed to in explaining why, given that the set-up was right for the change to occur, it *did* occur, and proceeded in the way it did. Given the strong similarity of A and B, and the view that efficacious properties are shareable and generally characterizable, it follows that any property efficacious in the production by B of a change in A is possessed in common by A and B. Hence granted a situation in which that change can occur in A, any reason that can be offered why B should bring about that change in A will be matched by a reason why A should bring about that change in itself. That is sufficient to give (1): if B can bring about a change in A, and A and B are strongly similar, then A can bring about that change in itself.

As one might expect, (1) is plausible of just such models of change for which the view about efficacy mentioned in the previous paragraph is plausible. An illustration would be Aristotle's model of agency as reproduction. Something produces an effect in virtue of the possession of a form, and the upshot of the activity is that the form is reproduced in what is affected.[63] Paradigm examples would be a hot thing heating, or a teacher teaching. There are background conditions that need to be fulfilled in order that a fire should heat up my milk, or a teacher should impart knowledge of geography. These will include the appropriate sort of contact between agent and patient: that the milk is on the fire, that teacher and pupil are within earshot. Those conditions are required for the change, and enable it to occur, but they do not explain why it occurs as it does. What is the source of the change, what one should cite as efficacious, is some form in the agent – heat in the fire, or knowledge in the teacher – which is reproduced in the object affected – the milk becomes hot, the pupils become knowledgeable. In each such case what renders the one object an agent at all, and able to produce a particular sort of change, is the possession of a form. The fire is a heater in virtue of its heat, the expert a teacher in virtue of possessing knowledge. That is what explains how the agent was able to produce the sort of change it did. Contact of the appropriate sort is a background condition, the obtaining of which enables what is affected to be affected, and enables the agent to produce the change it does in the way that it does.

Such examples manifest precisely the further view about change mentioned earlier. What is efficacious, the form, is both shareable and generally characterizable, and so would be possessed in common by objects which were strongly similar. Further features which are not generally characterizable, yet which are relevant, are considered background enabling conditions: conditions which are required for the change to come about, yet which are not productive of it. In consequence (1) is plausible of the types of change of which the examples mentioned above are a good illustration. Since fires warm milk in virtue of the heat they possess, it is as impossible that a fire should warm milk that is of the same temperature as itself as it is that the milk should warm itself. Since teachers teach their pupils in virtue of the knowledge they possess, it is impossible that any teacher should teach pupils already possessed of the knowledge of their teacher.

Correlatively, (1) will not be defensible as regards types of change for which the assumption about efficacious properties is not plausible. Suppose there are efficacious properties which are not both shareable and generally characterizable. Then it will not follow from A and B's being strongly similar that they have in common all the properties efficacious in this instance. Any property that is both efficacious and not generally characterizable could be possessed by B yet not by A, while it remains true that A and B are strongly similar. In that case it would not follow that there is as much reason for B to produce a change in A as for A to produce the change in itself. The case of mechanical collision provides a clear example. Suppose B collides with A and dents it, or alters its trajectory. B's having a direction of movement *towards A* is a property of B efficacious in the production of that change. It is not a background condition, the holding of which enables A to be affected by B. It is what would be cited, in some way, in a good explanation of how A came to be affected as it was. It is because B has that property, of moving towards A, that it produces the change it does in A: for example, that B changes the direction of A's motion in just the way it does. Further, that is a property of B that is not generally characterizable, for it is necessary to mention A in order to say what the property is. B's moving towards objects which are, to whatever degree, similar to A will not serve to explain how B produced the effect it did on A. Further still, it is not a property that A could possibly possess, and since it is not a generally characterizable property it will not follow from A's being strongly similar to B that it does possess it. So it will not follow from A's being strongly similar to B that A could dent itself, or alter its own trajectory. Hence the perfectly plain fact that A could not have these effects on itself will not tend to show that A could not be affected by objects strongly similar to it. In a world of strongly similar atoms – atoms of equal size, shape, weight and so on – there would be exactly this sort of mechanical action of one atom on another.

Now we have made some progress as regards the indifference argument with which we started. Whether there is a good indifference argument underlying the conditional

(1) if A and B are strongly similar and B can produce an effect on A then A can produce that effect on itself

depends on whether strong similarity between objects guarantees that there is as much reason for the one as for the other to produce an effect. If it does the argument is no more problematic than many another indifference argument. If the one can produce an effect so can the other, and if the one cannot nor can the other. What is stimulating about the argument are the issues about action and change which are connected with the underlying question about strong similarity.

4.5 Closing Remarks

There are other indifference arguments which could be discussed. Plato's argument at *Theaetetus* 209a–c, that if what I have in mind when thinking of Theaetetus holds no more of Theaetetus than of Theodorus, then my thought will not be a thought of Theaetetus any more than of Theodorus, has similarities to the argument discussed in the preceding section. The argument noted earlier in Parmenides, that if there is to be generation there needs be a reason for its being at one time rather than another, is also found in Aristotle.[64] There are certain types of argument used in rhetoric which Aristotle mentions.[65] If we do not find something where it is more likely to be found we can conclude that it does not exist where it is less likely to be found. If what is less likely turns out to be true we can conclude that what is more likely is true also. Granted, for example, that a man is more likely to be honest in his dealings with his own family than with complete strangers, if a man is not honest with his own family we can conclude that he is not honest with strangers. Similarly, since there is more reason to expect honesty in family dealings than in wider dealings, if someone *is* honest in their wider dealings one can conclude they are honest in family matters. The exposition of such inferences plausibly involves appeal to indifference reasoning. Suppose that it is equally likely that a man is honest in dealing with his sons as in dealing with his daughters. That is to say that there is no more reason for him to be honest in dealing with his sons than in dealing with his daughters. Then if he *is* honest in dealing with his sons we can conclude that he *is* honest in dealing with his daughters.

Each of these cases, and no doubt others also, would bear comment in their own right, and in each instance there are likely to be underlying points of independent interest to be identified. The identification of such points has been a principal aim in discussing some occurrences of indifference arguments in this chapter. Yet in order to maintain a balance between consideration of specific indifference arguments, and attainment of a more general perspective on the argument form, it is important now to turn to a more abstract discussion of indifference arguments. On that basis it will be possible to say something of fairly wide application about what makes an indifference argument a good or bad argument.

NOTES

1 The development of the *ou mallon* formula is the subject of de Lacy (1958). As his title indicates, de Lacy's main concern is with the development of the *ou mallon* formula characteristic of ancient scepticism. This chapter is not mainly concerned with scepticism, nor with giving a historical account of the use of the *ou mallon* formula.

2 Aristotle *Met* 1.4 985b7–9, DK 67A6, Luria §7: 'Since the void exists no less than body, it follows that what is not exists no less than what is' (διὸ καὶ οὐθὲν μᾶλλον τὸ ὂν τοῦ μὴ ὄντος εἶναι φασιν, ὅτι οὐδὲ τὸ κενὸν τοῦ σώματος). Plutarch *adv Col* 1108f, DK 68B156, Luria §7, reports use of *ou mallon* in giving the view of Democritus that 'the thing exists no more than the nothing, [Democritus] calling body thing and void nothing' (μὴ μᾶλλον τὸ δὲν ἢ τὸ μηδὲν εἶναι, δὲν μὲν ὀνομάζων τὸ σῶμα, μηδὲν δὲ τὸ κενόν).

3 ὁρᾶν... μᾶλλον ἢ μὴ ὁρᾶν, οὐδέ τιν' ἄλλην αἴσθησιν μᾶλλον ἢ μή.

4 οὐδὲν ἐπιστήμην μᾶλλον ἢ μὴ ἐπιστήμην.

5 *Meno* 74e, σχῆμά οὐδὲν μᾶλλον εἶναι τὸ στρογγύλον τοῦ εὐθέος, οὐδὲ τὸ ἔτερον τοῦ ἐτέρου.

6 *Meno* 78e, οὐδὲν μᾶλλον ὁ πόρος τῶν τοιούτων ἀγαθῶν ἢ ἡ ἀπορία ἀρετὴ ἂν εἴη...

7 523c, ἡ αἴσθησις μεδὲν μᾶλλον τοῦτο ἢ ἐνατνίον δηλοῖ. Similarly μηδὲν μᾶλλον ἓν ἢ καὶ τοὐναντίον φαίνεσθαι at *Republic* 7, 524e; see also *Republic* 5, 479b, *Hippias Major* 289c.

8   *Republic* 7, 523e3f, 6f.

9   *Republic* 5, 479c3–5.

10 *Phaedo* 75c, οὐ γὰρ περὶ τοῦ ἴσου νῦν ὁ λόγος ἡμῖν μᾶλλόν τι ἢ καὶ περὶ αὐτοῦ τοῦ καλοῦ...

11 Aristotle *de Caelo* 2.13 295b11–15, DK 12A26, translation after KRS: εἰσὶ δέ τινες οἳ διὰ τὴν ὁμοιότητά φασιν αὐτὴν [τὴν γῆν] μένειν, ὥσπερ τῶν ἀρχαίων Ἀναξίμανδρος. μᾶλλον μὲν γὰρ οὐθὲν ἄνω ἢ κάτω ἢ εἰς τὰ πλάγια φέρεσθαι προσήκει τὸ ἐπὶ τοῦ μέσου ἱδρυμένον καὶ ὁμοίως πρὸς τὰ ἔσχατα ἔχον· ἅμα δ' ἀδύνατον εἰς τἀναντία ποιεῖσθαι τὴν κίνησιν. ὥστ' ἐξ ἀνάγκης μένειν. See also DK 12A1, 11, and Kahn (1960, §10, pp. 53–5, 76–81).

12 *Phaedo* 108e, 109a; *Timaeus* 62e, 63a.

13 By Aëtius, DK 28A44, Luria §4. The misattribution to Democritus is perhaps suggested by the use of the argument form; the claim about Parmenides is more puzzling. The addition by Aëtius that the earth does not move but shakes is odd.

14 Robinson (1953), Furley (1987, ch. 3.2), Furley (1987a) deny that the argument gives a genuinely Anaximandrian account of the position of the earth. The doxographers are not wholly consistent. Theon Smyrnaeus DK 12A26, Kahn (1960, §10, p. 54), says that according to Anaximander the earth *moves* around the centre; Simplicius *in de Caelo* 532.14f, Kahn (ibid.), says that it also remains still because it rests on the air.

15 *Phaedo* 108e, 109a, translation after Gallop (1975).

16 109a, ὁμοιότητα τοῦ οὐρανοῦ αὐτοῦ ἑαυτῶι πάντηι.

17 109a, τῆς γῆς αὐτῆς ἡ ἰσόρροπια.

18 The condition that the earth is in the middle of something uniform ὁμοίου τινὸς ἐν μέσωι. I take to be the same as the uniformity of the heaven in every direction with itself.

19 Kahn (1960, §11, pp. 55f, 81f), from Hippolytus and pseudo Plutarch. The view which Freudenthal (1986, p. 214) notes is taken by many commentators – that 'Anaximander's argument for the stability of the earth . . . is not valid for a cylindrical earth whose surface is *not* equidistant from the circumference', and that in consequence a spherical earth is suggested by Anaximander's argument – is thus false.

20 Kahn (1960, §§13–16, pp. 57–61, 85f), DK 12A17a, 18, 21, 22, 13A12. The fact that the circles are uniform might be taken as ruling out the possibility that one part of the cosmic circumference should exercise an undue influence on the earth. There will be no more reason for one part to exercise a special influence than another, if the rings are homogenously fire.

21 This statement is intended to be non-committal on the question of whether the earth is attracted by the edges (in which case it will move towards A if closer to A) or repelled by the edges (in which case it will

move towards A if closer to B). Since the argument is so stated as to be neutral on that question, no difference will be revealed between the case in which the earth stays at the centre in an unstable equilibrium (as it will do if attracted by the edges) and that in which it stays there in a stable equilibrium (as it will do if repelled by the edges). In the former case it would move to the edge if displaced from the centre, in the latter it would return to the centre if displaced. There is no indication in the argument attributed to Anaximander of any awareness of this distinction, and I guess the argument is meant to be powerful independently of that issue being raised.

22 *de Caelo* 2.13 295b15–296a22.

23 *de Caelo* 2.13 295b30–4, as the Revised Oxford Translation.

24 *de Caelo* 2.13 296a4ff.

25 Compare the point added by Plato in his use of the argument at *Timaeus* 62e, 63a, that what is at the centre is something firm or hard, τι στερεὸν.

26 *de Caelo* 296a12–15. It is not clear why the purveyors of Anaximander's in-difference argument should be committed, as Aristotle charges here, to the view that fire at the centre will move as a whole to one point on the edge.

27 For the claim that the existence of void is a necessary condition for motion, see Melissus DK 30B7 (7), cited in Chapter 2.4 above.

28 *Phys* 4.8 215a9–11.

29 See Sorabji (1988, ch. 9) for discussion of such responses.

30 That Aristotle does not restrict these arguments is noted by Sorabji (1988, p. 148f). Sorabji's further point there that 'the arguments would be more persuasive if restricted to the behaviour of the entire physical cosmos in an extracosmic void' cannot, however, be correct, in the light of the points made above.

31 214b31–215a1, translation Hussey (1983).

32 215a19–22, translation Hussey (1983).

33 Melissus DK30B7 (7).

34 *Phys* 4.8 215a22–4, translation Hussey (1983).

35 *Phys* 4.8 214b32f, οὐ γὰρ ἔστιν οὗ μᾶλλον ἢ ἧττον κινηθήσεται.

36 There are questions, which I pass by, about whether this is a fair strategy for Aristotle to adopt against the atomists, and what it shows about the account Aristotle took the early atomists to have provided of the motion of atoms. See Furley (1976) for a discussion of this latter.

37 215a8f.

38 'Again, every body perceptible by sense is in place, and the kinds and varieties of place are: above, below, forward, backward, right and left. These are not determined only relatively to us, and conventionally; they

are so in the universe itself. But they cannot exist in the infinite' (trans. Hussey, 1983). There is a related indifference argument at *Phys* 3.5 205a12–19, concerning the possibility of infinite body. If there were an infinite body which was a single sort of stuff, then no part of it could have a natural motion. A part of that infinite body would have no reason to move in one direction rather than another in the infinite place required for the whole body. Any place would be as much its natural place as any other, since the whole body is homogeneous. If every place were its natural place, displacement would never be followed by natural motion back to a proper place. On the other hand, if no place were its natural place then there could be no natural motion.

39 Note the difference of emphasis between 215a8f, 'in as much as it is infinite, there will be no above or below or centre' (ἧι γὰρ ἄπειρον, οὐδὲν ἔσται ἄνω οὐδὲ κάτω οὐδὲ μέσον), and 215a9, 'in as much as it is void, the above will be no different from the below' (ἧι δὲ κενόν, οὐδὲν διάφορον τὸ ἄνω τοῦ κάτω).

40 Compare the example imagined by Aristotle for another purpose at *Phys* 4.5 212a32f.

41 *Phys* 4.1 208b1 on.

42 *Phys* 4.5 212a5f. At 212a6f he explains that what he means by what is surrounded (τὸ περιεχόμενον), and so what has a place, is a body which can be moved locally (σῶμα τὸ κινητὸν κατὰ φοράν). Complexities concerning the further requirement that something's place should be an unmoving surface (212a14–21) can be ignored for our purposes. The problems are clearly discussed in Sorabji (1988, ch. 11).

43 *Phys* 4.2 209b32f, 'That which is somewhere is always thought both itself to be something and to have some other thing outside it' (trans. Hussey, 1983); also 4.5 212b14ff.

44 *Phys* 4.4 211a29–31.

45 *Phys* 4.5 212b4f.

46 I pick the example of a fluid deliberately in order to make a point more easily which is clear enough in outline, although harder to put completely generally. A number of wooden cubes which fit together perfectly so as to fill a trunk completely will maintain their identity while in contact, and each will have a separate place. This is the sort of case Aristotle has in mind at *Phys* 212b6, when he says that things which are separate but touching, like a heap, will have a place actually.

47 *Phys* 4.1 208b8–11: the natural motions of the elements show both that place is something (ἐστί τι ὁ τόπος) and that it has some power (ἔχει τινὰ δύναμιν).

48 *de Caelo* 4.3 311a2–6; also 310a33f, the movement of something to its own place is a movement to its own form, τὸ εἰς τὸ αὐτοῦ εἶδός φέρεσθαι.

49 *Phys* 8.4 255b8–13.

50 *Phys* 4.8 215a24–216a21.

51 Compare Sorabji (1988, p. 158f) on Philoponus' response.

52 *GC* 1.7 323b3–6: τὸ μὲν ὅμοιον ὑπὸ τοῦ ὁμοίου πᾶν ἀπαθές ἐστι διὰ τὸ μηδὲν μᾶλλον ποιητικὸν ἢ παθητικὸν εἶναι θάτερον θατέρου (πάντα γὰρ ὁμοίως ὑπάρχειν ταὐτὰ τοῖς ὁμοίοις), translation after Williams (1982).

53 *GC* 1.7 323b18–21: τό τε γὰρ ὅμοιον καὶ τὸ πάντηι πάντως ἀδιάφορον εὔλογον μὴ πάσχειν ὑπὸ τοῦ ὁμοίου μηθέν (τί γὰρ μᾶλλον ἔσται θάτερον ποιητικὸν ἢ θάτερον;...,) translation after Williams (1982).

54 *MXG* 3 977a14–18, DK 21A28.

55 As stated at *GC* 1.7 323b23f, the claim under consideration is that it is similars *insofar as they are similar* that are active, τὸ ὅμοιον ἧι ὅμοιον ποιητικόν.

56 This fits with his overall strategy, to show that in disagreeing with one another his predecessors had each some partial grasp of the truth. Aristotle's own view is that agent and patient are similar in some respects, dissimilar in others.

57 Compare *Topics* 2.18 108b13f, where it is given as reputable (as an ἔνδοξον) that what holds of one of a group of similars holds also of the rest.

58 *GC* 323b21–4: εἴ τε ὑπὸ τοῦ ὁμοίου πάσχειν τι δυνατόν, καὶ αὐτὸ ὑφ' ἑαυτοῦ – καίτοι τούτων οὕτως ἐχόντων οὐδὲν ἂν εἴη οὔτε ἄφθαρτον οὔτε ἀκίνητον, εἴπερ τὸ ὅμοιον ἧι ὅμοιον ποιητικόν, αὐτὸ γὰρ ἑαυτὸ κινήσει πᾶν, translation after Williams (1982).

59 Compare the strongest relation of similarity Aristotle gives at *Met* 5.9 1018a15f: those things are similar whose characteristics are the same in every way, τά πάντηι ταὐτὸ πεπονθότα.

60 Williams (1982) diagnoses the argument of 323b21–4 as vitiated by ambiguity. On the one hand, if the claim under attack is that something can be affected by *whatever* is like it, it will follow that it could be affected by itself. However, it is unfair for Aristotle to foist that claim on his opponents. On the other hand, while they may well have supposed that something can be affected by *something* that is like it, it does not follow from that that it can be affected by itself. That diagnosis seems irrelevant to the truth of (1). The more important issue appears to be the understanding of similarity involved.

61 For a typical contemporary use of this distinction, see Jackson and Pettit (1990). What it is, they say, for a property to be efficacious is for it to be a property 'in virtue of whose instantiation, at least in part, the effect occurs'; a property whose instantiation 'helps to produce the effect, and does so because it is an instance of that property' (p. 108).

62 Causal relevance is of interest to contemporary philosophers because it might be held that higher level correlates of underlying properties (for

example, fragility) can be taken to be causally relevant, while it is the lower level underlying properties (for example, atomic structures) which are taken to be genuinely efficacious. This is relevant to questions in the philosophy of mind: could psychological states be causally efficacious, or does efficacy reside only in some underlying physical (neural) structure?

63 For example, *Phys* 3.2 202a9–12, *GC* 1.7 324a9ff, *de An* 2.5 417a17–20.

64 *Phys* 8.1 252a11–19; *de Caelo* 1.12 283a10–17. See Sorabji (1983, ch. 15) for the later developments and discussion of cosmological versions of this sort of argument.

65 *Rhetoric* 2.23 1397b12–27. There are also the inferences Aristotle discusses in *Topics* 5.8.

5

The Form of Indifference Arguments

◆

Earlier chapters have shown something of the prevalence of indifference arguments. The aim now is to see when use of an indifference argument is acceptable. 'Acceptable' is a deliberately wide term. By asking after the acceptability of an indifference argument I mean to consider whether its use in a particular context, to establish a particular conclusion, should be endorsed: whether the argument as used gives good reason to accept the conclusion. Consideration of that question involves investigation of the general structure of indifference arguments. What in general validly follows from an indifference premiss, from a claim that there is no more reason for p than for q? That is the question for discussion in this chapter.[1]

Now while the question to be considered is a general one, it will not, of course, be possible to give a purely *formal* analysis of indifference arguments, since the indifference argument structure is not a *formal* argument. Still, the driving assumption of this book is that there is some *common structure* to be discerned through all the various arguments picked out as indifference arguments. The point of earlier chapters was to direct attention to that common structure through identification of particular instances of the arguments. My intention is to say something enlightening about this common structure which will apply across the range of different sorts of indifference arguments. If that intention is to be fulfilled there are contrary dangers to be avoided. On the one hand it is important not to wed an account of indifference arguments too closely to some specific, and contentious, analysis of the central notions involved. These, as it will turn out, are notions of reasons and modalities.

Over-specificity would here be a vice just because it would manifest a failure to sustain the vagueness and ambiguity in the notion of a reason that is at the heart of the *general* argument structure. A consequence of that failure would be that the account of indifference arguments which resulted would be insufficiently sensitive to the breadth of the notion of a reason to do justice to the variety of plausible indifference arguments. On the other hand, if a general account of indifference arguments is to be engaging and genuinely enlightening it cannot simply reproduce what is confused and unclear about the notion of a reason. What is needed is an account of indifference reasoning which allows for sufficient breadth in the notion of a reason, while focusing on genuinely central and uncontentious features of that notion. Only such an account will enable us to see what is impressive and powerful about indifference reasoning, and to engage critically in the sort of arguments to which earlier chapters have directed attention.

5.1 Two Types of Argument

First it is necessary to separate two very different types of indifference argument. These are to be distinguished by the form of their indifference premiss. Generally an indifference argument will have a premiss of the form: there is no more reason for p than for q. This is to be taken symmetrically, as meaning that as regards the terms of the premiss, p and q, there is neither more nor less reason for the one than for the other. Such a premiss can be read in one of two ways: either epistemologically, as

(A) there is no more reason to say (assert, judge ...) that p than to say (assert, judge ...) that q

or non-epistemologically, as

(B) there is no more reason for p (to be true) than for q (to be true).

For the sake of brevity I will sometimes talk of A-form and B-form indifference arguments. An A-form indifference argument has an indifference premiss of form A, a B-form argument a premiss of form B.

The premiss forms (A) and (B) are given so as to emphasize the distinction between epistemological and non-epistemological arguments. No complexity internal to the terms of the premisses p and q is revealed. When we consider particular indifference arguments it will often happen that some internal complexity of p and q is revealed, and it will emerge that there are various ways in which an indifference premiss can be stated. Consider a situation where John has no more reason to drink milk than to drink wine. An indifference premiss could be stated in various ways. For example,

(a) John has no more reason to drink milk than to drink wine.
(b) There is no more reason for John to drink milk than for John to drink wine.
(c) There is no reason for John to drink milk rather than to drink wine.
(d) There is no more reason why John drinks milk than why John drinks wine.
(e) There is no more reason for 'John drinks milk' to be true than for 'John drinks wine' to be true.

The way in which the indifference premiss is stated will not affect the account to be offered of indifference reasoning. So such differences as those between factors which explain why John F-ed and factors which give John a reason to F can, for our purposes, be ignored. It is safe to ignore these differences because (a)–(e) are equivalent, in that they are all true or false together. For example, if (a) is false and John does have more reason to drink milk than to drink wine (he wishes to avoid intoxication) then (b) is false, since the desire to avoid intoxication is more reason to drink milk than to drink wine; and (c) is false since John's desire to avoid intoxication is reason for him to drink milk rather than to drink wine; and (d) is false since the desire to avoid intoxication gives more reason why John drinks milk than why he drinks wine; and (e) is false since John's desiring to avoid intoxication is reason for 'John drinks milk' to be true rather than for 'John drinks wine' to be true.

The equivalence of the forms (b) (there is no more reason for p than for q) and (c) (there is no reason for p rather than q) merits particular comment, since it will be of importance later. It may be impossible to say anything comprehensive and general about what is involved in the comparison of reasons. In part this will be because the breadth of the notion of a reason has to be retained in order to do justice to the range of indifference arguments. Nevertheless there are minimum constraints on what can sensibly be said. The equivalence of the forms (b) and (c) is one such constraint. If there were more reason for p than for q then that would be reason for p rather than q, and if there were reason for p rather than q then there would *ipso facto* be more reason for p than for q.[2] If someone were to deny that, what grasp would they retain of talk of *more* reason?

The distinction between A-form (epistemological) and B-form (non-epistemological) arguments is an important one, since parallel arguments of these different forms may well not be equally acceptable. Consider the following examples. I show you a coin and offer you this A-form argument. There is no more reason for you to say this coin will show heads when next tossed than for you to say it will show tails when next tossed, and so you should not say either of these things. That seems a good argument. Given the epistemological position you are in, faced with a seemingly fair coin, you have no grounds to make any declaration about what the coin will do when next tossed. But a parallel B-form argument would not be acceptable: there is no more reason for this coin to show heads when it is next tossed than for it to show tails when it is next tossed, therefore it will show neither.[3]

A-form indifference arguments seem more straightforward, and less contentious, than B-form arguments. I will reserve detailed comment on them until later. Here I will say only that an A-form argument is to be understood by reference to the justification of assertions by evidence. If some evidence justifies me in asserting p, but would also and to the same extent justify me in asserting q – that is, if an A-form indifference premiss is true – then that evidence cannot justify me in asserting p with the implication that q is false. So, on the basis of such evidence I should assert both p and q if I assert either. So if p and q are incompatible I should assert neither.

Since the distinction between A-form and B-form arguments is made by reference to the *premisses* of the arguments, it is possible that either form of argument should have either epistemological or non-epistemological *conclusions*. A-form arguments to epistemological conclusions are fairly common, and are illustrated by the coin example given earlier. On the other hand, A-form arguments to *non-epistemological* conclusions are far less common and far more contentious. A sorites paradox such as Wang's paradox might constitute an example.[4] The A-form indifference premiss is: for any number n, there is no more reason to say that n + 1 is a large number than to say that n is a large number. The support for that premiss is that the addition of 1 to any number can never give more reason to apply the predicate 'large' than there was before the addition of 1. The conclusion that appears to follow is paradoxical precisely because it appears to be non-epistemological: there *are* no large numbers. One might not endorse this argument. Many issues of substance are raised by the attempt to avoid doing so, and this is not the place to go into them. The point here is merely to illustrate the possibility of there being A-form indifference arguments to non-epistemological conclusions.

B-form arguments are more interesting. Their structure is more difficult to discern, and they are more likely to be dismissed as generally ludicrous. It is important to remember that central cases of B-form indifference arguments are presented as having not only non-epistemological premisses, but non-epistemological conclusions too. For example, we have seen that Democritus argues by indifference reasoning that the number of shapes in the atoms *is* infinite, and that there *are* infinite worlds. It is the claim that indifference arguments can lead from non-epistemological premisses to non-epistemological conclusions that is so provoking. Just as there could be A-form indifference arguments to non-epistemological conclusions, so too there could be B-form indifference arguments to *epistemological* conclusions. B-form arguments will seem less contentious if taken in that way than if taken as establishing non-epistemological conclusions. Consequently there is a temptation to interpret all B-form arguments as defensible only if taken as generating epistemological conclusions. For example, since there is no more reason for there to be atoms of this shape than atoms of that shape, it is *reasonable to believe* that there is an infinite variety of atomic shapes; since there is no more reason for there to be a world here than there in the void, it is *reasonable to believe* that there are infinite worlds, and so on.[5] Now it might be charged that no sense is to be made of B-form indifference arguments to non-epistemological conclusions, and that the best to be hoped for is to establish epistemological conclusions from B-form arguments.[6] It might further be charged that B-form arguments to non-epistemological conclusions are plausible only to the extent that they are confused with those to epistemological conclusions. Yet given what the arguments *claim* to show, this seems a despairing line to take. It is one that should be considered only when the general structure of B-form indifference arguments has been clarified, and it has been seen what there is to be said in defence of B-form arguments to non-epistemological conclusions. It is to that general structure I now turn.

5.2 Reasons and Modalities

One might wonder whether it is possible to establish anything of substance about reasons without commitment to a particular account of what reasons are. If it is not possible it will be hard to give a general account of indifference reasoning. For as noted above we want to avoid contentious commitments to specific accounts of the concept of a reason. Progress is possible, though, because something very general can be established: it is that a B-form indifference argument justifies equivalences between the terms of the indifference premiss, *taken modally.*[7] From

(1) there is no more reason for p than for q

there follow uncontentiously

(2) $Lp \equiv Lq$

and

(3) $Mp \equiv Mq$.

The argument for this is as follows. (1) is contradicted by

(4) $Lp \& \neg Lq$

since if p is necessary, while q is not, then *that* is more reason for p than for q. So (1) implies $\neg(Lp \& \neg Lq)$, and so $Lp \rightarrow Lq$. Similarly (1) is contradicted by $\neg Lp \& Lq$. So (1) implies $\neg(\neg Lp \& Lq)$, and so $Lq \rightarrow Lp$. So (1) implies (2).

(1) is also contradicted by

(5) $Mp \& \neg Mq$

since if p is at least possible while q is impossible, then *that* is more reason for p than for q. So (1) implies $\neg(Mp\&\neg Mq)$ and so $Mp\to Mq$. Likewise (1) is contradicted by $\neg Mp\&Mq$. So (1) implies $\neg(\neg Mp\&Mq)$, and so $Mq\to Mp$. Thus (1) implies (3).

Now this argument requires discussion, since it carries a good deal of weight in the account of B-form indifference arguments. It is important to be clear on what is being attempted. The inference from (1) to (2) or (3) is offered as uncontentious in two respects. First, it does not rest on any specific, and therefore potentially contentious, account of what constitutes a reason. Second, it is not limited in its application just to some particular reading of the modalities. For example, it will apply to both alethic and deontic modalities;[8] and the argument is not limited, more specifically, to logical, physical, temporal or any other sort of modality. Both these points are important if we are to say something *general* about indifference arguments. An account of indifference arguments which required some particular reading of the modalities, or some specific account of reasons, would not be satisfactory for its purpose. It would tell us nothing about applications of indifference arguments which did not concern modalities of that type, or which seemed not to derive from a context where that notion of a reason was operative. It would be insensitive to the richness of the indifference argument structure.

Indeed, the fact that we want a *general* account of indifference arguments suggests that we should focus on the implication by an indifference premiss of *modal* equivalences. In comparison with those implications, an argument from (1) to

(6) $p \equiv q$

could not be seen as persuasive independently of contentious questions about reasons. The point is clear as soon as one tries to offer the same sort of argument from (1) to (6) as led from (1) to (2) and (3). For the first step of that argument would be the claim that (1) is incompatible with

(7) $p\&\neg q$.

Now (1) and (7) *would* be incompatible *if* one held that there must always be a reason why things are as they are rather than any other way. For then if p is the case and q is not there must be a reason why p is the case rather than q; so if there is no more reason for p than for q – and hence equivalently no reason why p is the case rather than q – then it cannot be that p *is* the case and not q; so (1) would then imply ¬(p&¬q). But that principle about reasons is something like the Principle of Sufficient Reason, and while the Principle of Sufficient Reason might be true – though it seems implausible that it should be – still it is plainly contentious. An analysis of indifference arguments which required the truth of such a contentious principle about reasons would be unsatisfactory in a number of ways. First, since the Principle of Sufficient Reason is a general claim, an analysis of a form of argument which rests on its being true would not survive its turning out to be false. Second, indifference arguments would be of limited interest if tied to a contentious claim.

Since the argument from (1) to (2) and (3) could not be a purely formal argument it will have to be mediated by some principles connecting reasons on the one hand and modalities on the other. The best way to defend the move from (1) to (2) and (3) as plausible is first of all to identify certain highly *im*plausible or, at least, highly specific, principles which might be *thought* to be required for the move from (1) to (2) and (3), but which are in fact *not* so required. The inference from (1) to (2) and (3) then gains plausibility through being detached from contentious assumptions. With those assumptions out of the way it becomes clearer which relations between reasons and modalities *are* required for the move from (1) to (2) and (3). Since it is the move from (1) to (2) and (3) which underpins indifference reasoning we can then see what general features of the notion of a reason are relevant to indifference arguments *in general.* In this way we will avoid the opposed dangers mentioned earlier. On the one hand, the account to be offered of indifference arguments will not be over-specific, since the inference from (1) to (2) and (3) does not require any overly specific account of reasons. On the other hand, we can identify features of the notion of a reason which are required for the move from (1) to (2) and (3). In doing so we identify a core notion of a reason sufficiently broad to be relevant to a wide range of indifference arguments, but with sufficient content to illuminate the intuitive power of indifference arguments.

The first point to make is that something is required for (1) even to be sensible. Not every pair of sentences will be comparable with respect to their reasons. This is plain by example. There seems neither more nor less nor equal reason for me to go to the cinema tonight, than for me to learn Spanish, than for me to keep my promises, than for the spleen to function as it does, than for two plus three to be five ... Whether or not sentences *are* comparable is independent of whether they are necessary or merely contingent. It is one way necessary for two plus three to be five, in another way necessary for me to keep my promises, but those sentences do not seem comparable. It is necessary for two plus three to be five and necessary for two times three to be six, and those sentences are comparable. On the other hand, it is in one way necessary for the spleen to function as it does and merely contingent whether I learn Spanish, and those sentences do not seem comparable. Yet it is not the fact that one sentence is necessary and another contingent that prevents comparison in respect of reasons. If it *were* impossible to compare the necessary and the contingent in respect of reasons then the move from (1) to (2) would be trivial. Suppose there is a disease rampant which is bound to kill those who are not inoculated and catch it, and yet suppose the inoculation does not in all cases prevent the disease: rather, it greatly lowers the probability of catching the disease. Alan is not inoculated while Bobbie is inoculated, and yet both catch the disease and die. Then Alan's death was necessary, Bobbie's merely contingent, and there was more reason for Alan to die than for Bobbie to die.

The distinction between sentences which are and those which are not comparable with respect to reasons[9] rests on another distinction, between different types of modalities. The first distinction is no more or less clear than the second: p and q will be comparable so long as it is *appropriate* or *sensible* to suppose that p and q should be necessary (or impossible or merely possible) in the same sense of necessary (or the related modalities) – that is, so long as p and q are *modally homogeneous*. Examples suggest that this is on the right lines. There seems neither more nor less nor equal reason for me to go to the cinema tonight than for two plus three to be five since, while it is appropriate (and true) to suppose it logically or mathematically necessary for two plus three to be five, my visiting the cinema tonight would, if necessary at all, be a prudential necessity (for example, necessary for my cultural advancement) or perhaps a physical necessity (for example, necessitated by the laws of nature and the state of the universe). It would at any rate be inappropriate to suppose it logically necessary.

Of course it will not always be perfectly clear in what respect some sentence which we suppose necessary *is* necessary. Is it, for example, *logically* necessary that something is not both red and blue all over? Or is it, if these are at all different, *conceptually* necessary? Or is it *physically* necessary? If it is physically necessary, is that necessity derived from the laws of physics or from some higher autonomous science? To the extent that questions about types of modality do not admit of a determinate answer in a particular case, it will be equally indeterminate how a question about comparability is to be answered in that case. There is nothing surprising in that. Some of the sentences that I said above were *not* comparable might have struck some readers as *being* comparable. Still, if there is disagreement about comparability, what is at issue is modal homogeneity. My reason for saying that there is neither more nor less equal reason to keep my promises than to learn Spanish was that, while keeping promises might be thought of as a moral necessity, learning Spanish would appropriately be thought of as a prudential necessity. Someone might disagree: perhaps it seems that there *is* more reason to keep my promises than to learn Spanish. But if that is plausible, that is because we are thinking of both promise keeping and learning Spanish as appropriate instances of the same type of modality. The thought might be, for example, that, while it is appropriate to suppose it morally necessary to keep my promises, the learning of Spanish will never in fact be other than morally contingent: learning Spanish is allowed but not required. That thought is what supports the claim that there is more reason to keep my promises than to learn Spanish. The comparison is underpinned by some single type of modality. One might say that it seems quite generally that there is more reason for what is morally necessary that for what is prudentially necessary. That is because it is assumed that what is prudentially necessary is as such invariably morally contingent.

The issue here is connected with a matter discussed by philosophers interested in the contrastive theory of explanation.[10] That is the view that the canonical form of explanation involves a *contrast* in both explanans and explanandum. The proper form of an explanation is: p rather than q because r rather than s. In order to defend that claim it is necessary to say something about which contrasts are sensible and which not. It seems sensible to ask for an explanation of why Alice won the departmental prize rather than Billy, but not sensible to ask for an explanation of why Alice won the prize rather than the bank base rate falling below 5 per cent. Various accounts have been offered of what makes a contrast sensible. Many claim that a necessary condition of a contrast's being sensible is that explanans and contrast should be *incompatible*. It is sensible to ask why Alice won the class prize rather than Billy because it is impossible that they should both have won it. However, that suggestion has been convincingly disputed.[11] An alternative suggestion is that a sensible contrast requires a largely, or significantly, similar history or background against which some *difference* stands out, as calling for explanation. Chuck and Danny are of the same age, and have similar life styles, diet and so on. It is that background of similarities which gives sense to the question of why Chuck developed depression while Danny did not: there is no *incompatibility* in their both becoming depressed.

Given this view about the contrast between p and q, our earlier claim that p and q are comparable so long as they are modally homogeneous might seem far too loose. If 'there is (no) more reason for p than for q' is to make sense then 'there is (no) reason for p rather than q' will make sense too. But if 'there is reason for p rather than q' makes sense then it makes sense to suppose there should be an answer to the question 'why p rather than q?' – since a reason for p rather than q would provide an answer to that question. In that case, the *question* 'why p rather than q?' must also make sense. But that p and q should be modally homogeneous – that they should be appropriately thought of as qualified by the same type of modalities – is a far weaker requirement than anything plausibly offered as a condition for a sensible explanatory contrast.

It is important to say something about this point, since the significance of the 'p *rather than* q' locution in both indifference arguments and the contrast theory of explanation is apt to make misleading comparisons tempting. The rationale for the contrasive theory of explanation is epistemological. Giving explanations invariably involves selecting among an excess of whatever sort of item is reckoned to be provided in explanations: causes, perhaps, or true answers to 'why?' questions. If a request for an explanation of p properly had to be a request for an explanation of p *rather than q* then the need for selection would be emphasized in the very form of a request for explanation, and a way of making a selection would be suggested. It is not generally the case that whatever is relevant to p is equally relevant to p rather than q. So seeking an explanation of p rather than q will impose a selection on the plethora of factors relevant to p *simpliciter*. If that is the rationale for a contrastive theory of explanation, it is bound to be the case that p and q will be appropriate contrasts only so long as there is a good deal in common between them. For only if there is a good deal in common between them will the question 'why p rather than q?' succeed in narrowing attention to just part of the background of p.

In contrast, what is required for comparability is far more minimal. What is required is just that there should be sufficient similarity between the terms of the indifference premiss p and q that the whole background of reasons for p could be compared with and balanced in general against the reasons for q. That is secured so long as p and q are modally homogeneous. Whether or not reasons *have to* give rise to necessities, it is uncontentious that they *could* do so. So if p and q were modally *heter*ogeneous – that is to say, if they *could not* be necessary in the same sense – then the reasons for p and q *could not* 'balance' in the way asserted by an indifference premiss. If p and q were modally heterogeneous it would be impossible for the reasons for p and the reasons for q to render p and q necessary in the same way.

For example, suppose I pick a p and q that could both be appropriately thought of as physically necessitated. In that case I can see what the claim that there is no more reason for p than for q would come to. That indifference claim would advert to the same sort of reasons as regards p and as regards q: the laws of nature and the previous physical state of the universe. If I can say what an indifference premiss concerning p and q would come to I must suppose that the comparison of p and q in respect of reasons makes sense. That will be so however difficult it might be in a particular case to answer the question of whether there *is* more reason for p than for q. On the other hand, in the absence of even the minimal comparison between p and q which follows from their being modally homogeneous, there is no guarantee that an indifference premiss will have any content.

So, while the question 'why p rather than q?' will *make sense* so long as p and q are modally homogeneous, that is a fairly minimal claim. It is certainly far weaker than the claim that q in 'why p rather than q?' will be a *sensible contrast* for p in the context of a request for explanation.

What is required for p and q to be comparable in respect of reasons is that it be appropriate or sensible to suppose p and q necessary in the same sense. It need not be *true* that p and q are necessary in the same sense. So it will follow that there can be comparisons in respect of reasons between what is necessary and what is contingent. Such a comparison was illustrated earlier by example. Alan's death and Bobbie's death are comparable in respect of reasons because it would be appropriate in each case to suppose their deaths *physically* necessary. The two things compared are modally homogeneous. The fact that one actually is physically necessary while the other is not does not threaten that point.

From now on I will limit my attention to pairs of sentences which are comparable in respect of reasons. The move from (1) to (2) and (3) might still seem implausible. It is uncontentious that (2) and (3) will follow from (1) if (1) is incompatible with (4) and (5). Since I want to preserve a looseness in the notion of a reason in (1), it will be difficult straight away to offer a supplementary argument to show that (1) *is* incompatible with (4) and (5). An indirect strategy is preferable. What makes the claim that (1) is incompatible with (4) and (5) seem *im*plausible is confusion about the relation between reasons and modalities to which the claim is committed. Once those confusions are identified, it should no longer seem implausible that (1) is incompatible with (4) and (5).[12]

First of all the argument offered does not rest on the thought that a reason for p must render p necessary. Put another way it does not involve the equivalent thought that there is no reason for what is merely contingent. At the very least that would be a contentious view to hold about reasons. It is not *prima facie* a true claim. During dinner Charlotte eats a steak, and drinks port, and subsequently develops indigestion. It can surely be true that the reason for her indigestion was her drinking port (rather than her eating steak) without it being true that her drinking port made it necessary that she would get indigestion.

There are two grounds on which someone might doubt that my argument is innocent of commitment to the claim that a reason for p must render p necessary. One is fairly slight. Leucippus links reasons with necessity, and claims that nothing is contingent: the only words purporting to be a direct quotation from Leucippus run:[13]

Nothing occurs at random, but everything for a reason and by necessity.

Leucippus was an atomist, and atomists, as we have seen, were taken with indifference reasoning. So perhaps indifference reasoning goes along with the idea that nothing for which there is a reason is contingent.

The second point is more substantial. The assumption that a reason for p must render p necessary would support an argument from (1) to the falsity of (4); further, it is alleged, without that assumption no argument from (1) to the falsity of (4) would be plausible. The thought is that if

(4) $Lp \& \neg Lq$

is true then, on the assumption that reasons necessitate and that there is no reason for what is merely contingent, there will be *no* reason for q. But if

(1) there is no more reason for p than for q

then there will be no reason for p either. That, however, seems to sit ill with p's being *necessary*. In that case (4) will be false if (1) is true. On the other hand, if it is not assumed that there is no reason for what is contingent, then we cannot infer from $\neg Lq$ that there is no reason for q, and if we cannot make that inference the move from the truth of (1) to the falsity of (4) is blocked.

The first point raised should not detain us. No general conclusion about reasons could fairly be drawn from Leucippus' words. Nor should one be swayed by the second charge. The argument that (1) is incompatible with (4) does *not* require the assumption that there is no reason for what is contingent. The claim that if

(1) there is no more reason for p than for q

is true, then

(4) $Lp \& \neg Lq$

is false requires only that the necessity of p and the contingency of q is a reason for p rather than q, and thus is more reason for p than for q. It is not required that there be *no* reason for q, and so it is irrelevant that there *can* be reasons for what is merely contingent. Equivalently it is not required that whatever is a reason for p render p necessary. All that is asserted is that if p *is* necessary then that is reason for p rather than q. It is, to be sure, a further question whether that assertion is defensible. That will become clearer presently.

A second and possibly more influential error concerning the argument from (1) to (2) and (3) is this. It might be reckoned that the argument offered involves supposing that it would be a good *explanation* of p simply to say that p is necessary. That would be a cause for concern if it were so, since it is almost invariably not the case that citing necessity provides a good explanation. The most that can be said is that citation of the necessity of p might *sometimes*, in the context of *some* questions, give an explanation good enough for the purposes at hand. Suppose Donald has invited that roughneck Eddie to his party, and the question of why he has done so is raised, the questioner's interest being in whether Donald's action shows anything about Donald's tastes in friends. I might provide an explanation perfectly satisfactory for those purposes by saying that Donald *had to* invite Eddie, since by doing so I reveal Donald's action not to be freely chosen.

Even so there are two important points to make. First, such cases are likely to be pretty rare. It will always be the case that a further request for an explanation of the necessity is possible and in order. Why, for example, did Donald *have to* invite Eddie? Because Eddie made threats which no reasonable man could resist against Donald if Donald did not invite him. It will most usually be the case that a further explanation of the necessity will be required if much light is to be cast on what is to be explained. However, that will not undercut the argument offered for the incompatibility of (1) and (4). There is a second point to emphasize. (1) does not concern the balance of *explanations*. By an explanation I mean what is provided by the *citation* of a reason. (1) is the claim that there *are* no more reasons for p than for q, that there *is* no reason for p rather than for q. It is quite consistent to hold both the following. First, that if p is necessary and q is not there is therefore reason for p rather than q; and second that an explanation of p which simply cites the necessity of p need not provide a better explanation than an explanation of q which does not reveal q as necessary. I give a better explanation of why Fay asked Graham to the party if I cite Fay's feelings for Graham, and her hopes of the outcome of being at the party with him, than I do of Donald's asking Eddie to the party if I say just that Donald *had to* ask Eddie. The first is a better explanation than the second even though my explanation of Fay's inviting Graham leaves it a contingent matter that she did invite him. She might have reckoned that her hopes were as likely to be fulfilled had she not invited Graham, but visited him at home instead. What is at issue in the argument from (1) to (2) and (3) is not, however, whether citation of one factor or another provides a better explanation, but whether the necessity of one outcome is reason for that outcome rather than some contingent outcome.

What then *is* required for the move from (1) to the falsity of (4) and (5)? The argument will go through so long as it is plausible that the necessity of p and the contingency of q is a reason for p rather than q. That can be made plausible by reflection on the thought that while, as has been pointed out, citation of the necessity of p will not generally be giving a very *good* explanation of p, yet it will provide *some* explanation, however feeble. For if I cite the necessity of p I do more closely circumscribe p, to however minimal a degree, than if I say just that it is true that p. Citation of the necessity of p presents p in a certain light, and rules out certain ways of seeing p. Such circumscription of p is at the core of explanation. Giving an explanation of the state of affairs reported by p involves presenting p in a certain light, setting it in a certain position relative to a background of possibilities. That is why I can often explain an occurrence by *redescribing* it, for the redescription relocates what called for explanation against a background. For example, I redescribe a mark on someone's arm as a bruise, or some physical contact as an embrace. In doing so I explain something about the mark or the physical contact.

Similarly, if the necessity of p is cited then p is presented in a certain light, and some ways of viewing p are ruled out. It is ruled out that p is the case by luck, or by chance, or that p was very likely yet contingent. For example, suppose someone asks: 'why did Hedy die after drinking that wine?' It is something of an answer to reply: 'she had to, it was necessary, she had no chance.' That reply rules out some ways of looking at Hedy's death. It rules out that it was pure chance that she died after drinking the wine, or that drinking that wine made it merely *likely* that death would ensue, as would be the case if, say, she had an ulcer that would be aggravated by wine, and was *more likely* to rupture if aggravated. Of course, citation of a necessity will not give a very good explanation because bare citation of a necessity leaves so much still open. Anyone sufficiently interested in Hedy's death to ask in the first place why she died will want her death placed within far narrower bounds. That is to say, they will want to know *why* her death was necessary on drinking the wine. Was it that the wine was poisoned, or that something about her biochemistry made alcohol necessarily fatal, or that her ulcer was in such a condition that any more wine was *bound* to lead to rupture and death? If I am unable to answer those further questions and am unable to circumscribe the *necessity* of Hedy's death any further, there are grounds for criticism of my explanation. In that case my citation of the necessity of her death was a particularly feeble explanation. Nevertheless it remains the case that my citation of that necessity provided *some* explanation.

Now if citation of the necessity of p provides some explanation, however feeble, of p, then the necessity of p constitutes a *reason* for p. While we are maintaining some looseness in the notion of a reason, in order to allow for the variety of indifference arguments, it is a minimal requirement that a reason is precisely what can be cited in explanation, however poor the explanation might be.

Suppose this is granted. Still a worry remains. How will it follow that if p is necessary and q is not then there is *more* reason for p than for q? All that has been shown is that if p is necessary that is *a* reason for p.

What is significant is that there are no similar grounds for supposing that the contingency of q could be a reason for q. For citation of the contingency of q gives *no* explanation, however feeble, of q. The point may seem to be obvious, and labouring it to be perverse. Indeed it might seem hard to see *what* to say in its support. Nevertheless, the asymmetry between citation of the necessity of p and citation of the contingency of q cannot reside just in the fact that citing the necessity of p presents p in a certain way, and rules out some other ways of seeing p. For it is just as true that citing q's contingency rules out certain ways of viewing q. It rules out precisely that q *had* to come about, or was *bound* to be the case. Yet citation of the contingency of q still will not provide any explanation of q – though it is difficult to avoid circularity in expounding the point here. Asking for an explanation of q manifests an assumption. It is assumed that q was the case rather than not-q, and that *that* is what requires explanation.[14] Citation of the contingency of q could not explain that, since if q is contingent so too is not-q. In citing the contingency of q I am only pointing to the default assumption of asking for an explanation of q in the first place.

Consider an example. Answering the question 'why did Hedy die after drinking the wine?' by saying 'it was chance, she didn't have to, she might not have done' offers nothing in the way of explanation. It may of course be true that her death was contingent, and there will be a further question to ask about *why* it was contingent. That question will be worth asking if there is some presumption that it *shouldn't* have been contingent – 'given the amount of poison we put in the wine, how *could* it have been chance?' Yet pointing out that her death was contingent will not provide any explanation of why she died. Another way to put the point is that to describe something as contingent is not so much to give a *positive* characterization of it as to deny that it is either necessary or impossible. It is of course consistent with this to suppose that there can be all sorts of explanations, and good explanations at that, of what is contingent. That is why it was earlier shown that the argument from (1) to (2) and (3) does not imply that there are no explanations of what is contingent. The point here is that to cite contingency will not be to offer, or even gesture towards, such an explanation of what is contingent. Since citation of contingency does not provide any explanation, however feeble, q's contingency will not be any sort of reason for q.

It follows that the move from the truth of

(1) there is no more reason for p than for q

to the falsity of

(4) Lp&¬Lq

proceeds on the basis of a minimal assumption about reasons: that a reason can be cited in an explanation. For a consequence of that assumption is that, while the necessity of p is a reason for p, the contingency of q is not a reason for q. Suppose that p is necessary and q is not. Then q is either impossible or contingent. If q is impossible then, since the necessity of p constitutes a reason for p, while the impossibility of q can hardly constitute a reason for *q*, then there is reason for p rather than q. Likewise, as argued above, if q is contingent. So, if (4) is true there is reason for p *rather than* q; further there will not be reason for q *rather than* p, since p is *bound* to be the case. As noted earlier the claim that there is reason for p rather than q is to be taken asymmetrically (if there is reason for p rather than q there is not also reason for q rather than p), and is equivalent to the claim that there is more reason for p than for q.[15] So, if (4) is true then (1) is false, and if (1) is true then (4) is false.

There are no assumptions about a particular way of reading modalities built into this argument. So the argument should run for any and all modalities. As a consequence the account of indifference arguments which rests on this argument should apply generally. The crucial point required is that citation of necessity provides some sort of explanation while citation of contingency does not. The plausibility of that point can be illustrated as regards different types of modalities, and in cases involving both compatible and incompatible outcomes.

First *deontic* necessities. I have more reason to go to the seminar at noon tomorrow than to go to lunch at noon tomorrow (there is reason for me to go to the seminar at noon tomorrow rather than to go to lunch at noon tomorrow) if I *have* to go to the seminar (it is a demand of duty, required by my contract of employment) but don't *have* to go to lunch. In this case the outcomes are incompatible. The same holds in a case where the outcomes are compatible. I have more reason to return my overdue book to the library than to return it to Ian at the library (I have reason to return it to the library rather than to return it to Ian at the library) if I *have* to return it to the library (it is required of me as a borrower) while Ian is but one among many library assistants.

Second, *physical* necessities. In some cases outcomes are incompatible. There is more reason for the bridge to collapse under the weight of the lorry than for it to flex (there is reason for the bridge to collapse rather than to flex) if the weight of the lorry and the construction of the bridge are such that its collapse is physically necessary, determined by laws of mechanics. In others outcomes are compatible. There is more reason for James to die than for James to die at noon on 1.1.99 if it is physically (medically) necessary that humans are not immortal, while their precise times of death are not physically (medically) determined.

Finally, *logical* necessities. An example concerning incompatible outcomes: there is more reason for a random prime number greater than two to be odd than for it to be even (there is reason for a random prime number greater than two to be odd rather than even) since its logically necessary that a prime number greater than two be odd. The case of compatible outcomes can also be illustrated. There is more reason for a random prime number greater than two to be odd than to be between 10 and 20 (there's reason for a random prime number greater than two to be odd rather than between 10 and 20) since it is logically necessary that a prime number greater than two be odd.

The move from

(1) there is no more reason for p than for q

to

(3) Mp ≡ Mq

does not require such lengthy discussion, since some of the basic points have been clarified. That move proceeds by means of the contradiction between (1) and

(5) Mp&¬Mq

The argument here is in one way more difficult, in another way easier. It is not possible to offer an exact parallel to the argument concerning necessity. For while citation of the *impossibility* of q will indeed give an explanation, (however feeble), the explanation will be an explanation of *not-q*; and citation of the contingency of p will give no sort of explanation of p. Yet the indifference premiss is the claim that there is no more reason for p than for q, that there is no reason for p rather than q: it does not raise a question about the availability of reasons for *not-q*.

On the other hand, it is possible to argue more directly in this case from (1) to the falsity of (5). The more lengthy argument concerning necessity was required in order to make clear that the move from (1) to (2) did not involve the assumption that there is no reason for what is contingent. One could not conclude straight away from the contingency of q and the necessity of p that there was more reason for p than for q, since there could well *be* reason for q.

In the case of the move from (1) to (3), in contrast, a more direct argument is possible. It does not rely on the (false) thought that the possibility of p is a reason for p. All the argument requires is that citation of the contingency of p *along with the impossibility of q* should be an explanation, however feeble, of why p *rather than q*. Citing the impossibility of q makes it plain that q is not the case, that it *cannot* be the case; citing the bare possibility of p leaves it open that p should be the case. While citing the possibility of p will not explain anything about why p is the case, it will explain why p is the case rather than

q. So the possibility of p conjoined with the impossibility of q is reason for p rather than q. Of course it is not assumed that these reasons necessitate, and so p might not actually *be* the case. Still, there is reason for p to be the case, at least *rather than q*: and so the claim of the indifference premiss (1) that p and q are 'balanced' in respect of their reasons for obtaining is false.

Again this can be shown plausible by example, involving the various sorts of modality, whether outcomes are incompatible or compatible. First *deontic* possibilities. Incompatible outcomes: I have more reason to park my car in the supermarket car park than on the town hall lawn (there is reason for me to park my car in the supermarket car park rather than on the town hall lawn) since parking in the first is allowed, on the second forbidden. Compatible outcomes: I have more reason to get from here to London by travelling on the motorway than by cycling on the motorway (there is reason for me to get to London by travelling on the motorway rather than by cycling on the motorway) since the latter is forbidden while the former is permitted.

Second, *physical* possibilities. Incompatible outcomes: there is more reason for the coin to show heads when I toss it than for it to remain suspended in the air (there is reason for it to show heads rather than for it to remain suspended in the air) since the latter is physically impossible, the former physically possible. Compatible outcomes: there is more reason for the water to boil when heated at standard pressure than for it to boil at 50 °C when heated at standard pressure (there is reason for it to boil when heated at standard pressure rather than to boil at 50 °C when heated at standard pressure) since the latter is, while the former is not, physically impossible.

Finally, *logical* possibilities. Incompatible outcomes: there is more reason for a randomly picked triangle to have base angles summing to 120° than to have base angles summing to 180° (there is reason for a randomly picked triangle to have base angles summing to 120° rather than to 180°) since only the former alternative is a logical possibility. Compatible outcomes: there is more reason for a random prime number greater than two to be between 10 and 20 than to be even (there is reason for a random prime number greater than two to be between 10 and 20 rather than to be even) since the latter alternative, unlike the former, is logically impossible.

Now the advantage of basing an account of indifference arguments on the derivation of modal equivalences is manifest. For it is plain that there could be no similar argument from

(1)   there is no more reason for p than for q

to

(6) p ≡ q

since there is no contradiction between (1) and

(7) p&¬q

which could be derived as above. For citing p's *being the case* or q's *not being the case* could not constitute any sort of explanation, however feeble, of p or not-q. In such a case neither p nor not-q are put in any more specific a light than they are already in through the assertion that p or that not-q. Since the truth of (7) will not uncontentiously entail the falsity of (1), there will be no argument from (1) to (6).[16]

Still, it often seems that indifference arguments *do* aim for non-modal equivalences as conclusions. *How* could such conclusions be derived in general? There is an assumption which is both necessary and sufficient for an argument from (1) to (6), a strongly determinist assumption:

> D: for anything that does happen, or is the case, there is a reason for it, rather than anything else that could have happened or been the case, to happen or be the case.

D is sufficient for an inference from (1) to (6). Suppose

(7) p&¬q.

Since p is the case, then according to D there is some reason for p: call it Rp. Now consider q, which according to (7) is *not* the case. There are two alternatives. On the one hand, perhaps q *could have* been the case: but in that case according to D Rp will be reason for p rather than q – and so (1) will be false. On the other hand, perhaps q *could not have* been the case: but then, on the line of argument considered above, the impossibility of q plus Rp will be reason for p rather than q, and so there will be more reason for p than for q, and so (1) will be false.

D is also necessary for the inference from (1) to (6). For if D were not accepted that inference would not be justified. Suppose D were false. Then it would be possible that p should be the case without there being any reason for p being the case; and so it would be possible that there should be no reason for p rather than q, and yet for p to be the case rather than q. Hence if D were false then (1) could be true and

(7) p&¬q

true also, in which case (1) could not imply

(6) p ≡ q.

There is a great difference between D and the assumptions made about reasons in the argument from (1) to (2) and (3). While those assumptions were minimal and uncontentious, D is at least highly contentious and at most plainly false. As we shall see, though, we do not need to suppose that (1) should entail (6) in order to give an account of indifference arguments. All that is required for there to be acceptable indifference arguments is that the inference from (1) to (2) and (3) should be safe, and defensible on the basis of minimal assumptions about the notion of a reason and for various readings of the modalities. It has been the argument of this chapter that that inference is indeed safe. It is because that inference is safe, and is at the core of any indifference argument, that arguments of this sort have the intuitive appeal they do.

Indifference arguments as they are actually used, however, invariably do not aim for the sort of conclusions which I have argued follow uncontentiously from an indifference premiss. First, the conclusions are generally not equivalences at all. Second, the conclusions are not usually modal. An argument from an indifference premiss 'there is no more reason for p than for q' will typically proceed either to the conjunction of the terms of the premiss ('hence p and q...') or to the negated disjunction of the terms of the premiss ('hence neither p nor q nor...'). Democritus, for example, argues that there *are* an infinite number of worlds, rather than that there *have to be* or *can be*, or that one thing obtains if and only if another does; Anaximander's argument was that the world *will not* move; Zeno contended that a division of a homogeneous medium once started *will not* stop anywhere, and so on.

So there is a further question to ask. What has to hold of the terms of an indifference premiss in order that in a particular case there should be a legitimate move from the modal equivalence – which can be derived uncontentiously – to the non-modal conclusion typical of indifference arguments? Whether a particular indifference argument entitles me to a non-modal conclusion depends on how modal and non-modal propositions are related in the case in question. What is crucial is whether the terms of the indifference premiss are *non-contingent*. A proposition is *contingent* if and only if it is neither necessary nor impossible: that is, if it is both possible and non-necessary. Hence if p is *non-contingent* then in order to establish p it is sufficient to establish possibly p. For the claim that p is non-contingent is equivalent to the claim that possibly p implies necessarily p (viz. $Mp \rightarrow Lp$).[17] It is uncontentious, in the case of alethic modalities, that necessarily p implies p ($Lp \rightarrow p$). So, if p is non-contingent, then on establishing possibly p one can conclude that p. Similarly, and equivalently, if p is non-contingent then in order to establish p one has to establish necessarily p, since establishing p would *ipso facto* be establishing necessarily p. From the non-contingency of p there follows $Mp \rightarrow Lp$, and so, given the uncontentious $p \rightarrow Mp$, establishing p would license the conclusion Lp. Of course, whether it is legitimate in some specific case to take the terms of the indifference premiss as non-contingent depends on the particularities of the argument in question.

In some cases it will not be legitimate to take the terms of the indifference premiss as non-contingent. Such cases will strike us as Buridan's Ass or Aristotle's Starving Man typically do. If there is no more reason for an ass to move left than to move right it *will* follow that it is necessary that it move left if and only if it is necessary that it move right. If some assumption is made that an ass moves only of necessity, that there are no non-contingent ass movements – the assumption, for example, that an ass moves only for a reason and that reasons necessitate – then some conclusion will follow concerning the actual movements, or lack of them, of the pitiful ass. Since such an assumption about non-contingency is required in order to derive an unacceptable conclusion such as that the ass stays still and starves, the patent unacceptability of the conclusion can be used for one of two purposes: *either* to cast doubt on the assumption and to show that a necessitating reason is not required for every fine detail of what occurs; *or*, if there is confidence in the assumption on some other grounds, to undercut the indifference premiss – of course, it might be said, an ass will not stay still and starve, from which it must follow that there will always be some difference, even if not apparent, which explains why one outcome occurs rather than another.

In other cases the assumption about non-contingency will be held to be justified, and so an indifference argument will be defensible. A pair of scales with equal weights in each pan will not move. For if it were to move it would have to go down on either the left or the right. But when there is an equal weight in each pan there is no more reason for it to go down on the left than for it to go down on the right, and so it will not move. In this case the assumption required concerning non-contingency seems justifiable. The assumption is that there is no merely contingent movement of a pair of scales, in that a scale will only go down on one side if it *has* to go down on that side, and *must* go down on the side which is heavier. If some physical set-up were not like that it would not be much use as a pair of scales, since it would be possible that the scales should go down on one side even though that side were not the heavier. If a farmer wanted a way of ensuring hay bales to be of a standard size, weight, and so on, it would be foolish to try placing them equidistantly on opposite sides of a hungry ass until the ass stays still and starves. It is plain why that would be foolish. While it is reasonable to suppose that there is no merely contingent going down of a pair of scales, it would not be reasonable to suppose that there are no merely contingent ass movements. Whether or not the required assumptions about modalities are justifiable in a particular case will often call for considerable discussion, since the more interesting uses of indifference arguments will generally not concern such straight-forward, and much discussed, determinist assumptions as the illustrative examples cited above. Such discussion can turn up issues of great philosophical interest, reinforcing the conviction that indifference arguments are a rich source of philosophical stimulation.

Suppose that the required assumptions about modalities are reasonable in some particular indifference argument. Still a question remains about the relation between the modal *equivalences* and the non-modal conclusions usually drawn. Which conclusions can be drawn depends on whether the terms of the indifference premiss are incompatible or compatible.

Suppose they are incompatible, so that we have $\neg M(p\&q)$, not possibly both p and q. The indifference premiss gives $Lp \equiv Lq$. Together $Lp \equiv Lq$ and $\neg M(p\&q)$ imply $\neg(Lp \lor Lq)$, neither necessarily p nor necessarily q.[18] If the required assumption about non-contingency is legitimate then p will be the case only if Lp is the case. Thus from ¬(LpvLq) there follows ¬(pvq), neither p nor q. That constitutes the non-modal conclusion. For example, a ball-bearing will balance in a position of unstable equilibrium at the top of a steel hemisphere. For if it is to roll off it will have to roll off in some direction or other, and in a position of unstable equilibrium it has no more reason to roll off in one direction rather than in any other. Let p and q be random propositions concerning its motion in one direction or another, and let us accept the assumption that the ball-bearing will only move in some direction if determined and necessitated to move in that direction. If that were not the case there would seem to be no grounds for holding that there should be any position at which it will balance. Since p and q are incompatible (the ball-bearing cannot move in two directions at once) it will follow from the indifference premiss that neither can be necessary (¬(LpvLq) via Lp ≡ Lq); and from that it follows, on the basis of the assumption about non-contingency, that neither p nor q is the case, ¬(pvq). What that conclusion tells us is precisely what is observed. The ball *does not* move in any randomly picked direction, which is to say that it *does not* move at all.

The premisses of an indifference argument can, on the other hand, be compatible. Then we do not have ¬M(p&q). Hence it will not follow from Lp ≡ Lq that ¬(LpvLq). Suppose we replace a ball-bearing by a drop of fluid of the same shape, and at the same position on the steel hemisphere; p and q are random sentences concerning its motion in one direction or another. Owing to its position it has no more reason to go left than to go right (there is no more reason for p than for q). But since it can flow both left and right we have M(p&q). Granted that there is some movement, then for some p we have Lp, and so Lp&Lq, and so p&q; and indeed we would expect a drop of fluid at a position of unstable equilibrium on a steel hemisphere to flow equally down all sides.

The indifference premiss entails not only Lp ≡ Lq but also the equivalence Mp ≡ Mq. Since the terms of the indifference premiss have to be non-contingent in order for the argument to proceed to a typical non-modal conclusion, it does not much matter which of these equivalences we think about. For on the condition that both p and q are non-contingent, Lp ≡ Lq and Mp ≡ Mq are themselves equivalent, since from the non-contingency of p and q and the standard implication of possibility by necessity there follow Lp ≡ Mp and Lq ≡ Mq.[19] Should we choose to focus on the equivalence Mp ≡ Mq in exposition of an indifference argument, an assumption is required about possibility: namely, that in order to establish p it is sufficient to establish possibly p. Again it will be relevant whether the terms of the indifference premiss are taken as compatible or not.

An initial consideration of the Democritean argument for the infinite variety of atomic shapes will illustrate the point. Let p and q be random sentences of the form 'there is an atom of shape S'. Allowing that there is no more reason for p than for q it follows that Mp ≡ Mq. Allow that there are an unlimited number of *atoms*, this having been argued previously. Two further points follow. First, it follows that any such sentences p and q *could* be true together. There will never turn out not to be enough atoms to instantiate the possible atomic shapes. Second, it follows that *some* such sentence will be true, since any atom has to have some shape or other. From Mp ≡ Mq it therefore follows that Mp&Mq: that any and every shape is a *possible* shape for instantiation as an atomic shape. Now the shapes of atoms are not like the shapes of ordinary macroscopic things. A Democritean atom is indestructible and unalterable. If a Democritean atom ever *will* have some particular shape it has that shape now. Given that, a principle connecting possibility and actuality comes into view: if something remains possible throughout an infinite future then at some time in that future it is actual.[20] On the basis of that principle it follows that, since atoms are indestructible and eternal, if there *can* be an atom of a certain shape there *will* sometime be an atom of that shape. Further, since atoms cannot change their shape, if there ever *will* be an atom of a certain shape there *is now* an atom of that shape. Then since the indifference argument shows that there are an infinite number of shapes which are equally possible atomic shapes, it follows that the number of atomic shapes there are is infinite. For this to be a defensible argument requires, first, that the core indifference argument structure can generate the modal equivalences – and we have seen above that it can; second, that the underlying principle connecting possibility and actuality be defensible – we shall see below that a substantial defence can be mounted of that; and, third, that the indifference premiss is justified on the Democritean theory – that, given atomic indestructibility and impassibility, there are still non-question-begging grounds for asserting that there is no reason for there to be an atom of one shape rather than of another.

An example where the terms of the indifference premiss are *incompatible* is a Zenonian argument about division. Let p and q be random sentences of the form 'this magnitude is divided at such and such a point'. The indifference premiss that there is no more reason for p than for q follows from the homogeneity of the magnitude in question. Hence we get Mp ≡ Mq. For any two points you like, either it is possible to divide the magnitude at both or at neither of those points. Let us suppose, the argument runs, that any such p and q are compatible: that it is possible to divide the magnitude at any such possible points of division. There will be an infinite number of such points. In this case the assumption linking possibility and actuality is made explicitly. It is assumed that it is possible to actualize all those possibilities of division. But then an impossible result seems to follow, that the original magnitude could not be built up from the products of that division. Therefore it cannot be that *all* the possibilities of division are compatible. In that case, a random p and q will be incompatible, since supposing them compatible leads to contradiction. Hence, given Mp ≡ Mq and ¬M(p&q), there follows ¬(MpvMq). That is to say that the homogeneous magnitude is not divisible at any point. That is just the argument for the indivisibility of a homogeneous continuum seen earlier in some Eleatic philosophers. In addition to the core indifference argument structure, that argument requires for its success a number of more particular claims: first, that bodies are in general such as to render an indifference premiss true (that randomly picked bodies are homogeneous); second, the principle connecting possibility and actuality, that it is possible to actualize all the possible divisions; third, that such an actualization would lead to contradiction.

An account has now been provided of the general structure of indifference arguments. An indifference premiss 'there is no more reason for p than for q' justifies equivalences between the terms of that premiss *taken modally*. Independent of any particular (and therefore possibly contentious) account of reasons, and of any specific reading of the modalities, there is a defensible route from that indifference premiss to Lp ≡ Lq and Mp ≡ Mq. There is no similarly defensible move from 'there is no more reason for p than for q' to p ≡ q. Nevertheless, indifference arguments typically offer conclusions that are not themselves modalized. We have seen what is required for such conclusions to be justified in particular cases. Now it is possible to turn to some critical engagement in the indifference arguments which are of particular interest.

NOTES

1 This chapter expands on, and includes some revision of, the account of indifference arguments given in Makin (1986).

2 Hence there being reason for p rather than q is intended to be taken asymmetrically, so that if there is reason for p rather than q there cannot also be reason for q rather than p. So 'there is reason for p rather than q' means more than that there is a reason for p which is not a reason for q, since that relation is not asymmetric.

3 I do not deny that someone might find that B-form argument convincing. They might well do so if they believed that which face a coin will show when tossed is *determined*, for example by precise force of spin, air currents, and so on. The relevance of that determinist assumption to indifference reasoning will become clear presently. The point here is just that there seem *prima facie* to be cases where an A-form argument is defensible, and a parallel B-form argument not.

4 See Dummett (1975). See further chapter 6.4 on the issues raised by sorites arguments.

5 During an enlightening discussion of *ou mallon* (that is, indifference) arguments in Barnes (1982, pp. 557ff; and compare pp. 23–8), there is consideration of what non-epistemological interpretation of the indifference premiss could be given. But the conclusion Barnes gets from discussion of the atomist argument at DK67A8, 68A38, Luria §2, is *epistemological*: 'it is reasonable to believe in an infinity of atomic shapes'. No matter how well that conclusion might be supported, it is important to remember that it is not the conclusion that Democritus wants. I will return to more detailed discussion of why an epistemological reading of that argument could not be satisfactory in chapter 6.3.

6 As, for example, Barnes (1982, p. 559): 'In conclusion, I say first, that the epistemological Ou Mallon principle is a sound and important principle of reasoning; second that certain other Ou Mallon principles, which the Atomists may possibly have confused with it, are equally interesting, though more in need of elucidation.' I think that a similar predilection towards an epistemic reading is apparent in the discussion of symmetry arguments in van Fraassen (1989). Symmetry arguments proper, according to van Fraassen, rely on a meta-principle which he states informally as a slogan: 'Symmetry Requirement: Problems which are essentially the same must receive essentially the same solution' (p. 236). That requirement is also described as a principle of methodology. Symmetry is a concept which relates to the structure of models, and models are emphasized as part of a rejection of scientific realism. Van Fraassen's wider concerns are different to mine, and I cannot here do justice to the complexity of his discussion.

7 Some symbolism is inevitable in what follows. All symbols are explained in an appendix. For an account of *why* some formalism is required, see chapter 1.3.

8 Deontic modalities are modalities of obligation and permission: for example, *it is necessary (obligatory)* to drive on the left hand side of the road, *it is possible (permissible)* for public houses to remain open on Sundays. Alethic modalities concern what is true. There is a formal distinction. As regards alethic modalities necessity implies actuality (if it necessary that $2 + 2 = 4$ then it is the case that $2 + 2 = 4$) and actuality implies possibility (if it is the case that $2 + 2 = 4$ then it is possible that $2 + 2 = 4$). Those implications do not hold as regards deontic modalities (it is necessary (obligatory) for Bloggs to buy a television licence; it does not follow that Bloggs does buy a television licence. Bloggs steals your car; it does not follow that it is possible (permissible) for Bloggs to steal your car).

9 For the sake of brevity I will omit *with respect to reasons* from now on.

10 For recent discussions, see Temple (1988); Lipton (1990).

11 See Lipton (1990, pp. 250f, 258).

12 My experience has been that people who do find the move from (1) to (2) and (3) implausible do suppose that I rely on just such assumptions as those to be discussed below.

13 DK 67B2 = Luria §22: οὐδὲν χρῆμα μάτην γίνεται, ἀλλὰ πάντα ἐκ λόγου τε καὶ ὑπ' ἀνάγκης. For a discussion of what Leucippus could have meant by these words, see Barnes (1984).

14 Those who want to extend the contrastive theory of explanation to cases where there is no *obvious* contrast in view often suggest that the form 'why p?' should be understood as 'why p rather than not p?' For example, Lipton (1990, p. 260f) endorses and defends this claim. It should be particularly obvious for such theorists that citing the contingency of p could not provide *any* sort of explanation of p.

15 It does not, of course, follow from there being reason for p rather than q – there being more reason for p than for q – that q may not nevertheless be the case. That is precisely why 'there is no more reason for p than for q' will not straight off imply $p \equiv q$, since it will not contradict $p\&\neg q$, except on the basis of some very strong and contentious assumption. See further on this below.

16 The following diagrams make it clear that $Lp \equiv Lq$, $Mp \equiv Mq$ and $p \equiv q$ are all independent, in that none implies the others.

Diagram A:	p	q
World W1	F	T
World W2	F	F

Diagram B:

World W1	T	F
World W2	T	T

Lp is true in W1 (or W2) if and only if p is true in both W1 and W2, Mp is true in W1 (or W2) if and only if p is true in either W1 or W2. Then A renders Lp ≡ Lq true in W1 but p ≡ q and Mp ≡ Mq false in W1; and p ≡ q true in W2 but Mp ≡ Mq false in W2. B renders Mp ≡ Mq true in W1 but p ≡ q and Lp ≡ Lq false in W1; and p ≡ q true in W2 but Lp ≡ Lq false in W2. Since Lp ≡ Lq, Mp ≡ Mq and p ≡ q are all independent, the relation of each to the indifference premiss 'there is no more reason for p than for q' has had to be considered separately.

17 If 'it is contingent that p' is defined as Mp&¬Lp, then 'it is not contingent that p' is equivalent to ¬(Mp&¬Lp), which is equivalent to (Mp→Lp).

18 If Lp ≡ Lq is true then either both or neither of Lp and Lq will be true. If they were both true then p and q would both be true, but that is inconsistent with ¬M(p&q) being true; hence it remains that neither Lp nor Lq are true, in which case ¬(LpvLq) is true.

19 The point made earlier, in the course of offering separate arguments for the moves from 'there is no more reason for p than for q' to Lp ≡ Lq and to Mp ≡ Mq, was different. For those equivalences will follow separately from an indifference premiss regardless of whether the terms of the premiss are non-contingent; and, as seen in note 16, Lp ≡ Lq and Mp ≡ Mq can differ in truth value – in which case at least one of p and q will be contingent.

20 In chapter 7.1 we will see reason to suppose that Democritus did endorse this principle. See also chapter 2.4 on the relevance of this to one of Melissus' arguments.

6

Epistemological
Indifference Arguments

◆

6.1 Are All Indifference Arguments Epistemological?

As we have seen, it might be claimed that any intuitive appeal indifference arguments have is owing to the possibility of their being read on epistemological lines. Indifference arguments which seem not to be epistemological should be reinterpreted if they are to be revealed as good arguments. A typical non-epistemological (B-form) indifference argument will move from a premiss of the form 'there is no more reason for p than for q' to a conclusion C. An argument like that admits of an epistemological slant at two points. First, the premiss could be given an epistemological reading: there is no more reason *to assert* that p than *to assert* that q. Second, the conclusion could be taken epistemologically, as showing that one would be justified in *asserting* C.

An epistemological slant will be recommended first of all on grounds of charity: the (putatively B-form) arguments come out as *better arguments* if treated epistemologically. Second, counsels of metaphysical caution might appear to incline us towards an epistemological reading. Someone could reason along these lines. In sustaining a B-form indifference argument one is committed to some principle or other which mediates between necessity or possibility on the one hand, and actuality on the other; one also has to come to some view on the relation between how things are and *reasons*. But those matters involve metaphysical claims, and it is all too understandable that it could turn out that those metaphysical claims are false, or that we do not have any good grounds for supposing them true. It could, for example, turn out to be false that there is a sufficient reason for whatever is the case being the case. An A-form (epistemological) argument, in contrast, is not so much dependent on contentious metaphysics. An A-form argument involves commitment to some view about the relation between assertion and justification, as we shall see; and the view required will not be in the same way contentious. It is less likely to turn out false that one is equally justified in asserting what there is equal reason to assert.

The best way to approach this general preference for A-form indifference arguments is to ask what conclusions *could* be defensibly derived from an epistemological indifference premiss. If it emerges that an A-form indifference premiss does not achieve enough to provide a sympathetic reading of B-form arguments, that will be significant. It is useful to start at a general level. Then we can identify a particular sort of B-form argument as the only plausible candidate for an epistemological reading. The Democritean 'infinity' arguments, concerning worlds, atomic sizes, atomic shapes, and so on, are a paradigm instance of that sort of argument. In that case a more detailed discussion of those arguments is appropriate. That will reveal what the best epistemological reading allows us.

An A-form indifference argument has a premiss of the form

(1) there is no more reason to assert (say, judge...) that p than to assert (say, judge...) that q.

What, if anything, follows from (1)? Since reference to epistemological notions (asserting, saying, belief...) comes within the scope of the 'no more reason...' operator, we would expect that some sort of modal equivalence will follow in this case, just as with the B-form arguments. We might try making that point by introducing *epistemic modalities*, construed on the model of deontic modalities: for example, what I *can* assert, as what my epistemic obligations *permit* me to assert; and what I *must* assert defined in terms of what I *can* assert. But there are great complexities involved in making those concepts clear. It is better to avoid opening that can of worms, and to concentrate instead on an equivalence which is in *some* way modal, and which can be derived directly and uncontentiously from (1).

(2) I am justified in asserting that p ≡ I am justified in asserting that q

follows from (1) by an argument parallel to that by which Lp ≡ Lq and Mp ≡ Mq were derived from 'there is no more reason for p than for q'. If I were justified in asserting p and yet *not* justified in asserting q then (1) would be false. Reflection on the fact that assertion of p would, while assertion of q would not, be justified would assure me of there being more reason to assert p than to assert q: asserting p is asserting something justified, while asserting q is not. The argument from (1) to (2) follows then just as before.

What could legitimately be inferred from (2)? Some general distinctions are useful here. I will call a conclusion *epistemically strong* if and only if either the dominant operator in the conclusion is 'I am justified in asserting that...' or it is a quantification over a conclusion in which that is the dominant operator. A conclusion is *epistemically weak* if it is equivalent to the negation of an epistemically strong conclusion.

Further I will say that an epistemological indifference premiss concerns *epistemically compatible* terms just if

(3) I am justified in asserting M(p&q)

and *epistemically incompatible* terms just if

(4) I am justified in asserting ¬M(p&q).[1]

A general point can now be established. The most favourable case for sustaining an inference from (1) *alone* will be that in which the terms of (1) are epistemically incompatible. In that case, however, the conclusion is bound to be epistemically weak. Such an argument from an epistemological indifference premiss could not, therefore, constitute a charitable explication of a putatively B-form argument. First the argument, and then some illustration by examples.[2]

Suppose

(5) I am justified in asserting that p.

Given (2), there follows

(6) I am justified in asserting that q.

(5) and (6) together give[3]

(7) I am justified in asserting (p&q)

But in this case (7) is an unacceptable consequence, given the claim of (4) that p and q are epistemically incompatible. We are interested in what follows from the indifference premiss being true, so we should not escape trouble by denying (1). The only alternative is to deny the supposition (5). That gives the epistemically weak conclusion.

(8) it is not the case that: I am justified in asserting that p.

That argument structure is instantiated by some types of sceptical argument. Suppose the evidence I have gives me no more reason to say that this gem is diamond than to say that it is cubic zirconium. Then I will be justified in asserting that it is diamond if and only if I am justified in asserting it is cubic zirconium. Since I am justified in asserting that it cannot be both diamond and cubic zirconium, it follows that I am not justified in asserting that it is diamond; nor am I justified in asserting that it is cubic zirconium.

The upshot of such an argument will be a withholding of judgement on the question whether p or q, since the argument shows that I have no justification for the assertion of either. I will make some brief comment presently on the relation of the argument (1)–(8) above to the use of the *ou mallon* formula by classical sceptics. At present it is more to the point to note that no putative B-form argument to a non-epistemological conclusion could possibly be sympathetically explicated by an argument which gives only an epistemically weak conclusion.

Consider a fairly arbitrary example discussed earlier: Anaximander's argument for the immobility of the earth. An epistemological reading of the indifference premiss would be

(i) there is no more reason to assert that the earth will move in direction d_1 than to assert that the earth will move in direction d_2.

That gives

(ii) I am justified in asserting that the earth will move in direction d_1 $\equiv$ I am justified in asserting that the earth will move in direction d_2.

Since different directions are plainly incompatible, then

(iii) I am justified in asserting that it's not possible that (the earth will move in direction d_1 and the earth will move in direction d_2).

Now just suppose that

(iv) I am justified in asserting the earth will move in direction d_1.

That leads to the conclusion that I am justified in asserting that the earth will move in direction d_1 and the earth will move in direction d_2, which clashes with (iii). Hence I can reject (iv), which gives

(v) it is not the case that: I am justified in asserting the earth will move in direction d_1.

Since the particular direction d_1 is inessential to the argument, I can generalize over (v) to obtain

(vi) For all directions d it is not the case that: I am justified in asserting that the earth will move in direction d

which is an epistemically weak conclusion, equivalent to

(vii) it is not the case that there is some direction d such that I am justified in asserting the earth will move in direction d.

However, (vi) does not tend to give me any epistemic grounding for the conclusion that Anaximander's argument *seemed* to lead to, that the earth will not move. To be justified in asserting that conclusion I would require not the epistemically weak (vi) but the epistemically strong

(viii) for all directions d: I am justified in asserting that the earth will not move in direction d.

It is plainly impossible that any epistemically strong conclusion *could* follow by this argument. The argument is a reductio. In order to work it must derive an unacceptable consequence: the consequence that I am justified in asserting something that the epistemic incompatibility of the terms of the indifference premiss rules out. Only by making an epistemically strong assumption in the first place could I get that unacceptable consequence;[4] and the negation of an epistemically strong assumption cannot itself generally be epistemically strong.[5]

In place of (4) we will sometimes have p and q epistemically compatible,

(3) I am justified in asserting M(p&q).

In that case

(2) I am justified in asserting that p ≡ I am justified in asserting that q

will support an epistemically strong conclusion only so long as we make an epistemically strong assumption to start with. In the absence of (4) the argument will not proceed as a reductio. Hence the epistemically strong assumption will remain undischarged as a premiss of the argument, and thus will itself require support.[6] Suppose

(5) I am justified in asserting that p.

From (2) and (5) we can infer

(6) I am justified in asserting that q

and (5) and (6) will give

(7) I am justified in asserting (p&q).

(7) is an epistemically strong conclusion, yet can only be secured on the basis of an undischarged epistemically strong premiss concerning one of the terms of the indifference claim. If there is an *undischarged* epistemically strong premiss concerning one of the terms of an indifference premiss – in this case, premiss (5) – then (4) *could not* be true if the indifference premiss is true: the terms of the indifference premiss *could not* be epistemically incompatible. Hence there will be a valid A-form argument to an epistemically strong conclusion only if the epistemological indifference premiss concerns epistemically compatible terms. Since the only sort of A-form arguments that could plausibly sustain the conclusions

of putatively B-form arguments are those that issue in epistemically strong conclusions, we can see which *sorts* of B-form arguments – if any – will be amenable to an epistemological interpretation.

Those in which the terms of the indifference premiss are epistemically incompatible will not be amenable to that interpretation: such are Anaximander's argument for the immobility of the earth, Aristotle's Hungry Man, Aristotle's Hair, Buridan's Ass, and many others. But there will be plenty of other arguments in which the terms of the indifference premiss are epistemically compatible, and it remains to be seen whether a plausible epistemological reading is possible in those cases. The Democritean 'infinity' arguments – for the infinite variety of atomic shape and atomic size, and the infinite number of atoms, worlds and so on – provide paradigm illustrations here.

Let p, q... be sentences claiming that there are atoms of some particular shape: they will be epistemically compatible. In the absence of commitment to anything like a theory of basic shapes, Democritus has grounds to suppose that there *could be* any number of atomic shapes you like, and since the argument for the infinite variety of atomic shapes is subsequent to showing that there are an infinite number of atoms, there are grounds to suppose that there could never fail to be enough atoms to instantiate any variety of atomic shapes you like. The indifference premiss

(1) there is no more reason to assert that p than to assert that q

represents ignorance about the distribution of atomic shapes: all assertions about the instantiation of an atomic shape are on an epistemic level. But now a problem arises: for it might seem that any argument which could support an epistemically strong conclusion will be difficult to sustain. For *if* (1) is to lead to an epistemically strong conclusion, some undischarged epistemically strong premiss concerning one of the terms of (1) will be required – some premiss of the form that there is reason to assert that p. But that there should be an epistemically strong premiss available concerning one of the terms of (1) sits ill with the way in which Democritus is entitled to (1): namely, as an expression of epistemic indifference, consequent upon *ignorance* about the distribution of atomic shapes.

Democritus could respond to this challenge, and the response enables us to see more clearly what the logical structure of an A-form argument will *have* to be if there is to be any chance of its explicating the putatively

B-form Democritean indifference arguments. Ultimately the A-form reading will fail to deliver the goods for Democritus – and we shall see in the next chapter that a B-form argument is in fact far more plausibly defensible. However, in the course of this chapter the relation between this sort of A-form argument and *sorites* reasoning, and between A-form arguments and the quantifier rules, will come more clearly into view, and that will itself be of some interest.

6.2 Ou Mallon and Ancient Scepticism

Before turning to the Democritean arguments, however, this is an appropriate point at which to say something brief concerning the use of *ou mallon* in ancient scepticism. There is reason to think that something *should* be said. Yet it may seem surprising that it should be brief, and it may seem puzzling that, in a book on indifference arguments, there has been so little mention of ancient scepticism, since *ou mallon* (or *ouden mallon*, or related expressions) is most famously in the ancient world a sceptical formula.[7] It is found in early scepticism[8] and later Pyrrhonism.[9] So it might be expected that when we turn to *epistemological* arguments attention will turn to scepticism. Comment is in particular prompted now by reflection on the argument structure outlined in the previous section:

(1) there is no more reason to assert that p than to assert that q

therefore

(2) I am justified in asserting that p if and only if I am justified in asserting that q
(3) I am justified in asserting not possibly (p&q)

suppose

(4) I am justified in asserting that p

therefore

(5) I am justified in asserting that q

therefore

(6) I am justified in asserting that (p&q)

but (6) conflicts with (3), and therefore

(7) it is not the case that: I am justified in asserting that p.

That structure was illustrated earlier by a *sceptical* argument, concerning diamond and cubic zirconium. What is the more general relation of that structure to the procedures of ancient scepticism and how does the occurrence of (1) as a *premiss* above relate to the use of the *ou mallon* formula by the sceptics?

(1)–(7) is a schematic A-form indifference *argument:* (1) and (3) are premisses, and the conclusion (7) is supported in that (7) must be true if (1) and (3) are true. It is an argument that could be offered if someone wanted to be shown what the *rational* response *should* be if faced by balanced considerations in favour of an incompatible p and q. The requirement of *rationality* is this: one *should* suspend judgement, since one has no *justification* for either of the incompatible assertions.

It might seem as if (1)–(7) is instantiated then – particularly clearly – in the procedures of ancient scepticism. After all, the sceptics say *ou mallon*; and about opposed things,[10] as (3) would suggest; and the sceptic ends up suspending judgement.[11] But it would be very misleading to think of the sceptic as guided by an *argument* such as (1)–(7). If we pursue that point a little then we shall see why it is in fact to be wholly expected that a book on indifference *arguments* will not concentrate overly on ancient scepticism. Further, to the extent that indifference *arguments* are relevant to scepticism, it is as much B-form (non-epistemological) as A-form (epistemological) arguments that are to the point.

I simply accept without demur here an account of the sceptic's procedures along the following lines.[12] The description of the sceptic's way of life is the description of a causal progression. The sceptic speaks to someone who is perturbed by the conflicts and anomalies he finds around him.[13] The desire to resolve those conflicts and escape perturbation motivates enquiry, initially with the aim of finding determinate answers.[14] It soon becomes apparent, though, that on any particular question to which attention is turned there is a balance of opposed considerations.[15] That balance between opposed considerations, for and against, leads to suspension of judgement.[16] It then turns out, by chance and unexpectedly, that that suspension of judgement brings with it the very tranquility and freedom from disturbance, desire for which motivated enquiry in the first place.[17]

The above is simply a description of a causal progression – at least, so the sceptic would have us believe. The sceptic need not argue that if one comes upon opposed considerations concerning p and q – as one invariably will, the sceptic being skilled in providing them – one should suspend judgement, that one is under a logical obligation to do so. To do so would involve claiming that the premisses (1) and (3) are *true*, that the argument from (1) and (3) to (7) is *valid* and concluding that (7) is in consequence *true*. The sceptic's aim, however, is to avoid being committed to any claims that this or that is true. How then could (1)–(7) relate to the sceptic's way of going on? (1) need not function for the sceptic as a *premiss* at all, either in general or concerning some particular p and q. It is rather a formula expressive of the way the sceptic is affected, manifesting his feeling.[18] Sextus says explicitly that *ouden mallon* is not asserted. While it might *seem* like an assertion or denial, it is rather being used, as Sextus puts it, indifferently (ἀδιαφόρως): it is meant either as a question, or as an indication of what appears to the sceptic – that he does not know to what he should and should not assent.[19] Since (1) is not a sceptical premiss, then (1)–(7) will not give the structure of a sceptical *argument* for the conclusion that one should suspend judgement.

While *we* might ask whether suspension of judgement is the *appropriate* response to the balance of opposed considerations, the sceptical claim would rather be that it is the *inevitable* response. A mind faced with balanced and opposed considerations is in a similar position to a ball-bearing between two equally strong magnets: in the one case the mind, in the other the ball-bearing, hangs suspended.[20] Indeed, if an indifference *argument* were relevant here it would be a B-form argument. For the sceptic – in his desire to avoid recommending *belief* – will prefer to describe the causally necessary outcome of coming upon balanced considerations. There is no more reason for the mind to go this way than for the mind to go that way on the question. So the mind will be impelled to go the one way if and only if it is impelled to go the other way; yet it cannot go both ways at once (since the alternatives in question are incompatible). In this case the route from the modal equivalence, that the mind is *impelled* to go one way if and only if it is *impelled* to go the other, to the non-modal conclusion, that the mind will not go either way, is provided by the account of scepticism which emphasizes the passivity of the sceptic in respect of suspension of judgement: the mind will move to, assent to, a conclusion only if impelled to.

Now we can see why an interest in epistemological indifference *arguments* will not tend to direct our attention to ancient scepticism, even though the *ou mallon* expression is a significant sceptical formula. There is a B-form indifference argument which is relevent to the way that scepticism must be conceived if the sceptical ideal of life is to be coherent; but that is not an argument which raises *general* issues of any special importance. An interest in indifference *arguments* will direct us just as much – indeed, more fruitfully – to the sorts of examples I have concentrated on so far: the putatively B-form arguments found in Democritus and the Eleatic background to which he is responding.

6.3   A Democritean Argument

The general discussion earlier in chapter 6.1 narrowed the field of indifference arguments for which charity might recommend an epistemological reading. As a paradigm instance, consider the argument by which Democritus sought to establish the infinite variety of atomic shapes:[21]

> Leucippus ... held ... that the number of shapes in the atoms was infinite because nothing is rather thus than thus ... [Leucippus and Democritus] say that the number of shapes in the atoms is infinite because nothing is rather thus than thus.

What will the most charitable A-form (epistemological) reading of this argument be? Recall the general points that have been established. If an A-form argument is to stand any chance of providing a sympathetic explication of a putatively B-form argument it will have to proceed to an epistemically strong conclusion. In that case the argument will require an undischarged epistemically strong premiss. That premiss will concern one of the terms of the indifference premiss, and as a result the terms of the indifference premiss will have to be epistemically compatible.

Given that, what A-form indifference premiss is available for Democritus' argument? A first thought is that it should be a premiss directly about atomic shapes: something like 'there is no more reason to say that there is an atom of shape S than to say that there is an atom of shape S*'. But if that is the indifference premiss there will be no epistemically strong claim available concerning a term of that premiss. The sort of epistemically strong claim required would be something of the form 'it is justifiable to assert that there is an atom of shape S*'. But that Democritus should be entitled to an epistemically strong premiss like that is at odds with the indifference premiss being an expression of *ignorance* about the distribution of atomic shapes. Of course, there is some information about atomic shapes available to the Democritean – if ignorance were complete, *no* successful indifference argument would be possible. The information available is that there are atoms, and that atoms have some shape or other. That information will entitle him to *an* epistemically strong premiss: namely, that there is justification for asserting that there is some shape instantiated in the atoms. Yet that is not an epistemically strong claim which concerns one of the terms of the indifference premiss. For the indifference premiss being proposed is not that there is no more reason to say there are some atomic shapes than to say there are no atomic shapes: instead it is that there is no more reason to say there is an atom of *this* shape rather than to say that there is an atom of *that* shape. The undischarged epistemically strong premiss that is required is that there is some shape such that there is justification for asserting that *that* shape is instantiated in the atoms: and that epistemically strong claim is neither equivalent to, nor will it follow without fallacy from, the claim that there is justification for asserting that there is some shape instantiated in the atoms.[22]

Perhaps then the indifference premiss should concern not atomic shapes directly, but the *number* of atomic shapes. For example, it might be read: 'there is no more reason to say there are this many atomic shapes than to say there are that many atomic shapes'. One advantage of that suggestion will become clear presently. What is more, that formulation is consistent with taking the indifference premiss as an expression of ignorance: one does indeed know of no reason to prefer one number to another as being the number of atomic shapes. But again there will not be an epistemically strong premiss available which concerns one of the terms of that premiss. If one knows of no reason to prefer one number to another as giving the number of atomic shapes, there will be no number N such that it is justifiable to assert there are N atomic shapes. Further, the terms of that premiss are epistemically incompatible: it is justifiable to assert that it cannot be the case both that there are N atomic shapes and that there are N + 1 atomic shapes.

If the terms of the indifference premiss were of the form 'there are *at least* . . . atomic shapes' rather than the form 'there are (*just*) . . . atomic shapes', both those problems would be avoided. First, the terms of the premiss would then be epistemically compatible. Second, and more importantly, the information available concerning the atoms would then support an epistemically strong premiss respecting the terms of the indifference premiss. For given the information that there are atoms and that they have some shape or other, it does follow that it is justifiable to assert that there is at least *one* atomic shape. The indifference premiss would then read:[23]

(1) for all n (there is no more reason to assert that there are at least n atomic shapes than to assert there are at least n + 1 atomic shapes).

As seen earlier, (1) will give a biconditional

(2) for all n (it is justifiable to assert there are at least n atomic shapes ≡ it is justifiable to assert there are at least n + 1 atomic shapes)

and by taking one half of (2) we have a conditional

(3) for all n (it is justifiable to assert there are at least n atomic shapes → it is justifiable to assert there are at least n + 1 atomic shapes).

(3) is a generalized *material* conditional, claiming just that it is not the case *both* that it is justifiable to assert there are at least n atomic shapes *and* yet not justifiable to assert there are at least n + 1 atomic shapes. Democritus might hope that the indifference premiss, and hence (3), are plausible. If I am justified in asserting that there are at least n atomic shapes, then, whatever the reasons I have for that assertion, I will have as much reason (neither more nor less), given my state of knowledge

concerning the atoms, for asserting that there are at least n + 1 atomic shapes.

That hope turns out to be difficult to sustain. But before turning to that, notice that *if* (1) can be taken as true the Democritean can rule out one opponent straight away. Someone might seek to deny the claim that there are an infinite variety of atomic shapes by holding that for some specific n (say, 5927) there are exactly n (5927) atomic shapes. It follows straight away from (1) that there is no reason for asserting that there are n (5927) atomic shapes rather than n + 1 (5928) atomic shapes. But that is really a very weak conclusion: it rules out only the claim that for some specific n (e.g. 5927) it is justifiable to assert there are exactly n (5927) atomic shapes. Victory against an opponent foolish enough to make such a strong claim as that would be small gain for Democritus.

If Democritus' indifference claim is read as (1), what epistemically strong premiss can he offer? As noted above, the information that there are atoms and that each has some shape or other entitles him to

(4) it is justifiable to assert that there is at least 1 atomic shape.[24]

The trouble now, however, is that, given the information required to support (4), the indifference premiss (1) no longer seems true. (4) is supported by making the claim that there is at least *one* atomic shape epistemically privileged – there is more reason to say that than to say that there are at least *two* atomic shapes. For, granted that there are atoms and that each has some shape, it *could* turn out false that there are at least two atomic shapes, while it is *impossible* that it should turn out false that there is at least one atomic shape. So, it is epistemically preferable to assert that there is at least one atomic shape. Since (1) seems false, (3) is unsupported. Indeed (3) now seems false anyway: what is appealed to as justification for asserting that there is at least one atomic shape (the information that there are atoms and that each has some shape) will not give a justification for asserting that there are at least two atomic shapes.

The Democritean can at least avoid this difficulty by building some more information into the epistemic background. Suppose I also know that – to put it deliberately loosely – there are *quite a lot* of atomic shapes. There are good grounds for Democritus to make this claim. Even if it was not the *purpose* of the basic atomic theory to save the variety of phenomena from Eleatic criticism – even if we prefer the philosophical to the scientific Democritus – a variety of atomic shapes will give an explanation of the variety of experienced phenomena. Hence there is some reason to assert *some* variety of atomic shapes – that there is *more than one* shape instantiated in the atoms. Given that information, epistemic privilege is already removed from the assertion that there is at least one atomic shape. Further, since there is *quite a lot* of variety in the phenomena, there are grounds for asserting that there will be *quite a lot* of atomic shapes. Now an argument from the variety of the phenomena to the variety of atomic shapes is indeed attributed to Democritus.[25] It seems at first sight a weak argument, since while Democritus' view is that there is an *infinite* variety of atomic shapes, we clearly don't have experience of an *infinite* variety of phenomena.[26] It would, however, seem less weak if, while not itself justifying the conclusion of an infinite variety, it played a significant role in an argument which did.

Given the further information that there are quite a lot of atomic shapes, the indifference premiss is less vulnerable to the earlier objection. The grounds offered for treating the assertion that there is at least one atomic shape as epistemically privileged no longer apply. For given this further information I need not fear that it could turn out not to be true that there are at least *two* atomic shapes. For there to be at least one, but not at least two, atomic shapes would be for there to be just one atomic shape: and just one atomic shape is not quite a lot of atomic shapes. Hence I have as much reason – the background information gives me as much reason – for the assertion that there are at least two atomic shapes as I do for the assertion that there is at least one atomic shape.

Moreover, the Democritean might hope to run this argument for further claims of the form 'there are at least... atomic shapes'. Indeed it is necessary that he succeed in doing so. For, if he cannot, *some* assertion of the form 'there are at least... atomic shapes' will be privileged over, or epistemically preferable to, some other; and if that were the case the indifference premiss would not be true. On the other hand, *if* the indifference premiss (1) can be secured then from that and (4) there will indeed follow

(5) for all n (it is justifiable to assert that there are at least n atomic shapes)

and that is an epistemically strong conclusion, which gives a reasonable reading of the putatively non-epistemological conclusion, that there *are* an infinite variety of atomic shapes: that for all n – for every and any n you care to pick – there *are* at least that many atomic shapes. (1) gives

(3) for all n (it is justifiable to assert there are n atomic shapes → it is justifiable to assert there are n + 1 atomic shapes)

and (5) follows from (3) and

(4) it is justifiable to assert that there is at least 1 atomic shape

by repeated applications of *modus ponens*, as in reasoning by mathematical induction, with (4) as the basic step, and (3) as the inductive step. The reasoning here is a virtuous form of what is put to vicious effect in sorites paradoxes. Sorites paradoxes were cited earlier in Chapter 5.1 as an instance of a certain type of A-form indifference argument, and I will say something presently at some length about the general relation between sorites reasoning and A-form indifference arguments. Consider first, though, whether in this case the indifference premiss (1) can be sustained.

Democritus can argue that, just as I have as much reason for the assertion that there are at least two atomic shapes as I do for the assertion that there is at least one, given the information that there are quite a lot, so too I have as much reason for the assertion that there are at least three as for the assertion that there at least two. For the assertion that there are at least two would be epistemically preferable, on grounds of caution, to the assertion that there are at least three only if there were some probability of its being false that there are at least three, while being true that there are at least two, given the background information that there are quite a lot. But it will be false that there are at least three atomic shapes, while true that there are at least two, only so long as there are *just two* atomic shapes – and just two atomic shapes would not be quite a lot. Hence, given the background information that there are quite a lot, I am as safe in asserting that there are at least three atomic shapes as I am in asserting that there at least two.

In order to continue that line of argument, however, it would be necessary to proceed step by step, attempting to argue next in a similar way that I am as safe in asserting that there are at least three – since *just three* would not be quite a lot. But the attempt to carry that line of argument on step by step along the series 'at least four', 'at least five' ... relies on the plausibility of a sorites-type argument concerning the predicate 'quite a lot'. What is required for the argument that it is as safe to assert there are at least two atomic shapes as it is to assert there is at least one is that *just one* is not quite a lot; for the argument that it is as safe to assert that there are at least three as it is to assert there are at least two it is required that *just two* is not quite a lot. If *just two* is not quite a lot then neither is *just three*, and if *just three* is not quite a lot then neither is *just four*...; and in general if *just n* is not quite a lot, then neither is *just n + 1* – since there is no n such that just n is not quite a lot while just n + 1 is.

It is plain, however, that this Democritean argument for the infinity of atomic shapes cannot be successful. It is easy enough to think of cases structurally identical to the Democritean indifference argument, where it is clear that no conclusion parallel to (5) will follow. Suppose I know that Alana is going to bequeath me some money; and that since she is generous she will bequeath me quite a lot. Then

(i) it is justifiable to assert that Alana will bequeath me at least £1.

But if it were granted that

(ii) for all n (it is justifiable to assert that Alana will bequeath me at least £n → it is justifiable to assert that Alana will bequeath me at least £n + 1)

then it would follow (by parity with the Democritean argument) that it is justifiable to assert that I will receive an infinite amount of money – that

(iii) for all n (it is justifiable to assert that Alana will bequeath me at least £n).

But even if it were possible that I should receive an infinite amount of money (this being only a philosophical example), (iii) clearly isn't the possibility rendered epistemically preferable by the limited information that I will receive quite a lot of money.[27] So the Democritean conclusion

(5) for all n (it is justifiable to assert that there are n atomic shapes)

cannot be warranted by the limited information available about atomic shapes, that there are quite a lot. Yet (5) *would* be warranted if that information supported the indifference premiss (1) and the claim (4) – since (1) and (4) imply (5). Therefore it *must be* that the indifference premiss is not sustainable on the basis of the information required to warrant (4).

This conclusion would have been easier to force against a stubborn defender of the Democritean argument had the indifference premiss not been given as (1), but instead in terms of *non-adjacent* numbers:

(6) for any n and m, there is no more reason to assert there are at least n atomic shapes than to assert there are at least m.

For (6) seems straight away false: there *is* more reason to assert that there are at least 4 atomic shapes than to assert that there at least 4000, since the former is the epistemically safer assertion given just the information that there are quite a lot of atomic shapes. But once it is allowed that (6) is false, (1) cannot be sustained either. It would be necessary to go more into the entanglements of sorites paradoxes had (1) concerned not what there is reason to assert, but simply the application of the predicate 'quite a lot': that is, if it had involved the bare claim that for all n (if n is not quite a lot then n + 1 is not quite a lot). But since (1) concerns *reasons for asserting*, it invites a reaction along the following lines. (6) is false because there is some number – though not a least number – of atomic shapes (say 4000) which there is (justifying) reason to assert to be quite a lot of atomic shapes. Once the Democritean grants that, then he must allow that as N gets closer to (say) 4000 there is more reason to assert that N is quite a lot; but if there is more reason to assert that N is quite a lot, there is more reason to assert that there are at least N atomic shapes than to assert there are at least N + 1 atomic shapes, given just the information that there are quite a lot of atomic shapes. But in that case it has to be admitted that the indifference premiss (1) is false.

Even if that premiss *were* established as true, and the conclusion

(5) for all n (it is justifiable to assert that there are at least n atomic shapes)

could be defended, there would still be a gap between that and the conclusion that Democritus' B-form indifference argument seeks to establish: that there *are* an infinite variety of atomic shapes. That remains so in spite of the fact that the epistemically strong conclusion (5) is the most appropriate correlate of a non-epistemological conclusion that an A-form argument could support. For it is possible that I should be *justified in asserting* that there are an infinite variety of atomic shapes, and yet there not actually *be* an infinite variety. Indeed even the unreasonable opponent mentioned earlier could get it right, by accident: his assertion that there are 5927 atomic shapes is shown to be unjustified, but it could turn out – luckily, for him – that there *are* just 5927 atomic shapes.

Yet the Democritean indifference premiss appears to retain some power even in the face of that possibility. How could it be, one might ask, that there are just and precisely 5927 atomic shapes? Why are there just *that* many? But if there are a limited number, then for some N (even if not 5927) there will be just N. That response evidences an inclination to see the argument as more effective if read as a B-form argument, with *non*-epistemological premisses. Since charity does not recommend an A-form (epistemological) reading, it is now worth considering how far a B-form reading could be sustained.

Before turning to that, however, there are connections of interest to be drawn out between A-form indifference arguments and two more general areas: first, the relation between A-form arguments and sorites paradoxes, and second, the connection between A-form arguments and the logical quantifiers.

6.4 Sorites Arguments

The attempt to give the best epistemological reading of the Democritean indifference argument led us to connect the argument with the step-by-step procedure characteristic of sorites reasoning. Further, sorites paradoxes were cited in an earlier chapter as an instance of a certain type of epistemological (A-form) indifference argument. All this suggests that there should be a useful parallel to be drawn between some forms of indifference reasoning, and the way of arguing that underlies sorites paradoxes.

On the other hand, though, it might seem implausible that there should be such a parallel. Arguments containing the phrase *ou mallon* – indifference arguments – and sorites arguments are both described by ancient writers, who display no inclination to assimilate them.[28] Nor does the typical indifference premiss form appear in any statements of sorites paradoxes. These are reasonable worries to raise. Nevertheless it will emerge that there is an enlightening connection to be drawn between A-form indifference reasoning and a group of related types of reasoning, of which group sorites paradoxes form a part.

A sorites paradox is an argument by gradual progression. Given some ordering of objects, some predicate is granted to hold of one object in the series, and reckoned not to hold of a further object; and yet it appears to follow by repeated application of some conditional that if it applies to the one it must apply to the other. The form of argument is:

(1) a_1 is F
(2) (a_1 is F $\rightarrow a_2$ is F)
therefore
(3) a_2 is F
(4) (a_2 is F $\rightarrow a_3$ is F)
therefore
(5) a_3 is F
.

.

.

therefore
(6) a_i is F
but
(7) a_i is not F

There are two points to note. First, while the conditionals *may* be derived from some more general claim that for all n (a_n is F $\rightarrow a_{n+1}$ is F), they need not be: each could be offered separately, on independent grounds. It will be possible to run a sorites paradox in that way so long as only a finite number of conditionals are required in order to get to the particular case a_i in which the predicate is reckoned not to apply.[29] Second, in order that the argument be valid the conditionals *need* only be taken, as we would say, as material conditionals, as equivalent to negated conjunctions: not (a_1 is F and not a_2 is F).[30]

Now if confronted with such reasoning I am vulnerable to a paradox because the contradiction between (6) and (7) appears to be *forced* on me. What is it, then, that I hold concerning a predicate F and a series $a_1 \ldots a_n$ such that I am driven on *rational* grounds to the disastrous position where I seem committed to both (6) and (7)? That is a question worth pursuing. In answering it the relation of sorites paradoxes proper to other, non-vicious, forms of reasoning will emerge, the different uses to which sorites paradoxes can be put will become clearer, and we will see how various moves offered as solutions of the paradox achieve their purpose.

What is required first of all is that $a_1 \ldots a_n$ form some sort of ordered series. The series may be very strictly ordered (as, for example, a series of 1 stone, 2 stones, 3 stones... is ordered numerically) or ordered in a far less formal way (as, for example, the series of animals from human being, gorilla, chimpanzee, orangutang...). In the absence of any sort of ordering there will be no notion of adjacency in terms of which particular pairs of members of the group of a's are picked out, and so there will be no special plausibility attaching to conditionals whose antecedent and consequent concern adjacent a's: there will, for example, be no reason to take (a_1 is F$\rightarrow a_2$ is F) as more plausible than any other conditional concerning pairs of a's.

Further, some view is required about the *reasons* on the basis of which the predicate F is applied. By 'reasons' I mean just whatever I could cite in explanation of an application of F, what I could offer if asked why I had applied F in a particular case. For example, reasons for the application of a colour predicate ('red') are how something looks, that something looks a certain way to a sighted observer in normal lighting conditions; reasons for the application of the predicate 'human' might be that something has a certain chromosomal structure, or a certain parentage, or possesses certain psychological capacities. Associated with any predicate will be certain features, the possession of which by something provides reason for application of the predicate to that thing. These reasons might either be indicated in a general way – how something looks in normal light as reason to apply the predicate 'red', how something feels when picked up as reason to apply the predicate 'heavy' – or described more specifically – that something is an adult horse and male is reason for applying the predicate 'stallion'. It should not be thought that giving a more specific description of reasons for the application of a predicate shows that it is a determinate matter whether some particular falls under the predicate. It might be unclear whether some animal is a horse, or whether some horse is an adult. In what follows, talk about reasons for the application of a predicate will cover both general grounds (for example, how something looks) and specific characteristic features (for example, being an adult male horse).

Now the sorites paradox is not a purely formal paradox. It arises for particular predicates because of views about the semantics of those predicates: that is to say, whether or not a predicate admits of sorites reasoning depends on what are counted as reasons for the application of that predicate. It is a commonplace observation that the predicates vulnerable to sorites paradoxes are *vague* predicates. To call a predicate vague is to say something about the way in which what count as good reasons for its application do not completely determine its application or withholding in every instance, but admit borderline cases.

There is more to say. Genuine paradox threatens when the reasons I have for applying F in one case do not allow me to distinguish between that case and the adjacent case in the ordering. If, for example, I accept that n stones are few stones then I cannot see that I'm in *any* position to refuse to allow that n + 1 stones are few stones. This is an important point, and requires some care. Paradox would not threaten if I could see *more* reason to apply F to a_n than to a_{n+1}. That is why it constitutes a *response* to a sorites paradox to say that justification in the application of predicates comes in degrees, and that in consequence I have more reason to apply F to one than to an adjacent member of the series. Suppose, for example, that I have reason to accept, and would accept, £50 for a job; and suppose I see that I've got ever so slightly *less* reason to accept £49.99. Does sorites reasoning loom, threatening me with the paradoxical conclusion that I should be willing to accept £1? It does not seem so. For nothing forces me to accept such conditionals as 'if I would accept £30.00 then I would accept £29.99'. The obvious response to that conditional is: not so – since I've got less reason to accept £29.99 than to accept £30.00, perhaps I would accept £30.00 but not accept £29.99.

Still, the reader may be suspicious. It is likely to be talk of 'no more reason . . .' that brings reference to indifference arguments into the picture: yet the claim that a genuine sorites paradox arises when there is *no more reason* to apply F to one than to an adjacent member of a series seems perverse in two ways. First, it seems clear enough how a sorites paradox will arise even given that there is *less* reason to apply F to some a_{n+1} than to a_n. For the ordered series is such that adjacent members are similar enough that, while there is less reason to apply F to one than to an adjacent member, there is not *sufficiently* less reason to justify applying F to one while withholding it from the other. Second, there will in fact be precious few cases where it is plausible to suppose that there is no more reason to apply F to one than to an adjacent member of the series: in contrast, however, sorites paradoxes are common.

The connection between A-form indifference arguments and sorites reasoning remains, in spite of these two points. Take the first point first. What gets a sorites paradox going is the apparent impossibility of justifiably resisting the application of a predicate to one member of a series once its application to an adjacent member is allowed. That impossibility follows from views about what are reasons for applying the predicate. So what needs to be made clear about an instance of sorites reasoning is what the relation *is* between reasons for application in one case and reasons for application in an adjacent case which, once granted, *requires* that application be extended from the one case to the other. Only the claim that there is no more reason to apply the predicate in one case than in the other secures that consequence. For as was seen above, from the claim that there is no more reason to assert that some a_{n+1} is F than to assert that a_n is F, it follows that I am justified in asserting that a_{n+1} is F if and only if I am justified in asserting that a_n is F – the one assertion is justified if and only if the other is. In contrast no such consequence will follow once it is allowed that there is (say) *more* reason to assert that some a_n is F than to assert that a_{n+1} is F. So it will be reference to the A-form indifference premiss – that, for all n, there is no more reason to assert that a_n is F than to assert that a_{n+1} is F – which reveals what it is about sorites paradoxes that *forces* one to allow application of a predicate in one case on the basis of allowing its application in another.

This is borne out by examples, as we see if we turn to the second worry raised above. There are a number of sorites paradoxes where it seems natural to say that there is *no more reason* to apply a predicate in one case than in an adjacent case. I do not have any less reason to call n + 1 small than to call n small; nor any less reason to call one colour sample red than another which is visually indiscriminable from it; nor, in Carneades' ancient theological sorites, any less reason to call Poseidon a god than to call Zeus a god, nor any less reason to call Achelous a god than to call Poseidon a god[31] – nor in fact do I have any less reason to call a pile of n stones a heap than to call a pile of n + 1 stones a heap. This is because a sorites paradox looms for a predicate precisely when adjacent objects in a series are similar enough that what dissimilarities there are between them make no difference when considering the reasons we have for applying the predicate – when the reasons on the basis of which the predicate is applied are insensitive to the fineness of the distinction between adjacent members of the series.[32] It is of course true that reasons for calling something a heap concern how many stones it contains, and reasons for calling someone bald concern how few hairs there are on his head. But what is also true (and what is the source of trouble) is that the reasons for calling something a heap do not concern *exactly* how many stones it contains, and that the reasons for calling someone bald do not concern *precise* numbers of hairs: and since it is just at the level of precise numbers that n and $n + 1$ stones differ, that is to say that there is just as much reason to call n stones a heap as to call $n + 1$ stones a heap, no more reason to call a man with only n hairs bald than to call a man with $n + 1$ hairs bald.[33]

The way in which views about a series $a_1 \ldots a_n$, a predicate F and the reasons for applying that predicate combine to force one to a position where the contradiction between (6) and (7) results can now be set out as follows:

(i) if F is applied on the basis of certain reasons, there is no more reason to assert that a_n is F than to assert that a_{n+1} is F

(ii) F is applied on the basis of those reasons

therefore

(iii) there is no more reason to assert that a_n is F than to assert that a_{n+1} is F

(iv) it is justified to assert that a_1 is F

therefore (from (iii) and (iv))

(v) it is justified to assert that a_2 is F

.
.
.

therefore

(vi) it is justified to assert that a_i is F

but

(vii) it is justified to assert that a_i is not F.

So far this is simply an argument giving rise to a contradiction. If, being persuaded of (vi) and (vii), I assert what I am justified in asserting, I end up asserting both that a_i is F and that a_i is not F. The argument is valid. (i) and (ii) give (iii) by *modus ponens*; (iii) is an indifference premiss which, as shown earlier, gives the biconditional, that it is justifiable to assert that a_n is F if and only if it is justifiable to assert that a_{n+1} is F; that biconditional along with (iv) is enough to generate (v) ... (vi). The remaining premiss is (vii).

Setting out this argument makes it clear how contradiction derives from views about the grounds on which a predicate is applied (that is (ii)), the thought that, given those grounds, adjacent members of a series are indistinguishable with respect to justified application of the predicate (that is (i)), a conviction that there is some case in which the predicate is justifiably applied (that is (iv)) and a claim that there is some case in which it is justifiably withheld (that is (vii)).

It is left an open matter, in the case of a particular predicate, whether the reasons on the basis of which it is applied will cover a plurality of *related* factors (as '... is a Duke' applies to something if it is created a Duke, or is related in a suitable way to something which is created a Duke) or a plurality of *independent* factors (as '... is a work of art' might apply to something if it is sincerely declared to be a work of art by its creator, or if it is admired as a work of art by sufficient observers, or if it is found in a certain institution, or if it is entertaining...). Hence it can be allowed – as is plainly the case and was mentioned earlier – that a sorites paradox might rest on appeal to different reasons for extending application of F from a_1 to a_2 and for extending application from a_2 to a_3. The salient point is that, whatever those reasons might be, they are such that, in the case of each adjacent pair, there is no more reason for applying F to the one than to the other.

(i), (ii), (iv) and (vii) are the *premisses*, concerning use of the predicate F, through acceptance of which I am led to contradictory claims. So, granted the required rule of inference (*modus ponens*), contradiction will be avoided only by giving up one or another of those premisses. Now it will sound odd to describe some of those ways of avoiding contradiction as *resolutions* of a sorites *paradox* since there is a tendency to reserve the term 'sorites paradox' for cases where there is an agreed application of F – where (iv) is accepted – and an agreed withholding of F – where (vii) is allowed.[34] Resolving contradiction by dropping (ii), (iv) or (vii) appears more naturally to be either conversion of the threatened sorites paradox into some other non-vicious type of argument, or admission of defeat in the face of paradox. It is a beneficial consequence of identifying the underlying argument (i)–(vii) that it reveals the connections between sorites paradoxes proper and related but non-vicious forms of reasoning.

I will say nothing more about those responses to sorites paradoxes which involve dropping *modus ponens* as a rule of inference. It is hard to believe first of all that the motivation for abandoning *modus ponens* should be, wholly and solely, worries about sorites paradoxes, or that abandonment of *modus ponens* could be limited just to arguments which threaten sorites paradoxes in the application of particular predicates. In any case, the upshot of withholding general endorsement of *modus ponens* will be mirrored in the underlying indifference argument (i)–(vii) above, since in the absence of a general commitment to *modus ponens* no contradiction is guaranteed to follow from (i), (ii), (iv) and (vii).

Contradiction could be avoided by withdrawing from premiss (iv). Since (iv) represents the most well-grounded application of the predicate F, that response would be tantamount to abandoning all justified application of F. This is the response looked for when sorites reasoning is used destructively to undercut application of a predicate. The theological sorites offered by Carneades is presented by Sextus in this way.[35] 'If Zeus is a god . . . streams too would be gods . . . But streams are not gods' – so far this is the argument to the contradiction; 'Therefore Zeus is not a god either' – this move resolves the contradiction; 'but if there were gods, Zeus too would be a god' – this resolution of the contradiction drops the most well-grounded application of the predicate; 'Therefore there are no gods' – the price of dropping the most well-grounded application of a predicate is that there are then no justified applications of the predicate in question. Among contemporary philosophers Peter Unger has used sorites reasoning – a sorites of decomposition – to this effect, in order to argue that there are no such things as tables or chairs, stones, planets or persons; indeed to argue that he himself does not exist.[36]

Denying (iv) is, however, admitting defeat. A more resilient response would be to deny (ii). That would be the response called for if one admitted (or could not see a way to avoid) the step-by-step application of the predicate, and yet were convinced of some justified application and some justified withholding of the predicate. The upshot of this response would be to focus attention on particular grounds offered for application of the predicate. It might seem, for example, that the application of a colour predicate could be extended by sorites-type reasoning (from one sample to another that is indiscriminable in shade) in such a way as to generate contradiction. A response to that paradox would be to focus attention on the *semantics* of the colour predicate (and thus colour predicates in general). That is to say that one would revise a view about the grounds on which a colour predicate is justifiably applied: perhaps one would revise views concerning the *way* in which colour predicates are observational predicates. On this approach the contradiction is resolved by dropping a particular reading of (ii), a particular account of the reasons which sustain application of a predicate. An ancient example is provided by Cicero's account of the motive behind Carneades' theological sorites arguments.[37] According to Cicero the arguments are intended not to rule out application of the predicate 'god', but to show that the Stoic account of the application of the predicate is unsatisfactory. A contemporary example would be the gradual extension of the predicate 'living' from the healthy adult to the coma victim on a ventilator: the effect of sorites reasoning in this context would be to force critical attention to a particular account of the grounds on which the predicate 'living' is applied.

The relation between denials of (ii) and (iv) as strategies for resolution of the conceptual tension generated by sorites reasoning – between revising one's understanding of the grounds for application of the predicate and conceding the predicate to be inapplicable – is anyway complex and blurred. In some cases the conviction that the predicate *is* applicable will be robust, although unclarified. That may be sufficient to sustain application through realization of how poor one's understanding is of the grounds of application. Such is the case with colour predicates. Yet there remains a pressure to provide an account of the reasons underlying application of the predicate which do not render it vulnerable to sorites-type contradictions. In other cases the predicate itself may be sufficiently well understood, and the claim that there is anything falling under the predicate sufficiently weak, that (iv) is denied on the basis of acceptance of (ii). Such would be the case if one used sorites reasoning to rule out application of superlative terms such as 'the most beautiful picture', on the grounds that if application were allowed in one case it would be impossible to avoid the contradictory conclusion that it should be applied in some other instance also. But in many other cases one's view of a predicate that appears vulnerable to sorites-type reasoning falls between these two extremes. What we say concerning *rights bearers*, for example, is responsive both to common intuitions on 'central' cases – for example, that a fully functioning adult has a right to life – and to whether an account can be given of the grounds on which that predicate is applied which allows one to resist sorites-type extensions to unacceptable cases – slugs, or plants, or viruses or whatever.

A further way to avoid contradiction would be to withdraw from premiss (vii). To do so would be to accept that there is *no* case in which one is justified in withholding the predicate F. In that case there would be no sorites *paradox*, but rather a conversion of the threatened paradox into another form of reasoning, of precisely the sort discussed earlier in connection with Democritus. In that case the series $a_1 \ldots a_n$ was an ordered series of sentences (of the form 'there are at least... atomic shapes') and the predicate F was 'is assertable'. Since the argument built on the claim that there are atoms, the Democritean will hold on to (iv) – that there is some justified application of the predicate 'is assertable' to sentences of the form 'there are at least... atomic shapes'. The reasons for the application of that predicate which (ii) introduces concern the background information available to Democritus: that there are atoms which exhibit quite a lot of variety of shape. (i) corresponds to the claim that applying the predicate 'is assertable' to sentences about atomic shapes on the basis of that information does not allow one to draw any distinction between adjacent members of the series a_1 to a_n of sentences of the form 'there are at least... atomic shapes'. In this case, however, there is no threat of paradox – the paradox that (i)–(vii) manifests does not result – since there is nothing corresponding to (vii): there is no a_i (*no* sentence of the form 'there are at least... atomic shapes') such that one has any justification for withholding application of the predicate in question (in effect, for denying the sentence to be assertable). In that case application of the predicate could be allowed to extend *ad infinitum* along the series $a_1 \ldots a_n$ without fear of contradiction. The Democritean argument failed, not because it ran into paradox, but because the indifference premiss of that argument – what corresponds to (iii) above – could not be sustained. With an eye on (i)–(vii) we would expect that if (iii) could not be sustained that would be because either (i) or (ii) failed to hold. That expectation is indeed borne out. Sentences of the form 'there are at least... atomic shapes' are assertable on the basis of the background information about the atoms and their shapes – nothing else is relevant to their being assertable: and so (ii) is true. But (i) was seen to be false. Given the background information, it turned out to be false that there is no more reason to take 'there are at least n atomic shapes' to be assertable than to take 'there are at least n + 1 atomic shapes' to be assertable.

Sorites paradoxes proper need not in every case tend to show that a predicate can be applied in an infinite number of cases. In order to show that, the series $a_1 \ldots a_n$ would have to extend infinitely, and extension of application of the predicate from one member to another would have to be underpinned by some general claim: for all n (if a_n is F then a_{n+1} is F). It would be impossible to extend application of a predicate *ad infinitum* if in the case of each application one had to satisfy oneself of independent grounds for the extension. In some cases neither of those conditions is satisfied. On the other hand, when those conditions are satisfied an infinite extension of application of the predicate can be generated.[38] As noted previously, in sorites paradoxes proper it will usually be sufficient to go so far in extending application of the predicate as to secure a contradiction with an agreed case of withholding. Yet one could formulate a sorites paradox which made trouble for the application of a predicate just in virtue of justifying an infinite number of applications. Imagine someone who held that N is a natural number only if we are in practice capable of representing N in Arabic notation.[39] That position seems unsettling, and can be shown to be so by a sorites paradox. The predicate F is 'is a natural number', and the reason on the basis of which it is applied is the practical capacity to produce a name in Arabic notation. Clearly 1 counts as a natural number on those grounds, and the premiss (i) seems defensible too: if n is thus representable then so too is n + 1. A sorites paradox will make trouble for this position without any need to consider a *specific* number for which premiss (vii) holds. Given premisses (i), (ii) and (iv) it should follow that the totality of numbers practically representable in the Arabic notation is *infinite*; yet it plainly is not.

If (ii), (iv) and (vii) are allowed, the only way remaining to avoid contradiction is to drop (i). It is necessary that a cogent response to a sorites paradox should avoid commitment to (i). For in refusing to drop any of (ii), (iv) or (vii) one holds onto an account of the reasons for applying a predicate F, and allows clear cases of the application and withholding of F. Unless (i) is avoided, contradiction still threatens.

Some resolutions of sorites paradoxes do explicitly address (i). For example, one response is to emphasize that there are different degrees of justification, and that one is decreasingly justified in applying F as one considers successive members of the series $a_1 \ldots a_n$. Making that response involves dissent from (i). Since the response suggests no revision of the reasons for applying the predicate F, the antecedent of (i) is accepted; yet the consequent of (i) is rejected since it is denied that one's confidence in applying F to adjacent members of the series remains constant.

There are other responses to sorites paradoxes, which seem to be not so explicitly aimed at (i). Nevertheless, closer attention to them will often bring (i) into the picture. In the remainder of this section I will consider some other sorts of response offered to sorites paradoxes, and their connection with the indifference structure (i)–(vii). The first is the response made in the ancient world by Chrysippus.

Chrysippus' strategy was one of 'keeping quiet'.[40] A sorites paradox can be presented to an opponent as a series of questions: 'is a_1 F?', 'is a_2 F?'... What corresponds to the conditionals is the apparent inability to answer 'yes' to one question but 'no' to the next. Chrysippus' recommendation was simply to refuse to answer at some stage – and it seems, at a stage at which the answer, were one to be given, would be *clear*.

Commentators dispute the precise value of this as a response. If we look to (i)–(vii) we can see why it might seem of negligible value, as it did to Carneades.[41] (i)–(vii) is a threatening argument in that it issues in the conclusion that one is *justified* in both applying and withholding the same predicate in the same case – the clash is between (vi) and (vii). In that case it will seem irrelevant whether one actually *does* apply or withhold the predicate: as Carneades' response has it, 'why should your pursuer care whether he traps you silent or speaking?' Nor do constructive modern interpretations of the keeping-quiet strategy represent much of a gain for Chrysippus, so long as (i) is left in place. By ceasing to answer at one point while starting to answer again later on, Chrysippus reveals that he is certain that in some case the predicate F applies, while in some later case it does not apply – and so (as it might be) both Fa_9 and $\neg Fa_{20}$ are true. From that it follows that the general conditional 'for all n (if a_n is F then a_{n+1} is F)' is not true, and so in particular does not follow from an understanding of the concept F.[42] The value of this, however, is admitted to be limited, and the strategy fails to achieve anything just to the extent that it leaves (i) in place. For suppose it granted that a particular sorites paradox is not powered by a general conditional – for all n (if a_n is F then a_{n+1} is F) – which is true on conceptual grounds. Still, trouble looms so long as the reasons that *are* adverted to as the question of each application of F arises – which reasons can be admitted to be distinct, and independent of one another – justify one new application of F after another along the series $a_1 \ldots a_n$; that will be the case just so long as the (possibly independent plurality of) reasons render (i) true of each adjacent pair in the series $a_1 \ldots a_n$. The response to Chrysippus that Burnyeat envisages for Carneades comes down to precisely the recognition that trouble persists so long as (i) remains in place. Carneades is in effect able to say: 'I think we will find, as you take one a_n after another, and given the distinct features you will allow me to cite as reason for applying F, that there will be no more reason to assert that any a_n is F than to assert that a_{n+1} is F.' That is to say that Chrysippus' strategy is unsuccessful just to the extent that it fails to show a way to evade (i).

That being so, the question arises whether the strategy would be more successful if it *could* be taken as generating a way to avoid (i). Chrysippus' advice that one should stop answering the question 'is a_n F?' while it is yet plain what the answer is augurs modesty and caution. Now consider, for the moment, someone who was neither modest nor cautious. This man would still cease answering at some point, but just at the first question at which he comes to see *less* reason to apply F. One might, of course, doubt the feasibility of identifying any such question. For the present, however, that is not to the point. What is relevant is rather to see how that response, if it *could* be made, would be a cogent response and would achieve its purpose.[43]

This respondent – call him Bold – would achieve an advantage if he could fall silent at the first *a* at which there comes to be less reason to apply F. His staying quiet reflects the fact that he intends neither to apply F nor to withhold F. If new reasons are offered to him for the application of F in this case, Bold can acknowledge that they *are* reasons – after all, he does not disagree about (ii), on what count as reasons for applying F. His claim is only that these give *less* reason to apply F to this a than there were to apply F to the previous a. Further Bold can answer Carneades' questions about *why* he remains silent: if there is an answer to be given, what difference can it make whether or not it is actually given? Does Bold have a clear answer to give to the question of whether F applies in this case? Well, since *ex hypothesi* Bold has less reason to apply F in this case than in the previous case, it does not *follow* from his previous practice that he is justified in applying F. If the refusal to answer *were* just a device for remaining silent Carneades would be right: 'you achieve nothing, for why should your pursuer care whether he traps you silent or speaking?'[44] However, since he claims *less* reason to apply F in this case than in the one preceding, Bold is not vulnerable to the damaging charge that he is refusing to make claims that he can be *shown* to be justified in making.

There is some advantage in Bold's response, as can be illustrated by example. Suppose the predicate to be extended from case to case is 'not to be killed for human profit'. The argument goes:

An adult human is not to be killed for human profit; if an adult human is not to be killed for human profit then a baby human is not to be killed for human profit (since they both have the same capacities); if a baby human is not to be killed for human profit then a congenitally mentally limited baby is not to be killed for human profit (since they are both human beings); if a congenitally mentally limited baby is not to be killed for human profit then an adult higher ape is not to be killed for human profit (since they have the same level of inner mental life); if an adult higher ape is not to be killed for human profit then a dog is not to be killed for human profit (since they are both mammals capable of pain awareness) . . .

Imagine this argument run far enough that the respondent comes definitely to disagree – it issues in the conclusion (which he finds unacceptable) that a tree is not to be killed for human profit.

Bold ceases answering as soon as the grounds offered come to provide *less* reason to apply the predicate – say, at the extension from a congenitally mentally limited baby to an adult higher ape. His response does not involve disagreement about what *are* reasons for applying the predicate 'not to be killed for human profit'; he can well agree that facts about inner mental life are reasons for application. Nor does his response involve claiming that an adult higher ape *is* to be killed for human profit. Nor need it even involve claiming that there is a sharp cut-off point between organisms which can and organisms which cannot be killed for human profit. All Bold's response requires is the claim that a point can be identified at which the reasons offered for the application of a predicate become weaker – a point at which there comes to be *less* reason to apply the predicate than there was previously.

However, this still seems to require payment of quite a high price. One might doubt that there *is* any such point as Bold claims to identify, when there first comes to be less reason to apply the predicate F. After all, the series $a_1 \ldots a_n$ is so arranged that adjacent members seem barely distinguishable. On the other hand, one sees that (i) can hardly be allowed to stand. If the concern with Bold's strategy is his claim to *identify* a *first* case where there is less reason to apply F, perhaps something could be achieved by a more cautious version of that strategy. To use Chrysippus' analogy, Cautious (as we can call him) will stand to Bold as the charioteer who stops before the precipice to the one who goes right to the edge. But what does Cautious stand to gain? He does not dispute that there is (as it were) a precipice to tumble over – that is to say, a case where there comes to be less reason to apply F. His worry is rather that he might not recognize that case when it comes up. Cautious is concerned by the possibility that in some case he may *in fact* have less reason to apply F than previously although he *thinks* he has as much reason to apply F as previously. But this is, on the face of it, a hard possibility even to make sense of, and so an odd possibility to be concerned about.

If pressed to elucidate his concerns, Cautious might say that what worries him about Bold's strategy is that in attempting to follow it he could be lulled into thinking that he has more reason that he in fact does to apply F in some particular case by the similarity of that case to an adjacent one. Perhaps a_{n+1} so resembles a_n that on the basis of that resemblance there seems to be as much reason to apply F to a_{n+1} as to a_n. But once its allowed that a_{n+1} *does* so resemble a_n (rather than merely *seeming* to) then there *is* (rather than merely *seeming* to be) as much reason to apply F to a_{n+1} as to a_n. After all, Cautious's worry is not that their adjacency leads him to see a_{n+1} as more similar to a_n than it really is. So it turns out that the worry about Bold's response which seemed to recommend caution in fact leads to the total collapse of Bold's strategy. Similarity between a_{n+1} and a_n sufficient to produce error about whether there is more reason to apply F to the one that to the other is similarity sufficient to *provide* as much reason to apply F to the one as to the other – and in that case, contrary to what Bold claims, there just is no (as Cautious might fear, unrecognizable) case in which there comes to be less reason to apply F. So Cautious's strategy of advising silence *before* one gets to that case, but when one sees it coming up, is empty advice. On the other hand, if the dissimilarity between a_{n+1} and a_n is sufficient that there could be less reason to apply F to the one than to the other, then a_n and a_{n+1} are not so similar that there could *seem* to be as much reason to apply F to the one as to the other; and in that case too Cautious's grounds for suspicion of Bold's strategy no longer seem persuasive.

No cautious version of the keeping-quiet strategy will, then, provide a cogent way of avoiding (i). Where does that leave Bold's response? It is not so easy to dismiss Bold out of hand. Bold advocates silence as soon as there comes to be less reason to apply F, but he need not claim that at *that* point the predicate F ceases to apply: there may be less reason to assert that a_{n+1} is F than to assert that a_n is F, although a_{n+1} just as much as a_n *is* F. That is as we should expect, since the rationale of drawing attention to the *A-form* indifference argument underlying sorites reasoning is to indicate the *epistemological* claims which give rise to the trouble. While we came upon Bold by imagining how Chrysippus' strategy could provide a way of evading (i), and while for Stoics such as Chrysippus there is an associated *metaphysical* claim, that there is a sharp cut-off between the a's which are and the a's which are not F – that is, some last a which is, and some adjacent first a which is not, F – it is not necessary to take on board the metaphysics in order to avail oneself of Bold's advice. Perhaps, for example, I think that there is no sharp temporal boundary in the development of a human organism between what is and what is not a person. Does it follow that I am vulnerable to sorites reasoning on the predicate 'person'? Not if I could agree with Bold that, while up to a certain point there is not increasing reason to apply the predicate (there is no more reason to call a 20-minute-old embryo a person than to call a 19-minute-old embryo a person), there comes a first point at which there *is* more reason – at which it is just no longer *equally clear* that the developing human is not a person.

Bold's response now seems less unreasonable. We might grant the implausibility of the metaphysical picture: that there is a first stage at which something ceases to be, or starts to cease to be, a heap, or bald, or red. Yet once that metaphysical picture is detached from Bold's response, the implausibility of the metaphysics will not infect Bold. Bold's claim seems to involve fairly minimal requirements. Bold requires that the degree to which reasons can support the application of a predicate F will vary. That seems an unobjectionable requirement, and as noted earlier underpins a denial of (i) and hence an escape from the argument that forces one to the contradiction between (vi) and (vii). Bold further requires that in considering the application of F one can recognize how good are one's reasons for applying F. Again Bold can present that as a minimal requirement: it would be at odds with the role of reasons in guiding applications of a predicate to suppose that a user of the predicate could not recognize good and less good reasons. Bold does not require the implausible claim that the ability to distinguish good and less good reasons rules out puzzlement in some particular case about whether I have enough reasons to support an actual application of the predicate. Bold can allow, as well he ought, that I might not be sure whether a certain man is bald, a particular collection a heap or a specific shade red. These will be borderline cases. Bold's response is aimed not at the existence of borderline cases but at an *argument* which seems to *force* him to admit successive applications of a predicate F actually to be justified. To evade that argument Bold need only recognize that in a particular case he has *less* reason to assert that a_{n+1} is F than to assert that a_n is F – for in that case it will no longer *follow* from the application to a_n's being justified that the further application to a_{n+1} is justified also. The keeping-quiet strategy is an appropriate behavioural manifestation of Bold's recognition that in a certain case he has less reason to apply F than he did previously: recognizing that enables Bold to deny (i).

We might now guess that other proposed responses to sorites paradoxes, which do not appear to be at all related to the indifference structure (i)–(vii), will seem deficient to the extent that they do not suggest a way of denying (i). One response that is suggested to sorites paradoxes is a degrees-of-truth story. The idea briefly is that the sentences 'a_1 is F', 'a_2 is F'...'a_n is F' vary in truth continuously between the wholly true (value 1) and the wholly false (value 0); a method is provided of deciding the truth of conditionals, on which the conditional $(Fa_n \rightarrow Fa_{n+1})$ has the same truth value for any pair of adjacent a's, being very nearly wholly true;[45] that result answers well to the intuition that each conditional is very plausible, and seems to command our assent. Nevertheless the series $Fa_1 \ldots Fa_n$ can start with a wholly true sentence and end up with a wholly false sentence.

It is not to the point here to consider whether this is a plausible way of dealing with sorites paradoxes; so talk of a sentence being true to a particular degree, or a predicate applying to some degree, will be accepted without demur. The interesting question is how this strategy relates to the indifference argument (i)–(vii). It does not *seem* to relate to it at all, since it does not appear to turn on any epistemological considerations.

Still, one might ask what it would be natural to say if sympathetic to a degrees-of-truth approach when faced with an epistemological question about the application of predicates. Suppose Fa_n is more true than Fa_{n+1}, that F applies more to a_n than to a_{n+1}. Then I *could not* have as much reason to assert that a_{n+1} is F as I do to assert that a_n is F. For suppose I did have as much reason to assert the former as the latter; then reasons which are *ex hypothesi* just as good reasons for application of F will, at the very least, lead me more astray in one case than in another, since a_{n+1} is granted to be less truly F that a_n. Yet that is at odds with the initial supposition that I have *as much reason* to apply F to a_n as to apply it to a_{n+1}.

This is not, perhaps, surprising, but it does give the consequence that if one were sympathetic to a degrees-of-truth approach to sorites paradoxes one would also be committed to the denial of (i); and that consequence concurs with our earlier thought that a requirement on a cogent response to the sorites is that (i) should be denied.

Similar remarks are relevant to another popular contemporary way of dealing with sorites paradoxes: the supervaluational account of vague predicates offered by Kit Fine.[46] One might think of this as a partial divergence from the metaphysical picture associated with the Stoics. While it is not held that vague predicates mark out boundaries which are precise (though obscure to us), there is a crucial role for the notion of precision. Given some vague predicate there will be ways of making it precise or sharpening it. The predicate 'generous', for example, clearly applies to gifts of over £1000 and clearly does not apply to gifts of only £1, while a gift of £20 is a borderline case. A determinate boundary *could* be specified: one could just specify that a gift of £30 or over is generous while a gift of less than £30 is not. Of course, that particular precisification is arbitrary – there is no more reason to pick £30 than £40. But the supervaluational account aims to ameliorate that worry. A sentence containing a vague predicate is true if and only if it comes out true on *every* (admissible)[47] way of rendering it precise. That gives plausible results. '£1000 is a generous gift' comes out true, and '£1 is a generous gift' comes out false. A sentence like '£25 is a generous gift' does not come out true, since if 'generous' is made precise at £25 it would be true, while if made precise at £26 it would be false. Consider the conditional 'if £26 is a generous gift then £25 is a generous gift'. That will not be true, since it does not come out true on every way of rendering 'generous' precise: if 'generous' is rendered precise at £26 (so that gifts of that amount or more count as generous) then the antecedent of that conditional is true but the consequent false, and so the whole conditional is false on that precisification. So this account offers a way of avoiding (at least) one of the conditionals (a_n is $F \rightarrow a_{n+1}$ is F).

Adherence to this model is likely to relate to (i) in much the same way as adherence to the degrees-of-truth model. For one could use the apparatus of a variety of possible sharpenings of a predicate to motivate a degrees-of-truth account. One *could* claim that Fa_n is more true than Fa_{n+1} if and only if Fa_n comes out true on more (admissible) ways of rendering F precise than does Fa_{n+1}. The supervaluational account would claim not *that*, but rather that, of such an Fa_n and Fa_{n+1}, since neither is true on all (admissible) ways of rendering F precise, then neither is true. Still one can show that adherence to the supervaluational account involves denial of (i) by considering not the application of F to just any adjacent pair of a's but to the last a to which F applies on all admissible ways of rendering F precise, say a_i, and the a adjacent to that, a_{i+1}.[48] It is not possible that of those a's there could be as much reason to assert the one to be F as the other. A way of rendering F precise which makes a_{i+1} turn out to be not F is admissible, by hypothesis. But whatever dissimilarities there are between a_i and a_{i+1} are sufficient to render any way of making F precise which *fails* to make a_i turn out to be F *in*admissible. In that case those dissimilarities will be sufficient to provide *more* reason to apply F to a_i than to a_{i+1}. If they did not, a way of rendering F precise which made a_i turn out *not* to be F would not fail to be admissible. So since it will not be true of this a_i and a_{i+1} that there is no more reason to assert the one to be F than to assert the other to be F, the premiss (i) will not hold either. Just as in the case of the degrees-of-truth strategy, the supervaluational account allows one to avoid (i) and so avoid the contradiction which (i)–(vii) generate.

There are other, and interestingly different, lines of response that are taken to sorites paradoxes which might be considered, but any more lengthy a discussion would be inappropriate.[49] Some general conclusions about the relation between indifference arguments and sorites reasoning can now be drawn. The argument (i)–(vii) was intended to bring out the way in which views about the grounds on which a predicate is applied can generate conceptual tension. That tension is generated *via* the inference that lies at the core of epistemological indifference reasoning: the move from 'there is no more reason to assert that p than to assert that q' to 'it is justified to assert that p if and only if it is justified to assert that q'. By drawing attention to that argument we can see more clearly what are the various moves available to resolve the threat of contradiction. Some of these avoid paradox by converting a threatened sorites into a constructive form of reasoning, others represent the admission of defeat in the face of paradox, and still others involve revision of one's understanding of the reasons for applying a predicate. When sorites paradoxes proper loom, it is epistemological commitments which generate difficulty. A cogent response to a sorites will either address those epistemological issues directly, or can be shown to involve a way of addressing them.

Unsurprisingly, epistemological indifference reasoning is relevant to issues other than those connected with sorites reasoning. I will close this chapter with some – far briefer – comments on one more such issue.

6.5 Arbitrary Objects and Quantification

The previous section concerned the connection between indifference arguments and the possibility of extending application of a predicate infinitely along an *ordered* series of objects $a_1 \ldots a_n$. Indifference reasoning might also be expected to clarify a related procedure: the case in which application of a predicate is secured over a domain which may contain infinitely many objects, yet which are *not* presented in any ordered series. This is precisely the procedure encapsulated in the logical rule of *universal quantifier introduction*.

Suppose I want to establish that all Fs are Gs. I will not be able to do this in general by establishing of each F in turn that it is a G. I will not in general know, or need to know, whether the domain of Fs is empty, finite or infinite in extent. Further, even if I were to establish of each F in turn that it is a G, in order to be justified in concluding that all the Fs are Gs I would need to be justified in taking it that those *are* all the Fs. In the light of these points it might seem surprising that any universal conclusion *can* be established: for example, that all triangles have internal angles of 180° or that all books on Latin grammar bought since 1970 are on the computer catalogue. Universal conclusions are reached by finding a *single* argument which will serve to establish a general conclusion, in the following sort of way. Just consider some book on Latin grammar – any one you like. Then either it was bought by the main library, in which case it will have been put directly on the computer catalogue, or it was bought by a sub-library, in which case they will have informed the main library, in which case it will have been put on the computer catalogue, or it will have been donated by an alumnus, in which case it will have been sent to the main library, in which case it will be on the computer catalogue. So all books on Latin grammar will be on the computer catalogue. More formally, if I establish of an arbitrary triangle ABC that it has internal angles of 180° then I can conclude that *all* triangles have internal angles of 180°.[50]

Now one might ask what the justification is for that procedure. How should we unpack the thought, that *since* ABC is an *arbitrary* triangle, *then* if it is established that ABC has internal angles of 180° one is justified in concluding that all triangles have internal angles of 180°? In the course of answering that question some light is cast on the question of the status of the arbitrary triangle ABC.[51]

There is another way in which appeal to what is arbitrary appears in connection with quantifiers. Suppose one sought to draw a conclusion from the premiss that *some* F is G. The premiss might of course be false, and no F actually *be* G, but that does not tend to interfere with arguing validly to a conclusion from that premiss. Suppose I wish to argue that if some triangle has equal sides then not all triangles contain a right angle. Assume that an arbitrary triangle ABC has equal sides. In that case ABC will contain angles of 60°. Therefore ABC will not contain a right angle. If all triangles contained a right angle, then ABC would contain a right angle. Therefore not all triangles contain a right angle. Therefore, conditionalizing, if *some* triangle has equal sides then not all triangles contain a right angle.

Appeal to indifference arguments casts light on what is going on here. First, the case where I am to establish a universal conclusion. In providing a proof of a proposition I am giving reason to assert that proposition. If I have a proof, guaranteed to apply to each member $F_1 F_2 \ldots$ of the group of Fs, that each of them is G, then I have a proof which is sufficient to establish that all the Fs are G. If I can establish that an arbitrary F is G, I assuredly will have a proof guaranteed to apply to each member $F_1 F_2 \ldots$ of the group of Fs. This is because establishing that an *arbitrary* F is G entitles me to an indifference premiss: that there is no more reason to assert that F_1 is G than to assert that F_2 is G than to assert that F_3 is G $\ldots$ For the reason to assert that F_1 is G is the proof which results from replacing the term for the arbitrary

F by the name of F_1 throughout the proof that the arbitrary F is G. Suppose I introduce α as an *arbitrary* F. To say that α is an arbitrary F is to say that α is introduced as wholly *typical* of the kind F.[52] In that case, proofs that result from replacing α by any term for a particular F are sure to be equally cogent. So the proof that arbitrary α is G entitles me to the indifference claim that there is no more reason to assert that F_1 is G than to assert that F_2 is G than to assert that F_3 is G . . .

A modal equivalence follows from that indifference claim: it is justified to assert that F_1 is G if and only if it is justified to assert that F_2 is G if and only if it is justified to assert that F_3 is G . . . But it *is* justified to assert that F_1 is G, since replacement of α by F_1 throughout the proof that the arbitrary F, α, is G provides justification for the assertion that F_1 is G. Hence it follows that it is justified to assert of every F that it is G. Thus it is justified to conclude, once it is established that the arbitrary F, α, is G, that all Fs are G.

Does appeal to that indifference argument incline one towards any answer on the vexed question of the status of an arbitrary F? The weight of the explication rests on the thought that there is an arbitrary *name*, which can be replaced, without detriment to the proof, by a name of each F in turn. That is sufficient to convince me that there will be no reason for asserting one particular F to be G without there being equal reason to assert any other particular F to be G. Consequently it is not necessary to ask what the arbitrary name is a name *of*. It can more usefully be thought of as a place holder, available for replacement by names which are of particular Fs. In that case any worries as to what an arbitrary object could be are bypassed.

One might be tempted to hold that reasoning involving appeal to an arbitrary F is reasoning about some particular F by the thought that one is after all reasoning about *something* and there are no Fs other than particular Fs to reason about. It is precisely the thought that there are no Fs other than particular Fs which makes Fine's preferred account – that one is reasoning about a genuinely *arbitrary* object – seem so extremely implausible.[53] But one should not then conclude that what is significant about showing of an arbitrary F that it is G is that when I do so I am *ipso facto* showing of some *particular* F that it is G. That is, as Fine says, a very implausible suggestion, encouraged perhaps by over-concentration on geometrical examples, where the diagram which typically accompanies a proof is an (approximate) *instance* of the predicate F about which one is reasoning.[54]

The appeal to indifference reasoning is intended to shift attention from ontological questions altogether. I could use the *name* of a particular F in showing that all Fs are Gs, so long as in doing so I do not appeal to any assumptions about that particular F. For example, I could show that all students will either gain an honours degree or gain a pass degree or fail or drop out by showing of my favourite student Billy Briggs that *he* will either gain an honours degree or gain a pass degree or fail or drop out, so long as my drawing that conclusion about Billy Briggs does not rest on any assumptions which mention Billy Briggs. In that case use of *that* name was wholly arbitrary. I could have used the name of another F, or of some other kind of thing. What is important in making legitimate appeal to an arbitrary F is that I am guaranteed to be able to replace whatever name I use by the names of one particular F after another without detriment to the proof that the arbitrary F is G. That is sufficient to give the indifference premiss that there is no more reason to assert that F_1 is G than to assert that F_2 is G than to assert that F_3 is G ... So I can draw general conclusions about Fs without supposing that there *are* any particular Fs to reason about, or in the course of a reduction to *show* that there are no Fs.

Indifference arguments are involved in much the same way when I draw a conclusion from the premiss that *some* F is G, through reasoning about an arbitrary F. Establishing a conclusion C from the assumption that an arbitrary F is G is offering a proof involving an arbitrary (place holding) name for an F, of the conclusion C. Since that arbitrary name can be replaced by the name of any particular F, possession of that proof assures me of an indifference premiss: that there is no more reason to assert that since F_1 is G then C than to assert that since F_2 is G then C ... From that indifference premiss there follows an equivalence: I am justified in asserting that since F_1 is G then C if and only if I am justified in asserting that since F_2 is G then C ... Therefore given just that *some* F is G I can safely draw the conclusion C, since whichever F it is in virtue of which it is true that some F is G, I will be equally justified in drawing the conclusion C.

6.6 Conclusion

Before moving on to consider what is to be learned from a non-epistemological reading of the indifference arguments with which we started out, it is useful to draw the conclusions of this chapter together. The general thought, that indifference arguments should more charitably be taken as epistemological, has been found wanting. The paradigm arguments considered did not, in fact, fare particularly well when interpreted as epistemological arguments. Further, as will become apparent, they are neither less plausible nor less interesting when interpreted as non-epistemological. Nevertheless, connections of interest have emerged between A-form epistemological indifference reasoning and other forms of argument: in particular, sorites, and related, forms of reasoning; and the sort of reasoning by which quantifiers are handled.

NOTES

1 The terms of an epistemological indifference premiss may therefore be neither epistemically compatible nor epistemically incompatible: I may have no idea whether p and q are compatible or not. But I need not consider such cases at any great length, since – as will become plain – in such a case I will not be able to defend any significant inference from the epistemological indifference premiss.

2 The argument (1)–(8) that follows is very similar to the form of argument discussed by Barnes (1982, pp. 554–7) as a destructive use of indifference arguments. My discussion touches on that of Barnes at a number of points here. This is unsurprising. Barnes provides one of the few discussions of the *logic* of ancient indifference arguments of which I am aware.

3 This move is justified at least for this case, where there are two conjuncts. The completely general case is more complicated, owing to examples related to the lottery paradox. If there were 1,000,000 people in for a lottery, then I could be justified in asserting that ticket 1 will not win, and justified in asserting that ticket 2 will not win . . ., and yet *not* be justified in asserting the conjunction that (ticket 1 will not win and ticket 2 will not win and . . .). But the explanation of that result rests on there being a very large number of conjuncts. So the case above will not be affected.

4 Suppose that I make an epistemically *weak* assumption to start with: that I am not justified in asserting that p. The indifference premiss will then allow me to infer that I am not justified in asserting that q. But whether p and q are epistemically compatible or epistemically incompatible, there will be no absurdity in the conjunction that (I am not justified in asserting p and I am not justified in asserting q). Hence, while negation of the epistemically weak assumption would give an epistemically strong conclusion, there will be no route from an epistemically weak assumption to the position where the negation of that assumption is required.

5   I say *generally* because one can offer examples in which, due to particularities of the set-up, I can take it that establishing the negation of an epistemically strong conclusion will allow me to infer another epistemically strong conclusion. Consider a law court, where there is a default position – that *ceteris paribus* I am justified in asserting A is innocent. If the evidence offered to justify the assertion that Biggs is guilty would equally justify me in convicting Coggs, and yet I am justified in asserting that only one man committed the crime, I can conclude that I am not justified in asserting that Biggs is guilty (an epistemically weak conclusion); in this context I can then conclude that I am justified in asserting Biggs to be innocent (an epistemically strong conclusion). But there will not in general be a route from an epistemically weak conclusion to an epistemically strong conclusion.

6   A premiss is *discharged* if, having been assumed for the sake of a reductio, it is then negated. In that case what was originally assumed no longer remains as a premiss on which the conclusion rests. If a premiss is *undischarged* it is not merely assumed for the sake of a reductio, and the conclusion in which the argument issues rests on that premiss.

7   For one instance of the tendency of the sceptical connotations of *ou mallon* and related expressions to dominate over other uses, and the effect of that domination, see de Lacy (1964) on Plutarch's response to Colotes.

8   Diogenes *Lives* 9.76, LS 1G, concerning Timon.

9   See in Sextus Empiricus *PH* 1.14, 1.187. 11.188–91, 1.213; *M* 1.315; and, concerning Aenesidemus, the passage from Photius at LS 71C7.

10 Sextus *PH* 1.190.

11 Sextus *PH* 1.8 on the suspension of judgement, the adoption of ἐποχή.

12 For this account of the causal nature of the progression and our passivity in respect of suspension of judgement, see the opening of Barnes (1982a).

13 *PH* 1.12.

14 *PH* 1.7,26.

15 *PH* 1.190.

16 *PH* 11.8, 26.

17 *PH* 1.26–9. I do not claim that the matters laid out so briefly here are straightforward, nor that there is unanimity either among modern commentators or ancient sceptics. For example, Aenesidemus disagrees with Sextus as to the goal and the means of achieving it. Sextus' view is that the aim is freedom from disturbance, and that suspension of judgement is a way of attaining it hit upon by chance. According to Aenesidemus, in contrast, the goal is suspension of judgement itself, on which freedom from disturbance follows 'like a shadow'. See Diogenes *Lives* 9.107, LS 71A(3), and the comments of LS thereon. I do not pretend, though, to be *arguing* for a particular account of scepticism, so much as merely

describing why I have given such a scanty treatment of indifference reasoning in ancient scepticism.

18 *PH* 1.190.

19 *PH* 1.191.

20 Burnyeat (1980) emphasizes our passivity in respect to the suspension of judgement, and mentions the Stoic comparison at Cicero *Acad* 2.38, LS 40O, between the mind as affected by what is evident and a pair of scales.

21 Simplicius *in Phys* 28.4 on, Luria §2, DK 67A8, 68A38.

22 The charge of fallacy is levelled by Barnes (1982, p. 557f). It is a moot point whether the argument can in the end be sustained against that, or a similar, objection. But at least it can be given a better run for its money than the charge allows. See note 24 below.

23 It will become clear presently why *this* way of stating the indifference premiss gives the argument overall its best chance.

24 Since (4) implies

(i) for some n it is justifiable to assert there are at least n atomic shapes

another advantage of the 'at least' formulation becomes apparent. For (i) gives Democritus a premiss stronger than

(ii) it is justifiable to assert for some n there are at least n atomic shapes

without committing a quantifier shift fallacy in passing fallaciously from (ii) to (i). On that fallacy, see note 22 above.

25 See Aristotle *GC* 1.2 315b8 on, DK 67A9, Luria §240; also Simplicius *in Phys* 28.22–4, DK 68A38, Luria §318.

26 For this objection, see Epicurus *Ep Her* §42 = LS 12B.

27 Suppose I know that the devil will condemn me to quite a lot of days of pain: even though I allow it *possible* that he should condemn me to an infinite number, that information doesn't give me any epistemic preference for that alternative.

28 On ancient treatments of sorites arguments, see the passages collected by LS at 37B-H, 70D, E, and comments thereon; Barnes (1982b), and the collection of texts referring to sorites arguments cited at the end of that paper; Burnyeat (1982).

29 Compare the independent grounds offered in Carneades' sorites argument concerning the gods, Sextus Empiricus *M* 9.182–4, LS 70E: if Zeus is a god then Poseidon is a god (since they are brothers), if Poseidon is a god then Achelous is a god (since they are both large masses of water)...; see Burnyeat (1982) on the significance of this move, as an attempt by Carneades to evade Chrysippus' response to sorites paradoxes.

30 Sorites paradoxes are given in terms of negated conjunctions in ancient sources: Diogenes *Lives* 7.82, LS 37D. Modern commentators differ as to the precise significance of this for the resolution of sorites paradoxes, and how it relates to the first point noted above. Sedley (1977) holds that Stoic insistence on the use of the negated conjunction form is to indicate that the connection between antecedent and consequent is one of plausibility rather than necessity, in which case there is room to claim that one of the conditionals is in fact false (though one may be unable to recognize which); see further Sedley (1982a). Burnyeat (1982) relates preference of the negated conjunction form to the view that the sorites is not sustained on *conceptual* grounds (as it would be if the conditional were of the stronger form), and connects that with Chrysippus' 'keeping quiet' strategy for dealing with the sorites, Sextus *M* 7.416 = LS 37F, Cicero *Acad* 2.93 = LS 37H(3). Barnes (1982a) prefers to see adoption of the negated conjunction form as a preference for the weakest premisses required to get the argument going.

31 See reference at note 29 above.

32 Note Sextus' way of speaking at *M* 7.418ff, in showing how sorites reasoning makes problems for the Stoic notion of the 'cognitive impression' (καταληπτικὴ φαντασία): there is a 'great difference' (7.418 μεγάλη διαφορά) between 'fifty ... are few' and 'ten thousand ... are few', but there is 'nothing between' (7.419 οὐδὲν μεταξὺ) 'fifty ... are few' and 'fifty one ... are few'; the latter 'having no difference' (7.419 μηδεμίαν ἐχούσηι διαφορὰν) from the former; it is 'not at all different and remote' (7.420 οὐδενὶ δὲ [ἤδε] διέφερε καὶ ἐκεχώριστο) from it.

33 For a contemporary instance of exposition of sorites reasoning which refers to reasons for the application of a predicate, see this passage from Williamson (1990, p. 103): 'Let $x_1, \ldots, x_n$ be a sorites series for the predicate F: x_1 is clearly F, x_n is clearly not F, and for no value of i is there any reason to assert that x_i is F while x_{i+1} is not.'

34 In the ancient world the term sorites was reserved for a type of sophism or fallacy, and a sorites would have to issue in a false conclusion. See the passages cited by LS at 37C (Diogenes *Lives* 7.44), 37D (Diogenes *Lives* 7.82) and 37H(3) (from Cicero *Acad* 2.93). To some extent that is a matter of terminology. There is some purpose in taking the characteristic little-by-little reasoning as sorites *reasoning*, and calling sorites *paradoxes* those cases in which a false conclusion is established.

35 *M* 9.183 = LS 70E. Sextus summarizes the purpose of these sorites paradoxes as showing that there are no gods at *M* 9.190.

36 See Unger (1979 and 1979a). More recently sorites reasoning has been used by Heller (1990, especially ch. 3) in criticism of our standard ontology of temporally persistent three-dimensional objects.

37 *de Nat Deor* 3.44 = LS 70D. It is not relevant whether this is an *accurate* account of Carneades' purpose.

38 Compare this passage from Galen *On Medical Experience* 16.1–17.3 = LS 37E(3): '... you will not cease from denying, and will never admit at any time that the sum of this is a heap, *even if the number of grains reaches infinity* by the constant and gradual admission of more' (my emphasis). To return to an example already mentioned repeatedly, it might seem that there is little reason to suppose in advance that Carneades' theological sorites should even *tend* to show that the predicate 'god' applies in an infinite number of cases. Yet Cicero ends his presentation of Carneades' reasoning in this way: either the reasoning by which application of the predicate is extended will go on indefinitely, without end (*inmensum*), or no application will be allowed; the unlimited, infinite (*infinita*) claim of superstition cannot be admitted; hence no application will be allowed (*de Nat Deor* 3.52).

39 Compare Dummett (1975) on the strict finitist position: the example imagined above is an odder position than that, in that it specifies a notation in advance. But that does not affect use of the example to illustrate the point wanted.

40 See LS 37 F, Sextus *M* 7.416; LS 37 H (3), Cicero *Acad* 2.93–5.

41 LS 37 H (3), Cicero *Acad* 2.93.

42 See Burnyeat (1982) and Long and Sedley (1987) in comment on LS 37H3. Burnyeat makes the point that, to be fully appreciated, Chrysippus' strategy needs to supplemented with the advice that one should resume answering (in the negative) sometime after it has become plain that a negative answer is justified.

43 As Burnyeat notes, the report of the 'keeping quiet' strategy by Sextus, *M* 7.416, LS 37 F, concerns the Stoic Wise Man who keeps quiet when the last cognitive impression lies adjacent to the first non-cognitive impression.

44 This question, from LS 37 H (3), Cicero *Acad* 2.94, is in fact aimed not at someone like our Bold, but at the (seemingly historically more likely) person who refuses to reply to questions to which the answer is clear. I will say something later about whether there is an interesting cautious version of the Bold Response currently being considered.

45 $A \rightarrow B$ is assigned value 1 if $[A] \leqslant [B]$, and the value $1 - [A] + [B]$ if $[A] > [B]$. Suppose Fa_1 has value 1, and through a continuous decrease Fa_{50} has value 0. Pick any adjacent a_i, a_{i+1}. The value of a_i will be greater than that of a_{i+1} by 0.02, and so the value of the conditional $Fa_i \rightarrow Fa_{i+1}$ will be 0.98 – that is, very nearly wholly true.

46 Fine (1975); see the summary discussion in Sainsbury (1988, ch. 2).

47 Why this qualification? A way of making a predicate precise is *in*admissible if it excludes from the range of the predicate objects that clearly did fall

under the predicate prior to its being rendered precise. Some such qualification is required if the verdicts delivered by supervaluations are to correspond in any way to our prior intuitions. In the example in the text one way of making 'generous' precise would be to draw the boundary at £1001 – in which case '£1000 is a generous gift' would no longer come out as true on *every* way of making the predicate precise. Hence, drawing the boundary in that way is not an admissible way of making the predicate precise. See Tye (1990) on this.

48 Of course, one might be suspicious that there *is* any such last a. That is just the objection levelled against the supervaluational account by the more radical response of Sainsbury. See Sainsbury (1991 and 1991a). Again, though, the issue here is not the acceptability of the supervaluational account but the connection of it to our indifference argument (i)–(vii).

49 One particularly striking approach is that of Sainsbury, who denies that (most) predicates function by drawing boundaries. See the papers mentioned in note 48 above. While Sainsbury is explicit that his approach generates only a rather programmatic response to the sorites, he cites with approval the related more formal account offered in Tye (1990), which involves a three valued logic.

50 An ancient recognition of the importance of appeal to an arbitrary instance in establishing a universal conclusion may be seen at Aristotle *Post An* 1.4 73b32–74a3. Aristotle is discussing how one should establish that something holds universally. One condition is that it should be proved of a *chance* case (73b33, ἐπὶ τοῦ τυχόντος δεικνύηται).

51 This is a question which has excited a fair amount of discussion. See, for example, Fine (1985), and the symposium by Fine (1983) and Tennant (1983).

52 Compare Fine's formulation of his Principle of Generic Attribution (1983, p. 59): 'any arbitrary object has those properties common to the individuals in its range.' The same effect is achieved by the constraints included in rules for the use of arbitrary names in formal systems. For example, Lemmon (1965, p. 145f): I can pass from *Fa* (where *a* is an arbitrary name) to *(x)Fx* so long as the proof that *Fa* rests on no assumptions that mention *a*. For, as long as that is so, then replacing *a* by any proper name *m, n* ... is sure to give me a cogent proof that *m, n* ... is F. Replacing *a* by *m, n* ... can make no difference to the syntactic relation between the premisses and the conclusion *Fm, (Fn* ...), as *a* does not occur in those premisses.

53 For Fine's view, see this passage from the opening of Fine (1983, p. 55): 'In addition to individual objects, there are arbitrary objects; in addition to individual numbers, arbitrary numbers; in addition to individual men, arbitrary men ... an arbitrary number is odd or even, an arbitrary man is mortal, since each individual number is odd or even, each individual man

is mortal. On the other hand, an arbitrary number fails to be prime, an arbitrary man fails to be a philosopher, since some individual number is not prime, some individual man is not a philosopher.'

54 Fine (1985, pp. 136–8).

7

Indifference Arguments without Epistemology

◆

7.1 The Non-Epistemological Reading

The upshot of the previous chapter was that the strategy of interpreting all indifference arguments, including those which purport to be non-epistemological, in epistemological terms is not recommended on grounds of charity. A general account of the logical structure of non-epistemological (B-form) arguments was given in an earlier chapter. Now we can take a more constructive approach to the B-form arguments around which much of our attention has been focused so far: the Democritean arguments for the infinite variety of atomic shapes and sizes. By concentrating on these as a paradigm, general points about the structure of B-form indifference arguments can be made manifest, and points of independent interest will emerge as we consider how those arguments could be made most plausible.

The general account in chapter 5 suggests this approach to the Democritean arguments. If p, q . . . are sentences of the form 'there is an atom of shape S', then a non-epistemological indifference premiss is that as regards any such p and q there is no more reason for p than for q. From that there follows $Lp \equiv Lq$ and $Mp \equiv Mq$. Since it is granted that there are some atoms, there is some true sentence of the form 'there is an atom of shape S', and so there is some true sentence Mp. Since the sentences p, q . . . are all compatible, we will have Mp&Mq. That is, of course, not a conclusion anything like strong enough for Democritus. So far it is only the conclusion that, granted that there are atoms, if there is no more reason for there to be an atom of any one shape than of any another, then any shape you like is a *possible* shape for atoms. To get the conclusion that there are an infinite number of atomic shapes Democritus needs to establish that any shape you like is an *actual* atomic shape. That conclusion follows if a further claim is added, that some shape's being a possible atomic shape entails that shape's being an actual atomic shape. That further claim need not – indeed, most likely will not – rest on an indifference argument. Nevertheless, if Democritus did in fact make such a claim, the resources of the atomic theory would be sufficient to enable the indifference argument for an infinite variety of atomic shapes to succeed. Further, if such a claim were *true*, indifference arguments structurally similar to the Democritean argument with true premises would be sufficient to establish conclusions convincing to us. Even if there were no indifference arguments with true premises similar in structure to the Democritean argument, a claim that links possibility to actuality is of considerable interest in its own right.

The link between possibility and actuality is secured in this case by a principle we have come across previously in connection with Melissus: the principle of plenitude for eternal things (hereafter abbreviated to PPE).[1] The stronger principle of plenitude not limited to eternal things asserts that if something is possible now then it either is or will be actual:[2]

(a) $Mp \rightarrow (p \lor Fp)$

That rules out there being any possibilities which are not at sometime actualized. The weaker PPE allows that there can be possibilities which are never actualized, so long as they cease at some time to be possibilities. A partisan of PPE will not need to uphold (a) but only the weaker.

(b) $Mp \rightarrow (p \lor (Fp \lor F\neg Mp))$

Asserting (b) is sufficient to entitle the upholder of PPE to the claim that if something is possible and remains possible eternally, through an infinite future, then either it is or it will be actual.[3] Indeed, if something is to remain possible through an *infinite* future it will remain possible having been actual once, and so will be actualized again and again.

Why should we suppose that the Democritean indifference argument for the infinite variety of atomic shape should be interpreted by reference to PPE? One point is that, if the argument is to be charitably interpreted in line with the general account of indifference arguments offered previously, *some* bridge between possibility and actuality is required: and PPE is a principle interesting in its own right which would do the job admirably. There are more direct reasons than that, however, for finding PPE in atomist thought.

In *Physics* 3.4 Aristotle reports two arguments, without identifying their source:[4]

(A1) And if what is outside is infinite, then it is thought that there is infinite body and infinitely many world-systems, for why should these be *here* rather than *there* in the void? Hence [it is thought that] body with bulk is everywhere, since it is in one place.

(A2) And again, even if there is void, and place is infinite, there must be infinite body, since in everlasting things there is no difference between being possible and being.

The modal principle cited in (A2) is argued by commentators to give Aristotle's own view, the limiting qualification 'in everlasting things' being crucial.[5] It is not necessary to go into that issue here, nor to consider the difficult question of what understanding of the modalities would underpin Aristotle's commitment to PPE. The relevant question is, rather, whether the use of that principle in the argument of (A2) reflects some pre-Aristotelian – some Democritean – view. Three considerations make the supposition that it does reflect Democritean thought seem, on balance, reasonable.[6]

First, the occurrence of PPE in the context of (A2). Aristotle's concern at this point is with the grounds on which *others* have supposed the infinite exists. Suppose (A2) were an extrapolation by Aristotle from atomist premises to an atomist conclusion, proceeding on the basis of a principle peculiar to Aristotle. Then its relevance would be obscure. Without an atomist adherence to PPE, (A2) would show nothing about *atomist* grounds for belief in a real infinity. Nor would any *actual* pressures towards belief in a real infinity be revealed. (A2) would just be pointing out that accepting an atomist premiss which Aristotle reckons to be false (that there is an infinite void) plus a peculiarly Aristotelian premiss (PPE) would justify the conclusion that there exists infinite body.

Second, there is the relation between (A1) and (A2). (A1) is an instance of just the sort of indifference argument attributed to the atomists. Simplicius hesitantly attributes (A1) to Democritus.[7] We have seen that Philoponus cites an indifference argument for the infinity of worlds to Democritus.[8] Lactantius also reports an atomist argument along the lines of (A1):[9]

> Leucippus says that since the entirety of things is without bound, and nothing can be void, it is necessary therefore that there are innumerable worlds.

That (A1) is Democritean gives some reason to take (A2) as Democritean also: they agree in conclusion, and are conjoined by both Aristotle and Simplicius.

Third, there is evidence of pre-Aristotelian support for the modal principle cited in (A2), which would suggest some endorsement of PPE outside an Aristotelian context. Simplicius explicates (A2) without reference to Aristotle. The support he reports for the modal principle is fairly unsophisticated:[10]

> ... and in the case of eternal things what can come to be at all events will come to be, since were it not to come to be it is not possible that it come to be (for while, in the case of corruptible things, nothing prevents them perishing before what is possible comes to pass in the thing, in the case of eternal things this is impossible) ...

The argument is this. A possibility can fail to be actualized if its bearer is not eternal, since the bearer might cease to exist before the possibility becomes actual. My coat might wear out before it is cut up. But this is ruled out if the bearer is not going to cease to exist, if it is eternal. In that case, the thought goes, it is also ruled out that the possibility could fail to be actualized. So eternal possibilities will be actualized. That is not a strong argument, since it runs together *a* condition under which a possibility could fail to be actualized, that it ceases to be a possibility before it is actualized, with what is *required* for a possibility to fail to be actualized. In comparison with the support for PPE that would be available to Aristotle,[11] such argument strongly suggests a pre-Aristotelian origin.

It seems *reasonable* then, if no more, to take it that there is Democritean endorsement of PPE. So explication of the atomist indifference arguments by reference to PPE as the principle linking possibility and actuality has some historical plausibility. In that case, whether or not the Democritean arguments are good arguments for the conclusions they claim to establish depends on whether or not PPE is a defensible principle. At any rate PPE is a principle which exercises a perennial attraction, so that some discussion of grounds on which it might be supported is likely to be of interest.

7.2 An Argument for a Weak Principle of Plenitude

An argument can be offered which makes the weak principle of plenitude, for eternal things, appear fairly plausible. Even if this argument is not judged in the end to be convincing, it is sufficiently interesting and engaging to merit discussion, and it is instructive to see what would need to be assumed in order to render PPE acceptable.

We should expect an argument for PPE to reveal why it is only the weaker principle that is defensible. It is a matter of considerable debate precisely how the argument offered by Aristotle in *de Caelo* 1.12 is to be understood, and I do not intend here to add to that debate. It is appropriate to note, though, that were Aristotle's argument successful it would be extendable to transient things, and so would not provide support just for the weaker PPE. This point is made by Richard Sorabji, although his extension of Aristotle's argument, by reference to negative properties possessed for ever by things which have ceased to exist, seems unnecessarily complicated.[12] Far simpler is the following argument, on all fours with Aristotle's. Suppose Ann in the whole of her finite life never sings. Does she nevertheless have the capacity to sing or not? If so, then nothing impossible should result from the capacity's being exercised. Yet the supposition that it is exercised seems to lead to one of two impossible results. *Either* Ann sings while she is alive; yet it was assumed that she did not sing during her life, so that she would have to sing and not sing at the same time, which is impossible. *Alternatively* Ann sings while she is dead, in which case she sings and is dead at the same time, which is equally impossible. Since something impossible results in both cases, Ann does not have the capacity to sing if she does not sing once through the whole of her finite life. Hence, by contraposition, if she *does* have the capacity to sing then she *does* sing at some time in her finite life. That conclusion is the stronger principle of plenitude, rather than the weaker PPE. It is not that the argument for that conclusion is valid. It is, however, on all fours with Aristotle's *de Caelo* argument, and so would be defensible if the later were defensible. In that case the argument of *de Caelo* 1.12 will not justify a principle of plenitude which ruled out only eternal unactualized possibilities, and did not also rule out temporally limited unactualized possibilities.

In contrast, the argument to be discussed here, would, if successful, reveal more clearly *why* a plenitude principle is limited to eternal possibilities. It follows of course that the argument to be considered does not necessarily offer an underpining for PPE that is accurate to an *Aristotelian* understanding of PPE and the modalities PPE is concerned with.

Whether or not PPE is plausible depends on the view one takes of truths about the future. In particular it depends on what one supposes is required in order for it to be true *now* that it will *never* be that p – for example, for it to be true *now* that this tree will *never* bear fruit. The argument I will consider assumes that, in order for it be the case now that this tree will *never* bear fruit, it has to be the case now that it *cannot* bear fruit. Hence if this tree *can* bear fruit it is not the case that it will never bear fruit; so it follows that it will sometime bear fruit. But the initial assumption – that only if this tree cannot bear fruit could it be true now that it will never bear fruit – is plausible only on condition that any possibility of bearing fruit would remain a possibility through an infinite future. Suppose this tree were capable of bearing fruit only for a finite time. In that case it could be true now that this tree will never bear fruit without it being necessary that this tree will never bear fruit. The argument will tend therefore to support PPE, rather than any stronger claim about temporally limited possibilities.

That this argument is *valid* is plain if it is put formally. From

(1) $(n)\neg Fnp \rightarrow L(n)\neg Fnp$

there follows by contraposition

(2) $\neg L(n)\neg Fnp \rightarrow \neg(n)\neg Fnp$

and then

(3) $M(\exists n)Fnp \rightarrow (\exists n)Fnp$

The move from (1) to (3) involves putting L¬ for ¬M, an existential quantifier (∃n) for ¬(n)¬, and cancelling out doubled-up negations. An instance of (3) would be: if it is possible that this tree will sometime bear fruit then this tree will sometime bear fruit. Since the argument is plainly valid everything hangs on whether, and for what range of cases, (1) can be made plausible.

It is at this point that questions about future truths arise. What conditions need to be fulfilled in order for a future tense claim to be true? Two opposed answers are these.

First, a future tense sentence is true now if and only if the future state whose occurrence will render true the corresponding present tense sentence is now already bound to occur. For example, it is true now that this tree will bear fruit in the year 2000 if and only if it is necessary now that it bear fruit in the year 2000: if, as it might be, it is *causally* necessary now.

This first answer might, however, seem too stringent. An alternative is to allow that a future tense sentence can also be true in another way. A future tense sentence is true now if it just turns out in the future that the state whose occurrence is required to render the corresponding present tense sentence true does in fact occur. For example, it can be true now that this tree will bear 50 pounds of fruit in the year 2000 just so long as come the year 2000 it turns out that this tree does in fact bear 50 pounds of fruit.

It is helpful to adopt a device of Arthur Prior's in order to mark the difference between these two readings of the future tense: namely the distinction between the big letter 'it WILL be that p' and the small letter 'it will be that p'.[13] On the big-letter reading of the future tense, 'this tree WILL bear fruit' is true if and only if the bearing of fruit is already inevitable or settled, already 'present in its causes'. On the small-letter reading of the future tense there is an additional wait-and-seeish way for 'this tree will bear fruit' to be true. Future tense sentences behave differently depending on whether they are read in a big-letter or a small-letter way. Suppose that when the year 2000 comes around it turns out that this tree bears fruit. That in itself is sufficient for its being the case that the (small-letter) sentence 'this tree would bear fruit' was true earlier on. If 'this tree bears fruit' is true at some time, then 'this tree would bear fruit' was true at any earlier time. On the other hand, its turning out when the year 2000 comes around that this tree bears fruit is *not* sufficient for 'this tree WOULD bear fruit' having been true earlier. It does not follow from 'this tree bears fruit' being true at some time that 'this tree WOULD bear fruit' was true at all earlier times.

Return to our argument for PPE. The claim in support of (1) is that 'this tree will never bear fruit' is true only if 'it is necessary that this tree will never bear fruit' is true, regardless of the way in which the future tense operator is read, just on condition that any possibility of bearing fruit would remain a possibility through an infinite future. This can be seen by cases.

First take the big-letter reading. It follows directly that 'it WILL NEVER be that p' is true only if it is necessary that it will never be that p. So, 'this tree WILL NEVER bear fruit' is true now only if it is now necessary or inevitable that it never bear fruit: if, for example, it is now afflicted with disease, or past fruit-bearing age.

Next the small-letter reading. Here the matter is more problematic. There are *prima facie* two ways in which 'this tree will never bear fruit' can be true. It is either necessary, in which case the comments above concerning the big-letter reading apply, or it is true in the way peculiar to the small-letter reading – in a wait-and-seeish way. The charge, however, is that the latter way of being true does not apply if any possibility of the tree's bearing fruit would remain a possibility though an infinite future.

Contrast the case where we are not concerned with what remains possible through an infinite future. Suppose after ten years the tree dies. Then it is easy enough to say what is involved in its turning out that it is true now that this tree never fruits. It is its turning out after ten years that this tree has never fruited. The thought that this is a wait-and-see-ish way of being true is the thought that if we wait ten years we see that it was true that this tree would never bear fruit.

Suppose on the other hand that the possibility of bearing fruit remains a possibility through an infinite future. Then there is *no* waiting to see that the tree has *never* borne fruit. Any waiting to see will just be waiting some number of years N, and seeing that this tree has not *so far* fruited. All that gives us is that 'this tree will not fruit in the next N years' was true N years ago. There is no time at which what has to turn out to be the case, in order to render 'this tree will never bear fruit' true, does come to be the case. No such thing comes to be the case either now or at any time a finite distance from now, since by hypothesis nothing is established – either now or at any time a finite distance away from now – one way or the other about the eventual fruiting of this tree. Fruiting always remains an open possibility. So if the possibility of fruit-bearing remains a possibility eternally, 'this tree will never bear fruit' cannot be true in the way peculiar to the small-letter reading of the future tense.

So, whether the future tense is treated along big-letter or small-letter lines, the only way in which a sentence like 'this tree will never bear fruit' can now be true, is by now being necessary, just so long as any possibility of bearing fruit would be an eternal possibility. That gives an instance of (1) above, just in the case of eternal possibilities. So if it *is* possible through an infinite future that this tree bear fruit – that is, if it is *not* necessary that this tree never through an infinite future bear fruit – it follows that it is not the case that this tree will never bear fruit; and so this tree will sometime bear fruit. That gives an instance of (3), and so supports PPE.

The inference from (1) via (2) to (3) involves only logical moves concerning the interdefinability of the quantifiers, the interdefinability of the modal operators and the cancellation of doubled-up negations. It is important to note that no logical moves in this argument take place within the scope of the future tense operator. If the argument *did* rely on logical moves within the scope of the future tense operator, it could not proceed independently of deciding which reading of the future tense is to be preferred, without danger of equivocation. For in the case of the big letter WILL there is a logically significant distinction between an internal negation – 'it WILL be the case that the tree does not fruit in the year 2000' – and an external negation – 'it is not the case that it WILL be that the tree fruits in the year 2000'. The latter can be true, while the former is false. Suppose it turns out in the year 2000 that as a contingent matter the tree does not fruit. Then it could not earlier have been necessary that it would fruit in the year 2000, and so it would have been true earlier to deny that it WILL fruit: hence the external negation 'it is not the case that the tree WILL fruit in the year 2000' would earlier have been true. On the other hand, since its not fruiting was all along contingent, the internal negation 'it WILL be the case that the tree does not fruit in the year 2000' would earlier have been false.[14] While internal and external negations of the big-letter 'WILL' are not equivalent, in the case of the small-letter 'will' they *are* equivalent.

If any logical moves took place within the scope of the tense operator, this distinction would make trouble for the argument. The argument moves from 'it is not the case that it will never be that p' to 'it will sometime be that p'. Now that step might *seem* to involve a move from an external negation (not-will-never...) to an internal negation (will-not-never) to get the required conclusion (will-sometime). While that move would be acceptable as regards the small-letter 'will', it would not be justified as regards the big-letter 'WILL', since only in the former case are internal and external negations equivalent. Here is a case where formalization is enlightening. Attention to (1)–(3) makes it clear that no logical moves occur internal to, or within the scope of, the future tense operator, and so no equivocation can arise between internal and external negations of that future tense operator. The transition from $\neg(n)\neg Fnp$ to $(\exists n)Fnp$ will be justified whether the future tense operator $F..$ is read as 'will' or as 'WILL'.

This argument for PPE will not seem persuasive if neither of the two ways of taking the future tense which have been mentioned is found appealing. There are other accounts of the future tense which could be offered. One would be that it is true now that it will never be that p if and only if p is not true at any point in the actual (and possibly infinite) future. PPE will not seem plausible to one who accepts that account of the future tense, for there will not seem to be anything difficult in supposing that p should be possible though not true at every point in the actual (and possibly infinite) future. Yet one can see why the two accounts mentioned earlier should appear attractive. In each case future truth is explained in terms of some *present* state of affairs. The one case (the big-letter WILL) refers only to a present state which renders the way the future turns out necessary. The other case (the small-letter will) admits in addition a state which becomes present at some determinate point in the future: it is in virtue of that state, which will be present at a particular time, that future tense sentences about that time are now true. PPE is engaging because, given possibilities which remain open eternally, there is no particular time such that a present state obtaining at that time is sufficient to make true a sentence about the whole of the infinite future. If one feels any predilection for explaining the truth of future tense sentences by reference to present states which obtain at some particular time, an account in terms of the actual future will seem unexplanatory. For such an account would allow there to be facts about the actual future (for example, concerning what will contingently never be the case through the whole of the infinite actual future) to which no fact about the present state of affairs obtaining at any particular time corresponds. It is impossible to treat this large and difficult topic adequately here.[15] Nevertheless it is at least an advance to identify those views about the future which would be sufficient to support PPE, and to see that they have some plausibility.[16]

In the next section we will see how Democritus' arguments fare when based on appeal to PPE. Even if PPE is defensible it may be that Democritus' arguments are flawed in other ways. First, though, I will round off this discussion of plenitude by mentioning a sound indifference argument which involves appeal to PPE.

This is an argument about the occurrence of chemical elements in nature. Suppose we know of some reason why there is an upper limit to the atomic number of naturally occurrent chemical elements. Perhaps, for example, there are facts about electron configuration that make elements of a higher atomic number unstable. Consider all the atomic numbers below that upper limit. Suppose we think that for each of those numbers it is a matter of chance whether an element of that atomic number occurs naturally. For any such element it is neither necessary nor impossible that it should occur naturally. Suppose finally that these facts about atomic numbers and the natural occurrence of elements reflect laws of nature, so that it remains like this for ever given that this is how it is now.

It follows from all this that it is equally possible that each element below the upper bound should occur naturally. For there is no more reason for one to be naturally occurrent somewhere and sometime than for another to be naturally occurrent; and since at least one *is* occurrent the occurrence of each element below the upper bound is possible. Since that possibility is grounded in laws of nature it is an eternal possibility. So it follows by PPE that each of those possible elements will be naturally occurrent somewhere and sometime, for however short a time. Now that might not seem a terribly substantial conclusion, since it is quite compatible with there not being any of a particular element around right now, and with any number of the elements occurring only for a very short time. But there is another more significant conclusion that can be drawn.

It is a striking fact that the series of chemical elements is open ended *in principle*. We can construct diagrams of arrangements of nuclear particles and electrons without raising the question of whether elements of those structures occur in nature. In that case we could pick out elements by reference to such diagrams, without thinking that the elements so picked out occur in nature. Now let us allow that our initial supposition, that there is an upper limit to the atomic number of naturally occurrent elements, is true. Then the argument given can be used to show that there must be a *reason* for that, although it will not, of course, show anything about what the reason is. Suppose X is an occurrent element whose atomic number is just below the upper limit; and let Y be a non-occurrent element with atomic number just higher than that limit. Suppose there were *no* reason why only a limited number of elements were naturally occurrent. In that case there would be no more reason for X to occur somewhere and sometime than for Y to occur somewhere and sometime. It follows in a familiar way from that indifference premiss that it is possible that X occur if and only if it is possible that Y occur. Since X *is* occurrent it *is* possible that X occur, and so it is possible that Y occur: but by hypothesis there is no Y occurrent – Y is introduced precisely as a non-occurrent element of atomic number higher than the upper limit.

Now there is a dilemma. Either there is a cause for Y never being occurrent or there is not. But it is impossible that there should be *no* cause of Y *never* (for eternity) being occurrent. For if there were no cause Y's non-occurrence would be a matter of chance. In that case the occurrence of Y, which has been shown by an indifference argument to be possible, would also be a matter of chance. But PPE rules out possibilities whose actualization would be by chance, but which are never actualized though an infinite future. In that case it must be that there *is* a cause of Y's being non-occurrent. Then that cause provides a reason for the upper limit of atomic size being such as to exclude Y.

So, if there is an upper limit of atomic size for naturally occurring elements, there must be some reason for there being an upper limit to atomic size. That is a conclusion of some interest, which is generated by an indifference argument involving appeal to PPE.

7.3 The Democritean Arguments

The connection of PPE with Democritus' argument for the infinite variety of atomic shape is made plain if it is set out in this way:

(a) there is no more reason for there to be an atom of this shape than of that

(b) *therefore* for any p, q of the form 'there is an atom of shape S' there is no more reason for p than for q

(c) *therefore* possibly p if and only if possibly q

(d) since there are atoms (for which independent argument is offered) then for some shape there are atoms of that shape

(e) *therefore* for any p, q of the form 'there are atoms of shape S', possibly p and possibly q

(f) the atoms are eternal, so by the principle that what is forever possible is sometime actual, if it is forever possible that there be an atom of shape S there sometime will be an atom of shape S

(g) the atoms are immutable

(h) *therefore* if there ever will be an atom of shape S there is now an atom of shape S

(i) *therefore* if there ever can be an atom of shape S there is now an atom of shape S

(j) there are an unlimited variety of possible atomic shapes

(k) *therefore* there are now an unlimited variety of atomic shapes.

What is defensible in this argument? There is a valid argument from the indifference premiss (a) to the modal equivalence (c). Further, there is something to be said for the principle in (f) which connects possibilities with actualities. What might give pause is the question of whether the argument is sound: in particular, whether the indifference premiss (a) could be true, given further claims which an atomist needs to make in order that the argument be even minimally plausible.

No matter how many atomic shapes there are *now*, whether an infinite number, or a pretty small number, the fact that the atoms are immutable – premiss (g) of the argument – guarantees that there is a reason for there being just that many shapes, and just those shapes, rather than more besides or others instead. The reason is that there were just those shapes at some previous time. So the indifference premiss (a), that there is no reason for there to be an atom of this shape rather than that, does not seem true *now*; nor does it seem there ever was a time at which it *was* true.

There appears to be an obvious response. What (a) claims is that there is no reason for there *ever* being just this many atomic shapes, rather than more or less. It is hard to say how far Democritus would have wanted to make this response. Aristotle complains that Democritus appeals to the fact that things have always been thus and so to explain natural phenomena, while not offering any explanation of these temporal uniformities.[17] Suppose Democritus does deny that there are reasons for what is always the case. Where does that leave the indifference premiss (a)?

On the one hand it seems the indifference premiss (a) could be supported. If there is *no* reason for what obtains eternally, then for any number you like there could be no reason for there being that many atomic shapes, and so there can be no reason for there always being one number rather than another. On the other hand, the atoms are immutable, they *cannot* alter in shape; and they are eternal, they *cannot* come into or go out of existence. Those two facts entail that if at any time there is not *actually* an atom of a particular shape it is not at that time *possible* for there to be an atom of that shape. Suppose there were only a finite number of atomic shapes, and that shape S_1 is instantiated while shape S_2 is not. In that case it would not be possible that there should be an atom of shape S_2. So the modal equivalence (c) would not be true: it would not be true that it is possible that there is an atom of shape S_1 if and only if it is possible that there is an atom of shape S_2. Yet the supposition that there are merely a finite number of atomic shapes could be ruled out only by assuming the conclusion that Democritus' indifference argument aims to establish.

If the problem is due to premiss (g), concerning immutability, perhaps that premiss should be dropped. In that case, though, the situation is worse. It is not simply that any connection with the historical Democritean theory would be lost. More worryingly it could no longer be shown that there are *now* an infinite variety of atomic shapes. PPE and the indifference premiss would be compatible with there being at any one time atoms of only a single shape, with different shapes being instantiated at different times over an infinite future.

At this point a defender of Democritus might well feel impatient. It is hardly a criticism of Democritus' argument to point out that the indifference premiss (a) would be false if some shapes were and some were not found in the atoms – for that is just the negation of the conclusion Democritus aims to establish. All that shows is that if the conclusion of the argument were false at least one of the premisses would be false – the indifference premiss (a), as it seems. But that is just as one would expect if an argument is valid.

That response would be perfectly correct. Nevertheless it is a reasonable question whether Democritus has, or could have, said enough in support of the indifference premiss for the argument to render plausible the conclusion that there is an infinite variety of atomic shapes. The question might arise, whether there is any more reason to take this indifference argument as a demonstration of the conclusion rather than as a refutation of the (indifference) premiss.

The trouble concerns the sort of grounds that could be offered for the indifference premiss. Perhaps Democritus did think that there are no reasons for what is eternally the case. Perhaps the indifference premiss is intended to express something wholly negative, the complete absence of reasons one way or the other for what obtains eternally if at all. If that were so the argument would seem in a way more striking: out of that very negative indifference premiss comes the substantial conclusion that there is an infinite variety of atomic shapes. However, supporting (a) in that way threatens to undercut the whole indifference argument.

If all possible shapes are instantiated, that has always and necessarily been so. In consequence there would be no reason for all possible shapes to be instantiated, and so no more reason for that to be so than for there to be only, say, five atomic shapes instantiated – for there is no reason for there to be only five shapes instantiated either. Yet if the indifference argument were successful it would show that it *has* to be the case that all shapes are instantiated, and that it is *impossible* that only five should be. That, if anything, should count as reason for there to be an unlimited number of atomic shapes rather than only five. So it will not be possible both to run this indifference argument and to hold that there is no reason for what eternally obtains. In that case the indifference premiss could not be supported by, or express, the wholly negative point that there is no reason for whatever is eternal.

This might seem to be nit-picking. But there is a serious and general point to be made. An indifference premiss stands in need of some delineation of what would count as reasons for the terms of the indifference premiss. That is why certain indifference arguments strike us as powerful and persuasive. One can *imagine* what such a delineation could be in the Democritean case. For, contrary to what Democritus might have thought, it is not incoherent to offer reasons for, or explanations of, what is eternally the case. One might have a geometrical theory on which certain shapes are basic; that might provide a reason for there to be just those shapes eternally instantiated in the atoms. Or one might emphasize simplicity and fruitfulness as reasons for there being the minimum number of atomic shapes capable of giving rise by combination to some sufficiently large number of other shapes on the compound level. Doubtless Democritus would say that no such reasons hold in the mechanical atomistic universe. Yet saying even that would generate a more positive support for the indifference premiss (a). If there is a conception of what would constitute reasons, and grounds for saying that no such reasons apply in respect of the instantiation of atomic shapes, the indifference argument is stronger. For now it is possible for Democritus to allow that there can be reason for what is eternally the case, and yet claim that the indifference premiss (a) is true. It is true in that there are no reasons of the sort that would explain why one shape is, while another is not, instantiated. All particular atomic shapes are on a par as regards explanations of their instantiation. Nevertheless there *is* reason for there to be eternally an unlimited number of atomic shapes: the indifference argument provides just such reason.

PPE is relevant also to the indifference argument by which Democritus aims to show that the number of atoms and worlds is infinite. Philoponus reports the argument:[18]

> Democritus also holds that there are infinite worlds, holding that the void is infinite; for why would this part of the void be filled by a world but that part not? So, if there is a world in one part of the void, so too in all the void. So, since the void is infinite, worlds will be infinite too.

For any p, q of the form 'there is body at . . . in the void' we have an indifference premiss: there is no more reason for p than for q. Hence, on now familiar grounds, possibly p if and only if possibly q. Hence, since there *is* body somewhere in the void, possibly p and possibly q. So, as regards any part of the void it is possible that there be body *there*. Body and void are eternal, uncreated and indestructible. So according to PPE there either is or will be body at any point whatsoever in the void. The void is infinite. So it follows that body is infinite too.

While the conclusion is in this case an obvious *non sequitur*, it is instructive to see why. The problem is that nothing corresponds in the case of atomic position to the immutability of the atoms, and so there is no way to get from the claim that there either is *or will be* body at every point in an infinite void to the claim that there *is* infinite body. This argument will *either* be wholly consistent with there being only a finite number of atoms *or* will show that there is no void, since void would be now everywhere full of body.

Take the first alternative first. Since the atoms are constantly moving, the existence of a finite number of atoms would be sufficient to render it true that every part of an infinite void is filled by body either now or sometime in an infinite future. So it will not follow from there being an infinite void that there are an infinite number of atoms. Suppose, on the other hand, that there is a reply to that difficulty. Then another problem looms. The conclusion that there is an infinite amount of body will follow only if there is an inference from the possibility of there being body at some point in the void to there *now* being body at that point. But in that case an even more unacceptable conclusion follows. Consider again the passage cited earlier from Lactantius, in which he reports this atomist argument:[19]

> Leucippus says that since the entirety of things is without bound, and *nothing can be void*, it is necessary therefore that there are innumerable worlds.

It is surprising to read the words *nothing can be void* in the report of an atomist argument. In a way, though, Lactantius puts his finger on a serious problem. In order to get to the conclusion that there are an infinite number of atoms and worlds, and avoid the difficulty noted above, Democritus has to say that the possibility of there being body at some particular point in the void is actualized *now*. In that case, though, since every point in the void *can* contain body, there will be no points that do not *now* contain body; and while that will give the conclusion that there are an infinite number of atoms and worlds it will also imply that there is no void. The problem here is not with the indifference reasoning as such, nor with the principle which links possibility and actuality. It is rather in the move from the claim licensed by PPE, that for every part of the infinite void there either is or will be body there, to the position an atomist wants, that body and worlds are now infinite.

7.4 Looking Back

What has this detailed discussion of some of Democritus' indifference arguments achieved? There are two large points. One is about indifference arguments as a form of reasoning, the other concerns the nature of presocratic atomism.

The intention in giving an analysis of indifference reasoning was to provide as neutral an account as possible of what follows from an indifference premiss. The account offered was neutral because it did not rest on any overly contentious views about the nature of reasons. Such neutrality involves costs and benefits.

One signal benefit is that the account is comprehensive and unifying. Much the same structure can be seen in arguments about the movement of bodies, the distribution of shapes, the possibility of division, the asymmetry of agent and patient, choice between evidentially balanced alternatives, sceptical arguments and sorites reasoning. Another benefit is in respect of charity. In all these different cases some true conclusion will follow from a true indifference premiss. If there is no more reason for the earth to move to the right than for it to move to the left it can (or must) move to the right if and only if it can (or must) move to the left. If a body is homogeneous it can be divided at any one point if and only if it can be divided at any other. If two objects really were similar in the relevant way it would follow that the first could (or must) produce a change in the second if and only if the second could (or must) produce a change in the first. Faced with sentences where I have no more reason to assert one than the other it follows that I can assert (I would be justified in asserting) the one if and only if I can assert (I would be justified in asserting) the other. A third benefit is that the argument by which those conclusions are derived from an indifference premiss does not require large and contentious commitments, metaphysical or otherwise. I do not have to take the Principle of Sufficient Reason on board in order to endorse these arguments. I do not have to be party to any particular account of what reasons are or what counts as a justification for an assertion.

However, benefits are purchased at a cost. The main cost is that the conclusion which follows fairly uncontentiously from an indifference premiss – a modal equivalence – is often enough not the conclusion that the argument is used to support. What is said is that if the earth has no more reason to move left than right it will not move; that if there is no more reason for a homogeneous body to be divisible at one point than another it is indivisible; that one object could not produce a change in another sufficiently similar to it that there is no more reason for the first to produce a change in the second than *vice versa*; that if there is no more reason to say that this wine is sweet than to say that it is sour my senses cannot give me knowledge, at least of the taste of wine.

Sometimes these further conclusions will be reasonable, sometimes they will seem ludicrous, sometimes it will be unclear how to respond. What is plain is that there are no grounds for supposing that the route, from the modal equivalence which follows uncontentiously from an indifference premiss to the further conclusion the argument is used to support, will be the same in different cases. There is *something* general that can be said: in each case what is required is a link between possibility and actuality (so that something's being possible would be sufficient for its being actual) or a link between actuality and necessity (so that something will be actual only if it is necessary). But those links may well be made differently in different cases. The principle of plenitude for eternal things provides one route from possibility to actuality, and it supplements some of Democritus' indifference arguments. That principle has been discussed at length. It would be neither feasible nor profitable to repeat that sort of discussion for every other way of connecting possibility/necessity and actuality. There is no principled number of ways of making the connection, and considering one sort of case after another would simply generate an unstructured and indeterminately long string of arguments.

In some cases the issues that would need to be raised are thoroughly familiar. For example, we are, I think, sympathetic to Anaximander's argument about the earth's position to the extent that we provide him with the assumption that the earth's motion is determined by its position relative to the edges of the cosmos, so that it would have a unique direction of movement only if there were a unique direction of movement necessary for it. The question of whether the general assumption involved there is true is complex and not easily settled. Zeno's argument that what is homogeneous is indivisible, and the Democritean account of atomic indivisibility based on it, involve the assumption that there is no logically significant difficulty in moving from the claim that something is divisible at point a and divisible at b and divisible at c ... to the claim that it is divided at a and divided at b and divided at c.... Familiar questions about that assumption were first raised by Aristotle, in his discussion of Zeno's reasoning.

In other cases, in contrast, there would be more work involved in digging out and displaying the relevant connections between possibility/necessity and actuality. A case in point is Aristotle's argument about agent–patient asymmetries. Aristotle's assumption in that argument is that it could not be a merely contingent matter that one thing is active and another passive in a change rather than *vice versa*. That is not quite an assumption about determinism, which is a view about the relation between an effect and its causal antecedents. Still less does it manifest commitment to any general principle about the need to supply reasons. It is rather an assumption which is to be related in some way to further claims about the sort of properties that are efficacious in the production of changes – for example, to the claim that all efficacious properties are shareable and generally characterizable.

It is of course no accident that, with all the issues that could have been raised, the only principle connecting possibility and actuality discussed at length was one relevant to some Democritean arguments. Nor is it accidental that the analysis of indifference reasoning has been illustrated most fully by reference to atomist arguments. The reason is not simply that indifference reasoning is common in presocratic atomism. More significantly, emphasis on the importance of indifference reasoning in Democritus' thought presents his atomic theory in a particular light.

At the outset two characters were offered for consideration: the scientific Democritus and the philosophical Democritus. The former is someone motivated by the desire to provide a comprehensive theory of nature which avoids the threat posed by Eleatic argument. The latter is not so much a natural theorist as an indifference reasoner, aiming to see whether something reasonably acceptable can be derived from a form of argument already found in the Eleatics. The promise was that the philosophical Democritus would be taken more seriously than is usual in accounts of presocratic atomism. The cumulative effect of the discussion of Democritean atomism that has accompanied the analysis of indifference reasoning throughout this book should have been to make the philosophical Democritus an attractive figure.

Indifference reasoning is found in Zeno, and less explicitly in other Eleatics. So it is at least as reasonable to see Democritus as adapting Eleatic forms of argument as it is to view him as an anti-Eleatic proponent of a comprehensive theory of nature. Of course Democritus disagrees with the Eleatics: they are monists and atomism is a pluralist theory. That should not incline us against the philosophical Democritus, however. There are other reasons for rejecting monism than a desire to save and account for the world of nature. The bare fact that someone finds monism self-defeating allows us to predict very little about any pluralist theory they erect in its place. Anyone might reasonably reject Eleatic monism just on the grounds that it offers its proponents so few resources from which to construct any account of rival and non-respectable views of the world. The Eleatics have nothing of substance to say either about what the status of such views is, or how they are possible. The minimal adjustment necessary to repair that fault is the abandonment of monism.

What follows once monism is dropped? It follows trivially that there is more than one thing. In that case, given an Eleatic indifference argument from homogeneity to monism, it is necessary that any plurality exhibit heterogeneity: hence the distinction is introduced between the atomic stuff and the void. Given the same Eleatic argument, any homogeneous mass of atomic stuff will be indivisible in just as strong a way as the sole denizen of the Eleatic universe: hence there are some indivisible *atoms*. How much void and how many atoms? Indifference reasoning will suggest a void of infinite extent and an infinite number of atoms. How many sizes of atoms and how many shapes? By now the role of indifference reasoning in generating the basic atomic theory should be sufficiently familiar not to need repeating. In order to avoid the problem originally identified in monism, all that is now necessary is that the atomist has the wherewithal to say something about claims about the world which are not atomistically respectable. Once a plurality of atoms is introduced there will be compounds of atoms, relations between atoms and various relations between compounds of one sort or another. None of that is available to a monist. A distinction between what is real and what is conventional can be defined, in one way or another, in terms of atoms, relations and compounds. Once that distinction is secured it is possible to say something substantial from an atomist perspective about non-atomistic claims about the world. Along with that goes an atomist epistemology, into which indifference reasoning also enters. Finally an atomist can now embark on speculations about a theory of nature, while reserving the right to take a deflationary view, from a rigorously atomistic standpoint, of the status of claims about the working of the natural world.

That is a thumbnail sketch of a way in which the basic atomic theory could develop in reaction to Eleatic monism. There is a place for an associated theory of nature, and that theory of nature could well be in its own terms wide ranging and subtly nuanced. The motivations behind the atomic theory understood in that way, however, are very much those of the philosophical Democritus. The more indifference reasoning impresses us as stimulating and fruitful, the more charity should warm us to the philosophical Democritus. The analysis offered of indifference arguments allows us to be more confident in the judgement that these embody a powerful form of reasoning. More could be said, and in greater detail, about our understanding of presocratic atomism. It is clear enough already, though, that the philosophical Democritus is a figure of sufficient acuity to recognize the force and fecundity of indifference reasoning. I recommend him to you.

NOTES

1 Chapter 2.4 above
2 See the appendix for an explanation of the temporal operators used here, and the other tense operators used later in this chapter.
3 This is assured since (b) $Mp \rightarrow (p \vee (Fp \vee F\neg Mp))$ is equivalent to $Mp \rightarrow (GMp \rightarrow (p \vee Fp))$.
4 Physics 3.4 203b25–30, Luria §1: ἀπείρου δ' ὄντος τοῦ ἔξω, καὶ σῶμα ἄπειρον εἶναι δοκεῖ καὶ κόσμοι· τί γὰρ μᾶλλον τοῦ κενοῦ ἐνταῦθα ἢ ἐνταῦθα; ὥστ' εἴπερ μοναχοῦ, καὶ πανταχοῦ εἶναι τὸν ὄγκον. ἅμα δ' εἰ καὶ ἔστι κενὸν καὶ τόπος ἄπειρος, καὶ σῶμα εἶναι ἀναγκαῖον· ἐνδέχεσθαι γὰρ ἢ εἶναι οὐδὲν διαφέρει ἐν τοῖς ἀιδίοις. Translation as Hussey (1983).
5 See Aristotle *de Caelo* 1.12, especially 281b25; Sorabji (1980, ch. 8); for a more thorough discussion, Waterlow (1982).
6 A Democritean attribution is argued to be a 'very plausible guess' by Furley (1969). See also the arguments of Luria (1964).
7 *in Phys* 467.16, Luria §1.
8 *in Phys* 405.23 on, Luria §1.
9 *de Ira Dei* 10.10, Luria §1: Quoniam est omne, inquit [Leucippus], infinitum nec potest quidquam vacare, necesse est ergo innumerabiles esse mundos. I will say something more presently about the oddities of the argument Lactantius reports.
10 *in Phys* 467. 20–3: my translation.
11 As indicated by the sophistication of Aristotle's discussion in *de Caelo* 1.12.
12 Sorabji (1980, p. 129f).
13 Prior (1976).
14 It should not be surprising that the internal and external negations of WILL are not equivalent, since WILL involves necessity, and

plainly 'it is not necessary that p' and 'it is necessary that not p' are not equivalent.

15   For a recent discussion of questions about future truth, and their relation to the issue of fatalism, see Lucas (1989).

16   One might think – as for a long time I thought – that considerations about probability would support PPE: there *seems* to be an argument in the intuition that if it is possible that a die show a six, then sometime in an infinite sequence of throws a six will occur. It is notoriously difficult to get coherent intuitions about probability. In fact an argument for PPE from probability theory should *not* be persuasive, though large matters are raised by such arguments. For a good diagnosis of the issues see White (1985, ch. 8, plus Appendix).

17   *Phys* 8.1 252a34ff, DK 68A65, Luria § 14.

18   Luria §1, from *in Phys* 405.23 on; compare the passage cited earlier as (A 1) and (A 2) from Aristotle *Phys* 3.4 203b25–30.

19   *de Ira Dei* 10.10, Luria §1, emphasis added.

Appendix: Logical Symbols

◆

For the convenience of readers it may be useful to list and explain here the logical symbols that occur in the text.

&: and. Read p&q as: p and q
v: or. Read pvq as: p or q
¬: not. Read ¬p as: not p
→: if... then... Read p→q as: if p then q
≡: ...if and only if... Read p ≡ q as: p if and only if q
p→q is equivalent to ¬(p&¬q)
p ≡ q is equivalent to (p→q)&(q→p)

L: necessarily. Read Lp as: necessarily p
M: possibly. Read Mp as: possibly p
Lp is equivalent to ¬M¬p, not possibly not p
Mp is equivalent to ¬L¬p, not necessarily not p.

( ): universal quantifier.
For example, read (n) (it is justifiable to assert there are n atomic shapes → it is justifiable to assert there are n + 1 atomic shapes) as: *for all n* if it is justifiable to assert there are n atomic shapes then it is justifiable to assert there are n + 1 atomic shapes

(∃): existential quantifier
For example, read (∃n) (it is justifiable to assert there are at least n atomic shapes) as: *for some n* it is justifiable to assert there are at least n atomic shapes
F: non-metric particular future tense operator. Read Fp as: it will sometime be that p
G: non metric general future tense operator. Read Gp as it will always be that p

Fn . .: metric future tense operator. Read Fnp as: it will be in n units of time that p

Read (n)Fnp as: it will always be that p. (n)Fnp is therefore equivalent to the nonmetric Gp

Read (∃n)Fnp as: it will sometime be that p. (∃n)Fnp is therefore equivalent to the non-metric Fp

Read [A] ≤ [B] as: the value of A is less than or equal to the value of B

Read [A] > [B] as: the value of A is greater than the value of B

Lemmon (1965) is a clear introduction to the basics of logic – though not the only one – and goes well beyond anything required for this book. Hughes and Cresswell (1968) provides a good introduction to modal logic, and explains the assessment of modal formulae in terms of possible worlds (mentioned in chapter 5.2). McArthur (1976) is a useful text on tense logic.

Bibliography

◆

Abbreviations

CIAG   *Commentaria in Aristotelem Graeca* edition of the Greek Commentators on Aristotle (23 volumes plus 3 supplements); reference is to page and line number of this edition.

DK   *Die Fragmente der Vorsokratiker*, ed. H. Diels and W. Kranz

KRS   *The Presocratic Philosophers*, ed. G. S. Kirk, J. E. Raven, and M. Schofield

Luria   *Democritea*, ed. S. Luria

LS   *The Hellenistic Philosophers*, ed. A. A. Long, and D. N. Sedley

A: Ancient works referred to:

Alexander	*in de Sensu*	Commentary on Aristotle's de Sensu (CIAG vol. 3, pt 1)
	in Met	Commentary on Aristotle's Metaphysics (CIAG vol. 1)
Aristotle	*de An*	On the Soul
	de Caelo	
	GC	On Generation and Corruption
	Met	Metaphysics
	Part An	Parts of Animals
	Post An	Posterior Analytics
	Phys	Physics
	Rhetoric	
	Topics	

pseudo Aristotle	*MXG*	On Melissus, Xenophanes and Gorgias
Cicero	*Acad*	Academica
	de Fin	On Ends
	de Nat Deor	On the Nature of the Gods
Diogenes Laertius	*Lives*	Lives of the Philosophers
Epicurus	*Ep Her*	Letter to Herodotus
Galen	*de Elem Sec Hipp*	On the Elements According to Hippocrates
	On Medical Experience	
Hippolytus	*Ref*	Refutation of All Heresies
Lactantius	*Inst*	Divine Institutions
	de Ira Dei	On the Wrath of God
Lucretius	*de Rer Nat*	On the Nature of Things
Philoponus	*in de An*	Commentary on Aristotle's de Anima (CIAG vol. 15)
	in de Gen et Corr	Commentary on Aristotle's Generation and Corruption (CIAG vol. 14, pt 2)
	in Phys	Commentary on Aristotle's Physics (CIAG vols 16, 17)
Plutarch	*adv Colot*	Against Colotes
Sextus Empiricus	*PH*	Outline of Pyrrhonism
	M	Adversus Mathematicos, Against the Professors
Simplicius	*in de Caelo*	Commentary on Aristotle's de Caelo (CIAG vol. 7)
	in Phys	Commentary on Aristotle's Physics (CIAG vols. 9, 10)
Themistius	*in Phys*	Paraphrase of Aristotle's Physics (CIAG vol. 5, pt 2)
Theophrastus	*de Sens*	On the Senses

B: Secondary literature

Anton, J. P. and Kustas, G. L. (1971): *Essays in Ancient Greek Philosophy* (State University of New York Press, Albany, NY).

Balme, D. (1972): *Aristotle's de Partibus Animalium 1 and de Generatione Animalium 1*, Clarendon Aristotle Series (Clarendon Press, Oxford).

Barnes, J. (1979): 'Parmenides and the Eleatic One', *Archiv für Geschichte der Philosophie* 61, pp. 1–21.

— (1982): *The Presocratic Philosophers*, rev. edn (Routledge, London).

— (1982a): 'The beliefs of a Pyrrhonist', *Proceedings of the Cambridge Philological Society* 208 (New Series 28), pp. 1–29.

Barnes, J. (1982b): 'Medicine, experience and logic', in *Science and Speculation*, ed. J. Barnes, J. Brunschwig, M. Burnyeat and M. Schofield (Cambridge University Press, Cambridge) pp. 24–68.

— (1984): 'Reason and necessity in Leucippus', *Proceedings of the First International Congress on Democritus* (International Democritean Foundation, Xanthi, Greece), vol. 1, pp. 141–56.

Booth, N. B. (1957): 'Were Zeno's arguments a reply to attacks upon Democritus?', *Phronesis* 2, pp. 1–9.

Burnyeat, M. (1980): 'Can the sceptic live his scepticism', in *Doubt and Dogmatism*, ed. M. Schofield, M. Burnyeat and J. Barnes (Cambridge University Press, Cambridge), pp. 20–53.

— (1982): 'Gods and heaps', in *Language and Logos*, ed. M. Schofield and M. Nussbaum (Cambridge University Press, Cambridge) pp. 315–38.

Coxon, A. H. (1986): *The Fragments of Parmenides*, Phronesis Supplementary vol. 3 (Van Gorcum, Assen and Maastricht).

Curd, P. (1991): 'Parmenidean monism', *Phronesis* 36, pp. 241–64.

de Lacy, P. (1958): '*Ou mallon* and the antecedents of ancient scepticism', *Phronesis* 3, pp. 59–71.

— (1964): 'Colotes' first criticism of Democritus', in Mau and Schmidt (1964), pp. 67–77.

Denyer, N. (1981): 'The atomism of Diodorus Cronus', *Prudentia* 13, pp. 33–45.

Diels, H. and Kranz, W. (1952): *Die Fragmente der Vorsokratiker*, 6th edn (Weidmann, Zürich) [referred to as DK].

Dummett, M. (1975): 'Wang's paradox', *Synthese* 30, pp. 301–24; also in Dummett (1978).

— (1978): *Truth and Other Enigmas* (Duckworth, London).

Düring, I. (1969): *Naturphilosophie bei Aristoteles und Theophrast* (Lothar Stiehm Verlag, Heidelberg).

Fine, K. (1975): 'Vagueness, truth and logic', *Synthese* 30, pp. 265–300.

— (1983): 'A defence of arbitrary objects', *Proceedings of the Aristotelian Society Supplementary* 57, pp. 55–77.

— (1985): *Reasoning with Arbitrary Objects*, Aristotelian Society Series, vol. 3 (Blackwell, Oxford).

Forrester, J. (1973): 'The argument of the "Porphyry Text"', *Journal of the History of Ideas* 11, pp. 537–9.

Fowler, D. (1984): 'Sceptics and Epicureans', *Oxford Studies in Ancient Philosophy* 2, pp. 237–67.

Freudenthal, G. (1986): 'The theory of opposites and an ordered universe: physics and metaphysics in Anaximander', *Phronesis* 31, pp. 197–228.

Furley, D. (1967): *Two Studies in the Greek Atomists* (Princeton University Press, Princeton, NJ).

— (1969): 'Aristotle and the atomists on infinity', in Düring (1969), pp. 85–96.

Furley, D. (1976): 'Aristotle and the atomists on motion in a void', in Furley (1989), pp. 77–90.

— (1987): *The Greek Cosmologists*, vol. 1: *The Formation of the Atomic Theory and its Earliest Critics* (Cambridge University Press, Cambridge).

— (1987a): 'The dynamics of the earth: Anaximander, Plato and the centrifocal theory', in Furley (1989), pp. 14–26.

— (1989): *Cosmic Problems* (Cambridge University Press, Cambridge).

Gallop, D. (1975): *Plato's Phaedo* (Clarendon Press, Oxford).

Guthrie, W. (1969): *A History of Greek Philosophy*, vol. 2: *The Presocratic Tradition from Parmenides to Democritus* (Cambridge University Press, Cambridge).

Heller, M. (1990): *The Ontology of Physical Objects: Four Dimensional Hunks of Matter* (Cambridge University Press, Cambridge).

Hughes, G. E. and Cresswell, M. (1968): *An Introduction to Modal Logic* (Methuen, London).

Hussey, E. (1983): *Aristotle's Physics, Books III and IV*, Clarendon Aristotle Series (Clarendon Press, Oxford).

Jackson, F. and Pettit, P. (1990): 'Program explanation: a general perspective', *Analysis* 50, pp. 107–17.

Kahn, C. H. (1960): *Anaximander and the Origins of Greek Cosmology* (Columbia University Press, New York).

Kirk, G. S., Raven, J. E. and Schofield, M. (1983): *The Presocratic Philosophers*, 2nd edn (Cambridge University Press, Cambridge) [referred to as KRS].

Lee, H. D. P. (1936): *Zeno of Elea*, Cambridge Classical Studies (Cambridge University Press, Cambridge).

Lemmon, E. J. (1965): *Beginning Logic* (Nelson, London).

Lipton, P. (1990): 'Contrastive explanation', in *Explanation and its Limits*, ed. D. Knowles, Royal Institute of Philosophy Supplement vol. 27 (Cambridge University Press, Cambridge), pp. 247–66.

Long, A. A. and Sedley, D. N. (1987): *The Hellenistic Philosophers*, 2 vols (Cambridge University Press, Cambridge) [referred to as LS].

Lovejoy, A. O. (1936): *The Great Chain of Being* (Harvard University Press, Cambridge, MA).

Lucas, J. R. (1989): *The Future: An Essay on God, Temporality and Truth* (Blackwell, Oxford).

Luria, S. (1964): 'Zwei Demokrit-Studien', in Mau and Schmidt (1964), pp. 37–54.

— (1970): *Democritea* (Leningrad) [referred to as Luria].

McArthur, R. (1976): *Tense Logic* (D. Reidel, Dordrecht).

McKim, R. (1984): 'Democritus against scepticism: all sense impressions are true', *Proceedings of the First International Congress on Democritus* (International Democritean Foundation, Xanthi Greece), vol. 1, pp. 281–9.

Makin, S. (1986): 'Buridan's ass', *Ratio* 28, pp. 132–48.

Makin, S. (1988): 'How can we find out what ancient philosophers said?', *Phronesis* 33, pp. 121–32.

— (1989): 'The indivisibility of the atom', *Archiv für Geschichte der Philosophie* 71, pp. 125–49.

Mau, J. and Schmidt, E. G. (1964): *Isonomia* (Akademie Verlag, Berlin).

Mourelatos, A. (1970): *The Route of Parmenides* (Yale University Press, New Haven and London).

O'Brien, D. (1981): *Theories of Weight in the Ancient World: Democritus, Weight and Size*, Philosophia Antiqua Monographs, vol. 37 (E. J. Brill, Leiden).

Owen, G. E. L. (1957): 'Zeno and the mathematicians', in Owen (1986), pp. 45–61 (orig. pubd in *Proceedings of the Aristotelian Society* 58, pp. 199–222).

— (1960): 'Eleatic questions', in Owen (1986), pp. 3–26 (orig. pubd in *Classical Quarterly*, NS 10, pp. 84–102).

— (1986): *Language, Science and Dialectic: Collected Papers in Greek Philosophy*, ed. M. Nussbaum (Duckworth, London).

Prior, A. (1976): 'It was to be', *Papers in Logic and Ethics*, ed. P. T. Geach and A. Kenny (Duckworth, London), pp. 97–108.

Rescher, N. (1991): *G. W. Leibniz's Monadology* (Routledge, London).

Robinson, J. (1953): 'Anaximander and the problem of the earth's immobility', in Anton and Kustas (1971), pp. 111–18.

Ross, W. D. (1936): *Aristotle's Physics: A Revised Text with Introduction and Commentary* (Clarendon Press, Oxford).

Sainsbury, M. (1988): *Paradoxes* (Cambridge University Press, Cambridge).

— (1991): 'Concepts without boundaries', *Inaugural Lecture, King's College, London, Department of Philosophy*.

— (1991a): 'Is there higher order vagueness?', *Philosophical Quarterly* 41, pp. 167–82.

Schofield, M. (1970): 'Did Parmenides discover eternity?', *Archiv für Geschichte der Philosophie* 52, pp. 113–35.

Sedley, D. (1977): 'Diodorus Cronus and Hellenistic philosophy', *Proceedings of the Cambridge Philological Society* 203 (new series 23), pp. 74–120.

— (1982): 'Two conceptions of vacuum', *Phronesis* 27, pp. 175–93.

— (1982a): 'On signs', in *Science and Speculation*, ed. J. Barnes, J. Brunschwig, M. Burnyeat and M. Schofield (Cambridge University Press, Cambridge), pp. 239–72.

— (1992): 'Sextus Empiricus and the atomist criteria of truth', *Elenchos* 13, pp. 21–56.

Sinnige, T. (1971): *Matter and Infinity in the Presocratic Schools and Plato*, 2nd edn (Van Gorcum, Assen).

Solmsen, F. (1971): 'The tradition about Zeno of Elea re-examined', *Phronesis* 16, pp. 116–41.

Sorabji, R. (1980): *Necessity, Cause and Blame* (Duckworth, London).

Sorabji, R. (1982): 'Atoms and time atoms', in *Infinity and Continuity in Ancient and Medieval Thought*, ed. N. Kretzmann (Cornell University Press, Ithaca and London).

— (1983): *Time, Creation and the Continuum* (Duckworth, London).

— (1988): *Matter, Space and Motion* (Duckworth, London).

Tarán, L. (1965): *Parmenides* (Princeton University Press, Princeton, NJ).

Temple, D. (1988): 'Discussion: the contrast theory of why-questions', *Philosophy of Science* 55, pp. 141–51.

Tennant, N. (1983): 'A defence of arbitrary objects', *Proceedings of the Aristotelian Society Supplementary* 57, pp. 79–89.

Tye, M. (1990): 'Vague objects', *Mind* 99, pp. 535–57.

Unger, P. (1979): 'I do not exist', in *Perception and Identity*, ed. G. F. McDonald (Macmillan, London), pp. 235–51.

— (1979a): 'Why there are no people', *Midwest Studies in Philosophy* 4, pp. 177–222.

van Fraassen, B. (1989): *Laws and Symmetry* (Clarendon Press, Oxford).

Wardy, R. (1988): 'Eleatic pluralism', *Archiv für Geschichte der Philosophie* 70, pp. 125–46.

Waterlow, S. (1982): *Passage and Possibility* (Clarendon Press, Oxford).

White, M. J. (1985): *Agency and Integrality* (D. Reidel, Dordrecht).

Williams, C. (1965): 'Aristotle and corruptibility', *Religious Studies* 1, pp. 95–107 and 203–15.

— (1982): *Aristotle's de Generatione et Corruptione*, Clarendon Aristotle Series (Clarendon Press, Oxford).

Williamson, T. (1990): *Identity and Discrimination* (Blackwell, Oxford).

Index

Aëtius, 56, 63, 67
agency, 115–22; Aristotle's account of agency, 120–1; Democritus on agents, 115; similarity of agent and patient, 116–20, 225–7
Anaximander: position of the earth, 101–5, 151, 163–4, 226; shape of the earth, 102
arbitrary numbers, 5
arbitrary objects, 197–200
Aristotle: on agents, 115–22, 226–7; on Anaximander, 101, 104–5, 107; on atomism, 17–18, 50–4, 63–5, 100, 105, 109–10; on atomist epistemology, 65–6, 79, 84; on continuity, 60, 111; on an Eleatic argument against plurality, 27–8, 50; on motion, 108–15; natural places, 104–5, 109–10, 112–13; on partless entities, 56–7; on place, 110–12; on Plato, 57; on plenitude, 210–13; potential and actual places, 111–13; 'starving man', 104, 152, 166; 'unbreakable hair', 104, 166; on void, 105–15; 'Why not sooner?', 122
atomism, 8–14, 17–18; and agency, 121; and indifference reasoning, Ch. 3 passim, 170–8, 219–24, 228–9; see also atoms, Democritus
atoms: contact, 13–14, 52–3; hardness, 55–6, 61–2; homogeneity, 13–14, 50–9, 61–2; immutability, 155, 220–1; indivisibility, 13, 49–62, 226, 228; number, 62, 64–5, 166, 223–4, 228;

partlessness, 52, 54–62, 63; physical/conceptual indivisibility, 54–6; shapes, 49, 62, 64–5, 133, 155, 166–7, 170–8, 187–8, 208–10, 219–23, 228; sizes, 63–5, 166, 228; solidity, 54–6; and void, 22, 24, 62, 98, 105, 223–4, 228; see also atomism, Democritus

balance, 153–4, 169–70
Buridan's Ass, 6, 152–3, 166
Burnyeat Myles, 190

Carneades, 182, 185–6, 189–91
cause, see explanation, reasons
causal efficacy/causal relevance, 118–19
charity, in interpretation, 12–14, 23, 38, 64, 65, 67
Chrysippus, 189–90, 192–3
Cicero, 67, 186

Democritus: on agents and patients, 115; basic atomic theory, 9–14, 49, 50, 71, 84, 173–4, 228–9; cosmogony, 64, 79; and Eleatics, 9–14, 17–18, 22, 24, 49–50, 53–4, 71, 173–4, 227–9; epistemic reading of Democritean indifference arguments, 170–8, 187–8; epistemology, 49, 65–84, 228–9; FUND (fundamental) defined, 72–3; INT (intrinsic) defined, 73–4; and Leucippus, 1; on macroscopic objects, 13–14, 71–2, 74–80; on the

Democritus (*cont'd*)
number of worlds, 64–5, 133, 223–4; on partlessness, 57–62; on perception, 11, 63, 64–7, 79–84; philosophical and scientific Democritus contrasted, 9–14, 49, 71, 84, 173–4, 227–9; and plenitude, 155, 208–12, 219–20, 223–4, 226; on real and conventional, 67–81; *see* FUND and INT; scepticism, 66–8, 80–4; theory of nature, 9–14, 49, 228–9; *see also* atoms, atomism, indifference arguments
Diodorus Cronus, 51–2, 56
Diogenes Laertius, 63, 67
Dionysius, 63

Eleatics: against coming and ceasing to be, 13, 76–8; and atomists, 9–14, 17–18, 49–50, 53–4, 71, 173–4, 227–9; monism, 17, 22, 25, 28, 33–4, 49–50, 54, 227–8; *see also* Melissus, Parmenides, Zeno
Empedocles, 50
Epicurus, 56, 63
equilibrium, 3, 102, 154
explanation, 8; citation of contingency 145–7; citation of impossibility, 148–9; citation of necessity, 143–7; contrastive theory of explanation, 138–40; and reasons, 143–5; *see also* cause, reason

Fine, Kit, 195, 199
future tense, 213–18

Heraclitus, 98
homogeneity, 111; of atoms, 13–14, 50–9, 61–2; Melissus, 33–8; Parmenides, 22, 29–33; Zeno 22–8, 49–50, 226

indifference arguments: A and B form distinguished, 130–4; epistemically strong/weak conclusions, 162; epistemological interpretation, Ch. 6 *passim*, 161–7, 170–8, 187–8, 200–1; from homogeneity to indivisibility, 22–4, 25–8, 29, 33–4, 49–62, 156, 225–6; general structure, 6–8, Ch. 5 *passim*, 225–7 metaphysical commitments, 1, 160–1

non-epistemological interpretation, Ch. 7 *passim*; parity of reasoning, 100–1; and plenitude, 39–41, 155, 209, 218–24, 226; and quantifier introduction/elimination, 197–200; rationality of belief, 2–3, 133–4; and sufficient reason, 2–5, 7–8, 135–6, 150–1; validity and soundness, 6–8; as used by Anaximander, 101–5 (*see under* Anaximander), Aristotle, 105–23 (*see under* Aristotle), Democritus, Ch. 3 *passim* (*see under* Democritus), Melissus, 33–41 (*see under* Melissus), Parmenides, 28–33 (*see under* Parmenides), sceptics, 167–70 (*see under* scepticism), Zeno, 18–28 (*see under* Zeno); *see also* indifference premiss, *ou mallon*
indifference premiss: defined, 6, 161–7, 170–8; comparable terms, 136–41; compatible/incompatible terms, 147, 149, 153–6; Democritus and indifference premisses, 171–7, 222–3; statement of indifference premiss, 131–2; epistemic and non-epistemic, 130–1; epistemically compatible/epistemically incompatible terms, 162; establishes equivalences between terms taken modally, 7–8, 134–49, 225–6; modal homogeneity of terms, 137–8, 140–1; non-contingent terms, 152–3; and non-modal equivalences, 135–6, 149–51; *see also* indifference arguments
Insufficient Reason, Principle of, 2; *see also* indifference arguments

Lactantius, 211, 224
Leibniz, G. W., 2, 5
Leucippus, 1, 22, 51, 62, 141–2, 170, 224

Melissus: against coming and ceasing to be, 38–9, 76–8; on division, 35–7; on homogeneity, 33–8; indifference reasoning, 33–41; on infinity, 19, 21, 34; on monism, 33–4; on motion, 35–7, 52, 108–9; on pain, 37–8; on possibility and plenitude, 38–41, 209; *see also* Eleatics, indifference arguments

minimal parts, 25–7, 58
modality, 8, 134–56, 161

necessity: deontic, logical and physical,
137–8, 147; and explanation, 143–7;
and Leucippus, 141–2; and reasons,
134, 141–5

ou mallon, 8, 98–101, 163, 167–70,
178–9; *see also* indifference arguments,
scepticism

Parmenides: against coming and ceasing
to be, 76–8; cosmology, 12; and
Democritus, 10, 17–18, 71; on
division, 28–33; on homogeneity, 22,
29–33; indifference reasoning, 28–33,
41–2; monism, 32–3; 'why later
rather than earlier?' argument, 28–9,
122; and Zeno, 17–19, 32–3, 41–2;
see also Eleatics, indifference arguments
partlessness, 20–1, 54–62, 63
Philoponus, 13–14, 62, 65, 211, 223
Plato, 17, 83; atomism, 53, 56–7; use of
indifference reasoning, 98–102, 104,
122
plenitude, principle of: in Aristotle,
210–11, 212–13; defended, 212–18;
in Democritus, 155, 208–12, 219–20,
223–4, 226; in Melissus, 38–41, 209;
strong and weak forms, 40–1, 212–18
Plutarch, 69, 73, 76–8
Porphyry, 24, 52
Prior, Arthur, 214
Protagoras, 66, 81

quantifiers, introduction and
elimination, 197–200

rational belief, 2–3, 134–5
reasons, 2, 8, 118, 160; comparability
with respect to reasons, 136–41;
Democritus on reasons, 222–3;
determinist assumption about reasons,
150–1; and explanation, 143–5;
Leucippus on reasons and necessity,
141–2; and modality, 134–56;
necessity is a reason, 134, 143–5;
reasons for application of a predicate,
180–5; reasons need not necessitate,
141–2; width of notion 129–130; *see*

also cause, explanation, indifference
arguments, indifference premiss
rhetoric, 99, 122–3

scepticism, 167–70; and atomism,
67–84; *see also ou mallon*
Sextus Empiricus, 67, 68, 71, 169, 185
Simplicius, 18–20, 24–5, 27, 52, 55–6,
62, 211
Sorabji, Richard, 212
sorites paradoxes, 5, 132–3, 178–97;
Chrysippus' 'keeping quiet' response,
189–94; and degrees of truth, 194–5;
and *modus ponens*, 184–5; relation to
indifference reasoning, 181–3, 196–7;
relation to other forms of argument,
184–8; how sorites paradoxes arise,
179–85; and supervaluations, 195–6;
underlying indifference argument,
183–5
Sufficient Reason, Principle of, 2–5,
7–8, 136, 225
symmetry, 1–2, 5, 6, 103, 116

Unger, Peter, 185

void: Aristotle's arguments against,
105–15; atoms and void, 10, 22, 24,
62, 98, 105, 223–4, 228; emptiness,
uniformity and infinity contrasted,
105–6; extra cosmic and intra cosmic
void, 106–7; and motion, 35, 52, 105,
107–10, 113–15

Wang's paradox, 132–3; *see also* sorites
paradoxes
Wardy, Robert, 13

Xenophanes, 115

Zeno: atomist response to Zeno, 9–14,
17–18, 22, 24, 49–50, 53–4;
assumptions about divisibility, 18–22;
dichotomy, 51–3; on homogeneity,
22–8, 49–50, 151; indifference
reasoning, 9, 11–12, 18–28, 41–2,
49–50, 156, 226–8; against motion,
14, 51–2; and Parmenides, 17–19,
32–3, 41–2; against plurality, 9, 17,
18–28; on separation 23–4; *see also*
Eleatics, indifference arguments

Index Locorum

◆

(see Bibliography for abbreviations)

indicates reference at which a passage is reproduced

Aëtius: III.10.5, 95 n.103; IV.9.1, 91
  n.75; IV.9.8, 91 n.87, 92 n.88
Alexander
  in de Sensu, 24.14 on, 95 n.106
  in Met: 35.24 on, 87 n.29, 87 n.30;
    36.25–7, 89 n.49
Aristotle
  de An: 1.2 404a27f, 96 n.109; 2.5
    417a17–20, 128 n.63; 2.7 419a15f,
    93 n.98; 3.3 427a25–427b5, 96
    n.109
  de Caelo: 1.7 275b31–3, 87 n.28; 1.12,
    212–3, 229 n.11; 1.12 281b25, 229
    n.5; 1.12 283a10–17, 128 n.64;
    2.13, 108; 2.13 295b11–15, 101*,
    124 n.11*; 2.13 295b15–296a22,
    125 n.22; 2.13 295b30–4, 104*,
    125 n.23; 2.13 296a4ff, 125 n.24;
    2.13 296a12–15, 125 n.26; 3.1, 57;
    3.1 299a6–7, 88 n.44; 3.1 299a11,
    57; 3.1 299a26 on, 88 n.46; 3.1
    300a1, 88 n.45; 3.7 306a26–306b2,
    89 n.53; 3.8 307a24–30, 100; 4.3
    310a33f, 126 n.48; 4.3 310b3–5,
    110; 4.3 311a2–6, 126 n.48
  de Part An, 1.1 640b29ff, 94 n.100*
  de Sensu, 2, 438a5 on, 95 n.106
  GC: 1.1 315b9 on, 89 n.54; 1.2,
    53–6, 60–1; 1.2 315a15–317a2, 60;
    1.2 315b8 on, 203 n.25; 1.2

315b9f, 96 n.109; 1.2
316a14–317a2, 85 n.3, 85 n.17; 1.2
316a15–16, 86 n.18, 86 n.19, 86
n.21, 86 n.24; 1.2 316a17, 86 n.19;
1.2 316a18, 86 n.19; 1.2
316a24–316b8, 86 n.20; 1.2
316a26–8, 86 n.22; 1.2 316a28–30,
86 n.23; 1.2 316b15–16, 86 n.24;
1.2 317a2–17, 86 n.19; 1.7, 115;
1.7 323b3–6, 115*, 127 n.52*; 1.7
323b18–21, 115*, 117, 127 n.53*;
1.7 323b21–4, 116*, 127 n.58*; 1.7
323b23f, 127 n.55*; 1.7 324a9ff,
128 n.63; 1.8, 17, 27, 50–4, 64; 1.8
325a4–5, 85 n.11; 1.8 325a5–12,
27*, 44 n.28*, 85 n.4; 1.8 325a6
on, 52; 1.8 325a8–12, 44 n.28, 86
n.25; 1.8 325a18–23, 43 n.13; 1.8
325a23–325b5, 85 n.2; 1.8 325a24
on, 63; 1.8 325a27–8, 85 n.12; 1.8
325a28–9, 85 n.2*, 87 n.29; 1.8
325a30, 63; 1.8 325a32–4, 88 n.43;
1.8 325b33, 57; 1.8 326a32–4, 88
n.43, 89 n.50
Metaphysics: 1.4 985b5–7, 84 n.1, 87
n.29, 87 n.32; 1.4 985b7–9, 123
n.2*; 3.4 1001b7–13, 42 n.11, 44
n.26; 4.5, 65, 80, 81, 84, 92 n.93;
4.5 1009b2, 91 n.70; 4.5 1009b4
on, 91 n.70; 4.5 1009b9–12, 65*,

79*, 91 n.69; 4.5 1009b13ff, 96
n.109; 4.5 1010b4ff, 95 n.105; 5.9
1018a15f, 127 n.59; 7.13 1039a11,
85 n.16

Physics: 1.2 184b21, 87 n.28; 1.3
186a23, 85 n.7; 1.3 187a1–3, 51*,
85 n.5; 3.2 202a9–12, 128 n.63; 3.4
203b 25–30, 210*, 229 n.4*, 230
n.18; 3.5 204a20–6, 91 n.68; 3.5
205a12–19, 125 n.38; 3.5
205b31–206a1, 109, 125 n.38*; 3.6
206b34–207a2, 46 n.41; 4.1 208b1
on, 126 n.41; 4.1 208b8–11, 126
n.47; 4.2 209b32f, 126 n.43*; 4.4
211a29–31, 126 n.44; 4.4 212a5f,
126 n.42; 4.4 212a14–21, 126 n.42;
4.5 212a32f, 126 n.40; 4.5 212b4f,
126 n.45; 4.5 212b6, 126 n.46; 4.5
212b14ff, 126 n.43; 4.6 213a24–5,
93 n.95; 4.7 214a6–7, 93 n.95; 4.8,
105, 106; 4.8 214b31–215a1, 107*,
109, 110, 125 n.31; 4.8 214b32f,
125 n.35*; 4.8 215a1–14, 109; 4.8
215a8f, 125 n.37, 126 n.39*; 4.8
215a9, 126 n.39*; 4.8 215a9–11, 25
n.28; 4.8 215a19–22, 107*, 113,
114, 125 n.32; 4.8 215a22–4, 108*,
114, 125 n.34; 4.8 215a24–216a21,
127 n.50; 6.1, 56–7; 6.1 231a24–6,
88 n.42; 6.9 239b19, 22, 85 n.8;
8.1 252a11–19, 128 n.64; 8.1
252a34ff, 230 n.17; 8.4 255b8–13,
127 n.49

Post. An., 1.4 73b32–74a3, 206 n.50
Rhetoric, 2.23 1397b12–27, 128 n.65
Topics: 2.18 108b13f, 127 n.57; 5.8,
128 n.65

(pseudo-)Aristotle
   MXG: 974a12–14, 34*, 38, 47 n.43*,
   47 n.44*; 976a31–3, 47 n.42;
   977a14–18, 127 n.54

Cicero
   Acad: 2.38, 203 n.20; 2.55, 90 n.65;
   2.73, 91 n.77, 96 n.108*; 2.93–5,
   205 n.40; 2.93, 204 n.30, 204 n.34,
   205 n.41; 2.94, 205 n.44; 2.125, 91
   n.66
   de Fin, 1.6, 87 n.29
   de Nat Deor: 3.44, 205 n.37; 3.52, 205
   n.38

Democritus (DK numbering): fr.5 c,
e–i, 92 n.90; fr.6, 91 n.72, 91 n.81,
96 n.108*; fr.7, 91 n.82, 95 n.107*;
fr.8, 91 n.83; fr.8a, 92 n.90; fr.9,
68*, 91 n.78, 91 n.85; fr.10, 91
n.73, 91 n.84, 94 n.101; fr.11, 82*,
95 n.107, 97 n.110*; fr.11 b–i, 92
n.90; fr.117, 83*, 91 n.76, 97
n.112*; fr.125, 95 n.107*; fr.156,
91 n.71, 123 n.2*; fr.164, 92 n.89;
fr.165, 91 n.77, 94 n.100*, 96
n.108*

Diels-Kranz: 12 A1, 124 n.11; 12 A11,
124 n.11; 12 A17a, 124 n.20; 12
A18, 124 n.20; 12 A21, 124 n.20;
12 A22, 124 n.20; 12 A26, 101*,
124 n.11*, 124 n.14; 13 A12, 124
n.20; 21 A28, 127 n.54; 28 A44,
124 n.13; 28 B1.30, 92 n.92; 28
B2.1–4, 30*, 32, 45 n.35; 28 B6.4
on, 92 n.92; 28 B8.3, 32; 28
B8.5–6, 43 n.16*; 28 B8.7–8, 32;
28 B8.9–10, 28*, 45 n.29; 28
B8.13–14, 32; 28 B8.22, 43 n.16*,
44 n.21; 28 B8.22–5, 29*, 30, 31,
45 n.30*, 45 n.36, 46 n.38, 87
n.34; 28 B8.29–30, 32; 28 B8.32–3,
45 n.36; 28 B8.38b–41, 92 n.92;
28 B8.42–9, 45 n.36; 28 B8.46–8,
29; 29 A21, 42 n.12, 43 n.13; 29
A16, 42 n.12; 29 B1, 19–24, 57–8,
60; 29 B1.4–12, 21*, 43 n.14*; 29
B1.7–9, 89 n.48; 29 B2, 19, 20–3;
29 B2.6f, 20*, 42 n.11*, 44 n.26;
29 B2.19, 42 n.4; 29 B3, 23; 29
B3.5–10, 23*, 43 n.17*; 30 A5,
34*, 47 n.43*; 30 B1, 38; 30 B2,
46 n.40, 46 n.41, 47 n.51; 30 B3,
42 n.6, 46 n.40; 30 B4, 46 n.40,
46 n.41*; 30 B5, 34*, 42 n.6, 46
n.39*, 47 n.42; 30 B6, 34*, 38, 42
n.6, 46 n.39*; 30 B7, 38; 30
B7.6–8, 94 n.99*; 30 B7.10–12, 94
n.99*; 30 B7 (2), 37*, 38*, 47
n.50*, 48 n.52*; 30 B7 (3), 48
n.54; 30 B7 (4), 37*, 47 n.49*; 30
B7 (7), 35*, 47 n.46, 85 n.11, 125
n.27, 125 n.33; 30 B7 (7)–(10), 47
n.47; 30 B8, 92 n.92; 30 B9, 42
n.6, 42 n.10, 89 n.47; 30 B10, 35*,
42 n.6, 47 n.45*, 47 n.48*; 59

Diels-Kranz (*cont'd*)
A96, 91 n.75; 67 A1, 90 n.63, 95
n.102; 67 A6, 84 n.1, 87 n.29, 87
n.32, 123 n.2*; 67 A7, 88 n.43; 67
A8, 62*, 89 n.54*, 157 n.5, 170*,
203 n.21; 67 A9, 89 n.54, 96
n.109, 203 n.25; 67 A13, 87 n.37,
88 n.39, 90 n.60; 67 A14, 87
n.29*, 87.30*; 67 A19, 87 n.28; 67
A29, 95 n.106; 67 A32, 91 n.87,
92 n.88; 67 B2, 141*, 158 n.13*;
68 A1, 87 n.32, 88 n.38, 90 n.56*,
90 n.63, 92 n.88; 68 A37, 87 n.29,
88 n.43, 90 n.61; 68 A38, 62*, 89
n.54*, 157 n.5, 170*, 203 n.21, 203
n.25; 68 A40, 90 n.64; 68 A42, 85
n.16; 68 A43, 87 n.32, 88 n.38, 90
n.57*; 68 A47, 88 n.38, 90 n.58*;
68 A48, 87 n.37; 68 A49, 90 n.60,
91 n.87; 68 A65, 230 n.17; 68
A81, 90 n.65; 68 A83, 90 n.63; 68
A94, 95 n.103; 68 A101, 96 n.109;
68 A110, 91 n.75; 68 A112, 65*,
79*, 91 n.69; 68 A113, 96 n.109;
68 A114, 91 n.71; 68 A121, 95
n.106; 68 A122, 93 n.98; 68 A125,
87 n.29; 68 A135, 91 n.69*, 91
n.86, 91 n.87, 93 n.96, 94 n.101,
95 n.106; 68 B5c,e–i, 92 n.90; 68
B6, 91 n.72, 91 n.81, 96 n.108*;
68 B7, 91 n.82, 95 n.107*; 68 B8,
91 n.83; 68 B8a, 92 n.90; 68 B9,
68*, 91 n.78, 91 n.85; 68 B10, 91
n.73, 91 n.84, 94 n.101; 68 B11,
82*, 95 n.107, 97 n.110*; 68
B11b–i, 92 n.90; 68 B117, 83*, 91
n.76, 97 n.112*; 68 B125, 95
n.107*; 68 B156, 91 n.71, 123
n.2*; 68 B164, 92 n.89; 68 B165,
91 n.77, 94 n.100*, 96 n.108*; 70
A6, 89 n.55
Diogenes Laertius
Lives: 7.44, 204 n.34; 7.82, 204 n.30,
204 n.34; 9.31 on, 90 n.63, 95
n.102; 9.44, 87 n.32, 90 n.56*, 92
n.88; 9.45, 90 n.63; 9.72, 83*, 91
n.76, 97 n.112*; 9.76, 202 n.8;
9.107, 202 n.17

Epicurus
Ep. Her. 42, 203 n.26; 55–6, 90 n.59

Galen
de Elem Sec Hipp, 1.2, 90 n.60, 91
n.87
On Medical Experience, 16.1–17.3, 205
n.38*

Hippolytus
Ref, 1.13.2, 90 n.64

Lactantius
de Ira Dei: 10.5, 90 n.60; 10.10, 211*,
224*, 229 n.9*, 230 n.19
Inst, III 17.22, 87 n.29, 90 n.60
Leucippus (DK numbering), fr.2, 141*,
158 n.13*
Long-Sedley: 1 G, 202 n.8; 12 A, 90
n.59; 12 B, 203 n.26; 12 C 1–2, 90
n.62; 37 B–H, 203 n.28; 37 C, 204
n.34; 37 D, 204 n.30, 204 n.34; 37
E, 205 n.38*; 37 F, 204 n.30, 205
n.40, 205 n.43; 37 H, 204 n.30,
204 n.34, 205 n.40, 205 n.41, 205
n.42, 205 n.44; 40 O, 203 n.20; 70
D,E, 203 n.28, 203 n.29, 204 n.35,
205 n.37; 71 A3, 202 n.17; 71 C7,
202 n.9
Lucretius
de Rer Nat, 2.478–99, 90 n.62
Luria: 1, 62*, 89 n.55*, 210*, 211,
223*, 224*, 229 n.4*, 229 n.7, 229
n.8, 229 n.9, 230 n.18, 230 n.19; 2,
62*, 89 n.54*, 157 n.5, 170*, 203
n.21; 3, 65*, 79*, 91 n.69; 4, 124
n.13; 6, 90 n.65, 91 n.66; 7, 123
n.2*; 11, 92 n.89; 14, 230 n.17; 22,
141*, 158 n.13*; 23, 90 n.63; 48,
91 n.72, 91 n.81, 96 n.108*; 49, 91
n.82, 95 n.107*; 50, 91 n.83; 51,
83*, 91 n.76, 97 n.112*; 54, 91
n.75; 55, 68*, 91 n.73, 91 n.78, 91
n.84, 91 n.85, 94 n.101; 57, 91
n.74; 58, 91 n.77, 96 n.108*; 59,
91 n.87; 60, 91 n.87; 61, 68*, 91
n.79; 65, 94 n.100*; 67, 96 n.109;
69, 96 n.109; 70, 96 n.109; 71, 93
n.96; 73, 96 n.109; 76, 91 n.71; 78,
91 n.71; 79–80, 95 n.107*; 83, 82*,
95 n.107, 97 n.110*; 90, 91 n.87;
93, 92 n.88; 95, 91 n.87, 92 n.88;
96, 96 n.109; 106, 87 n.37; 112, 90
n.60; 113, 87 n.29, 87 n.37, 88

n.39, 90 n.60; 123, 89 n.49; 124,
87 n.36; 141, 91 n.67; 172, 87
n.29; 173, 84 n.1, 87 n.29, 87 n.32;
184, 88 n.38, 90 n.56*; 204, 90
n.61; 206, 90 n.61; 207, 88 n.38,
90 n.57*, 90 n.58*; 211, 85 n.16;
212, 87 n.29, 87 n.31, 87 n.32, 87
n.35, 88 n.40, 90 n.60; 214, 87
n.29*, 87 n.30*; 215, 87 n.32; 218,
87 n.29, 90 n.60; 219, 87 n.32;
223, 87 n.28; 236, 88 n.43; 240, 89
n.54, 203 n.25; 261, 87 n.28; 293,
88 n.43; 301, 87 n.29; 316, 92
n.89; 318, 203 n.25; 349, 90 n.64;
369, 91 n.86; 382, 90 n.63, 95
n.102; 405, 95 n.103; 441, 91 n.87;
468, 93 n.98; 477, 95 n.106; 478,
95 n.106; 484, 94 n.101

Melissus (DK numbering): fr.1, 38; fr.2,
46 n.40, 46 n.41, 47 n.51; fr.3, 42
n.6, 46 n.40; fr.4, 46 n.40, 46
n.41*; fr.5, 34*, 42 n.6, 46 n.39*,
47 n.42; fr.6, 34*, 38, 42 n.6, 46
n.39*; fr.7, 38; fr.7.6–8, 94 n.99*;
fr.7.10–12, 94 n.99*; fr.7(2), 37*,
38*, 47 n.50*, 48 n.52*; fr.7(3), 48
n.54; fr.7(4), 37*, 47 n.49*; fr.7(7),
35*, 47 n.46, 85 n.11, 125 n.27,
125 n.33; fr.7(7)–(10), 47 n.47; fr.8,
92 n.92; fr.9, 42 n.6, 42 n.10, 89
n.47; fr.10, 35*, 42 n.6, 47 n.45*,
47 n.48*

Parmenides (DK numbering): fr.1.30, 92
n.92; fr.2.1–4, 30*, 32, 45 n.35;
fr.6.4 on, 92 n.92; fr.8.3, 32;
fr.8.5–6, 43 n.16*; fr.8.7–8, 32;
fr.8.9–10, 28*, 45 n.29; fr.8.13–14,
32; fr.8.22, 43 n.16*, 44 n.21;
fr.8.22–5, 29*, 30, 31, 45 n.30, 45
n.36, 46 n.38, 87 n.34; fr.8.29–30,
32; fr.8.32–3, 45 n.36; fr.8.38b–41,
92 n.92; fr.8.42ff, 42 n.7; fr.8.42–9,
45 n.36; fr.8.46–8, 29

Philoponus
in de An, 71.19, 96 n.109
in de Caelo, 39.4 on, 90 n.61
in de Gen et Corr: 12.2, 91 n.67; 23.2,
96 n.109; 158.26, 88 n.43; 160.10,
88 n.43.

in Phys: 42.9 on, 43 n.13; 80.23–81.7,
42 n.5, 42 n.12, 43 n.20, 44 n.27;
405.23 on, 62*, 89 n.55*, 223*,
229 n.8, 230 n.18
Plato
Charmides, 160b,c, 98
Hippias Major, 289c, 123 n.7
Meno: 74 d,e, 99, 123 n.5*; 78e, 99,
123 n.6*
Parmenides: 128d, 97 n.111; 144c, 42
n.12; 165e, 42 n.12*
Phaedo: 75c,d, 100, 124 n.10*;
108e–109a, 102*, 124 n.12, 124
n.15, 124 n.16, 124 n.17
Republic: 5, 479b, 123 n.7; 5, 479c,
124 n.9; 7, 523b on, 99, 123 n.7*;
7, 523e, 124 n.8; 7, 524e, 123
n.7*
Theaetetus: 182e, 98, 123 n.3*, 123
n.4*; 209a–c, 122
Timaeus, 62e, 63a, 124 n.12, 125 n.25
Plutarch
adv Col: 1108F, 123 n.2*; 1109A, 91
n.71; 1110E, 68*, 91 n.79

Sextus Empiricus
Outlines of Pyrrhonism: 1.7, 202 n.14;
1.8, 202 n.11, 202 n.16; 1.12, 202
n.13; 1.14, 202 n.9; 1.26, 202 n.14,
202 n.16; 1.26–9, 202 n.17; 1.187,
202 n.9; 1.188–91, 202 n.9; 1.190,
202 n.10, 202 n.15, 203 n.18;
1.191, 203 n.19; 1.213, 202 n.9
Adversus Mathematicos: 1.315, 202 n.9;
7.117, 92 n.89; 7.126–34, 92 n.91;
7.135–40, 71; 7.135, 68*, 91 n.78,
91 n.80; 7.136, 91 n.73, 91 n.85,
94 n.101; 7.137, 91 n.72, 95
n.107*, 96 n.108*; 7.138f, 95
n.107; 7.139, 82*, 97 n.110*;
7.140, 92 n.91; 7.141–9, 92 n.91;
7.369, 91 n.75; 7.389–90, 91 n.71;
7.416, 204 n.30, 205 n.40, 205
n.43; 7.418–20, 204 n.32; 8.184,
91 n.74; 9.133, 90 n.63; 9.182–4,
203 n.29, 204 n.35; 9.190, 204
n.35
Simplicius
in de An, 193.27, 91 n.87
in de Caelo: 242.18, 87 n.29*, 87
n.30*; 295.12–14, 88 n.43; 532.14f,

124 n.14; 609.17, 87 n.29, 88 n.40, 90 n.60

in de Gen et Corr, 294.33, 90 n.61

in Phys: 28.4 on, 62*, 89 n.54*,170*, 203 n.21; 28.22–4, 203 n.25; 81.34 on, 87 n.29; 82.1, 87 n.31, 87 n.32, 87 n.35; 82.4 on, 89n.51; 139.19, 42 n.5; 139.27–32, 25*, 26, 44 n.24*, 85 n.14; 140.1–6, 24*, 26, 43 n.19*, 47 n.44, 85 n.14; 140.21, 43 n.20; 467.16, 229 n.7; 467.20–3, 211*, 229 n.10; 512.28, 91 n.87; 925.10, 87 n.37, 90 n.60; 925.15, 88 n.39

Themistius
in Phys, 12.1–3, 42 n.5
Theophrastus
de Sens: 50, 95 n.106; 61, 93 n.96; 62, 91 n.86; 63f, 93 n.96; 67, 93 n.96; 69, 91 n.69*, 93 n.96; 71, 91 n.87; 73, 94 n.101; 74, 94 n.101

Zeno (DK numbering): fr.1, 19–24, 57–8, 60; fr.1.4–12, 21*, 43 n.14*; fr.7–9, 89 n.48; fr.2, 19, 20–3, 42 n.9; fr.2.6f, 20*, 42 n.11*, 44 n.26; fr.2.19, 42 n.4; fr.3, 23; fr.3.5–10, 23*, 43 n.17*